The waterfall and shade garden, the Jack Warner Garden. (Photograph by Mr. George Waters)

Left: Brick Court, the Jack Warner Garden. The single tree and the cupid riding a swan are whimsical performers within the calm scene of the villa and its pool. (Photograph by Mr. George Waters)

Below: The view from the front door, the Jack Warner Garden. The small basin at the top of the hill echoes the large pool in the foreground. (Photograph by Mr. George Waters)

Right: The Seahorse Terrace shaded by leaning sycamores, the Jack Warner Garden. (Photograph by Mr. George Waters)

A sunny, flowered entrance and inviting patio for a contemporary house, the Frank Work Garden. (Photograph by Mr. George Waters)

Landscaping the American Dream

Landscaping the American Dream

THE GARDENS AND FILM SETS OF
FLORENCE YOCH: 1890–1972

James J. Yoch

A Ngaere Macray Book

Harry N. Abrams, Inc./Sagapress, Inc.
New York

Library of Congress Cataloging-in-Publication Data

Yoch, James J., 1938–

    Landscaping the American dream : the gardens and film sets of

    Florence Yoch / by James J. Yoch : photographs by George Waters.

      p. cm.

    Bibliography: p.

    Includes index.

    1. Yoch, Florence.   2. Landscape architects—California-

-Biography.   3. Landscape gardening—California.   4. Gardens-

-California—Design.   I. Title.

SB470.Y66Y663   1989

712'.6'0924—dc19   88–13895 CIP

ISBN 0–8109–1273–2

Edited by Barbara Probst Morrow

Design and Composition by The Sarabande Press

Printed in The United States

First Printing

Contents

Illustrations

Preface

This study began several years ago when John Peirce, a landscape architect who had worked with my cousin Florence Yoch, took me to several of her surviving California gardens. Since then, other friends have helped discover more than 250 of her jobs, the inventions of a long career beginning in 1915 and continuing to 1971, her eighty-first year, when she wrote, "I am having fun this year doing the garden for the oldest wooden house in Monterey."[1]

As a student in the landscape gardening program at the University of Illinois, Urbana-Champaign, she spent weekends with her cousins, my grandparents, and stories about her work came down to me through the family. Intrigued by them, I visited her in California in the 1960s when, after the death of her partner, Lucile Council, she was living alone in Carmel. When she met my plane, she ordained the title "Aunt," which she felt suited the half-century difference between our ages. Aunt Florence was generous with time and with books; she shared her favorites, including Edith Wharton's *Italian Villas*. We traveled to look at gardens and scenery in the Monterey area, and she reviewed trips and designs she had made. We worked our way through her collection of photograph albums, and I particularly remember her good-spirited description of her exploratory trip in 1935 for sets in *The Garden of Allah*. Her touring car had broken down in the sands of the Sahara, and Bedouins rescued her and Lucile by pushing the car across the desert dunes. Travel, which she continued even in the final years of her life, was a serious pursuit, the major source of inspiration, she claimed, for the originality in her work. For a three-month trip to Italy in 1971, she gave me infallible advice about Italian villas to visit, although it has taken time and exploration to appreciate the wisdom of her choices, which favored subtle design on a difficult and confined site.

Florence Yoch and Lucile Council worked together throughout most of their careers. Yoch designed the gardens, and Council at times contributed planting schemes, supervised the work, and discussed ideas from the early 1920s until the early 1960s. Garden plans before and after this period of collaboration have only Florence Yoch's name on them, and in plans mutually issued, her name is always first. Having this evidence and the comments of the majority of clients that Florence Yoch did their gardens, although the firm name was Yoch and Council, I have often referred only to Yoch, when, of course, she was part of a team. My primary interest is in the gardens and the way Florence Yoch achieved them, studied plants and gardens, and wrote about them. Her dear friend was a major influence and a close companion in these enterprises, and without Lucile it seems unlikely that these gardens would have taken shape. I accept the oral and written attributions to Florence Yoch, but I occasionally use both names to remind readers of their bond. Their landscape designs depended, also, on the insights of sensitive and well-traveled clients, especially those who commissioned several gardens from Florence Yoch and whom she might have said worked *with* her.

To write this book, I gathered evidence from many sources, including interviews with clients and coworkers, office records, family stories, published commentaries on Yoch and Council gardens, and visits to many of her gardens that still exist. The work of her own hand survives in several places, and I have drawn on her sketchbooks, letters, and sets of seasonal horticultural instructions for clients as well as the many notes she intended to turn into a book on landscaping. Illustrations come from her snapshots, professional records, movie stills, and her own slides of gardens she designed and those she admired. To spare readers the distraction of innumerable footnotes, I have included a bibliography of sources, including interviews and letters used in preparing this study of Florence Yoch's gardens.

It is a pleasure to record some of the many kindnesses that have made the discovery of this material possible. First, Mr. Thomas Moore cared for the most extensive collection of plans, documents, and memories of Florence Yoch's work. Mr. John Peirce provided invaluable leads on her jobs, her own homes, and her movies. Florence Yoch's nieces, Mrs. Constance Ward and Ms. Elizabeth Lewton, shared pictures and memories of their aunt. From her wedding trip in 1900, my grandmother, Florence White Yoch, had several stories of her visit to the Santa Ana and Laguna Beach homes of her aunt and uncle, the parents of Florence Yoch. My parents recalled their visit to Florence Yoch in 1937, when they met with her on the site of the Warner estate. Several members of the firm of Yoch and Council have shared their memories of its methods: I am particularly indebted to Mrs. Margaret Pashgian, Mr. James Ross, Mr. Alex Salcido, and Ms. Emilie White.

Many owners of Florence Yoch gardens have scrupulously cared for or restored her work and generously permitted me to see and to photograph their grounds as well as to review plans and sketches in their collections. Although this book could not have been written without their help, I have not separately listed their names, because most wish to remain anonymous. Representative of the graciousness of these clients, the late Mr. George Cukor encouraged me to come at will to study his garden and his files, where he had carefully saved Florence Yoch's sketches; he was insightful in discussing her and described her as "a distinguished American artist."

Many other people have helped with this project, including those who showed me the first Florence Yoch garden I saw, those who arranged for me to give lectures on her work, to live in a house adjoining one of her gardens, those whose chance remark led to the discovery of one of her own homes, who found her plans and photos in a chest or an attic, and whose enthusiasm and field trips helped complete my task. These include Mr. William Aplin, Mrs. Florence Banning, Mrs. Grayson Carter Barber, Mr. Fred Boutin, Mr. and Mrs. Henry Braun, Mr. Herb Bridges, Mrs. Catherine Andrews Britton, Mr. Edward Carpenter, Ms. Virginia Crockett, Mr. and Mrs. Edwin C. Davis, Mr. Glen Dawson, Mr. and Mrs. Muir Dawson, Mrs. Harriet Doerr, Mr. Gep Durenberger, Mr. and Mrs. David Dvorak, Mr. Bob Easton, Contessa Barbara Emo, Mrs. Alice Everett, Mrs. Elizabeth de Forest, Dr. and Mrs. Richard Hambleton, Prof. Eric T. Haskell, Mrs. Carol Hotchkis, Mr. and Mrs. George Huntington, Mrs. A. Parley Johnson, Mr. and Mrs. Allen D. Krieg, Mr. A. James Lyons, Ms. Joyce MacRae, Ms. Penny McKenzie, Mrs. Catherine Millar, Mr. Herbert Nusbaum, Mrs. Ruth von Platen, Mr. Stephen A. Roake, Dr. Donald Scanlon, Mr. Daniel Selznick, Mr. Jeffrey Selznick, Ms. Ruth Shellhorn, Ms. Millie Smith, Mr. William J. Tomkin, Mrs. Georgie Van de Kamp, Mrs. Micheline A. Vogt, Mrs. Ann Warner, Mrs. Nancy Wilder. For their help in reconstructing Florence Yoch's plans, I am indebted to Ms. M. Jana Pereau and Mr. Timothy Scott.

At the Huntington Library I received invaluable support in my research, particularly from Ms. Jane Evans, Ms. Janet Hawkins, Ms. Noelle Jackson, Mr. Alan Jutzi, Dr. Myron Kimnack, Mr. John C. MacGregor IV, Ms. Barbara Quinn, Ms. Virginia Renner, Mr. Robert Schlosser, Ms. Elsa Sink, Ms. Doris Smeads, and Ms. Mary Wright. At the University of California at Los Angeles, Mr. Martin Lovell, Mr. James Mink, Mr. Jeffrey Rankin, and Dr. David Zeidberg were helpful. Other individuals and their institutions who contributed significantly to this project include Mr. Val Almendarez and Mr. Scott Busby, the Academy of Motion Picture Arts and Sciences; Ms. Claire W. Bogaard, Pasadena Heritage; Dr. W. H. Crane, Hoblitzelle Theatre Arts Library, Humanities Research Center, University of Texas at Austin; Mr. James V. D'Arc, Arts and Communications Archives, Brigham Young University; Ms. Ilse Davis, Architecture Library, University of Oklahoma; Dr. David Gebhard, University of California at Santa Barbara; Ms. Mary Corliss, the Museum of Modern Art; Mr. J. Larry Gulley, University of Georgia Libraries; Mr. Ronald Haver, Los Angeles County Art Museum; Mrs. Lothian Lynas, New York Botanical Garden; Ms. Ann Scheid, Keeper of Historic Records, City of Pasadena; Ms. Joanne L. Yeck, American Film Institute; the staff of the Pasadena Public Library, especially Ms. Cynthia Carey; and my colleagues at the University of Oklahoma Library. I am especially indebted to Dr. James R. Estes, Curator of the Bebb Herbarium at the University of Oklahoma.

At the University of Oklahoma, Dean Kenneth Hoving, Vice-Provost of Research Administration, the Research Council of the University of Oklahoma, Dr. Eddie C. Smith, Associate Dean of the Graduate College; and Dr. Alan R. Velie and Dr. George Economou, Chairs of English, kindly arranged for generous support of travel, photography, and duplication in this project. Proposal Services assisted in the preparation of the list of Florence Yoch's commissions. Information Processing Services typed the manuscript with notable care. The support of Provost Joan Wadlow for the Instructional Services Center and the help of Ms. Margaret A. Smith, Coordinator, have been invaluable for the production of photographs.

Editors, colleagues, and friends who have read portions of the manuscript have offered suggestions that greatly improved it: Mr. Stanley Baron, Ms. Sara Blackburn, Prof. Clay Lewis, Mr. Savoie Lottinville, Mr. Sam Marx, Ms. Mary Hall Mayer, Mr. Ray Merlock, Dr. Rogers Miles, Prof. Robert Nye, Mr. Thomas Radko, Prof. Joanna Rapf, Mrs. Kathleen Upshaw, and Mr. Hugh Van Dusen. Ms. Ngaere Macray, Ms. Mary Martin, and Ms. Barbara Morrow made extensive and thoughtful suggestions. Ms. Anna Holloway and Ms. Rebecca Kanost assisted in editing.

Most of Florence Yoch's gardens have not been published in depth, and none of her work in the 1950s and 1960s has been published before. The choice of gardens included in this book represents the variety in style and location of her work in a career continually adventuring into new areas. The examples depend on the available evidence, which is considerable for many Yoch and Council gardens, even those from the 1920s. A few keystone commissions, including Mrs. Howard Huntington's garden as well as other major projects such as the C. W. Gates garden, seem to have few surviving records. I would be glad to hear from those who have information about any garden she worked on in order to assemble a complete record of her work. I have used the historical present to describe the gardens as though they are all seen in their prime, something that only a very few loving owners manage today.

My cousin spent more than a decade reviewing her ideas about garden design and drafting a first chapter for her intended book on landscaping. That my study of her work has reached completion would have been impossible without her inspiration and the cheering help of Nancy, Michael, and Stephen.

James J. Yoch, Jr.

With special thanks to Mr. Thomas C. Moore, whom Florence Yoch's gardens inspired. After meeting and working with her during the last two decades of her life, he carefully saved many of her drawings, plans, records, notes, and correspondence, all of which he has most generously shared with me and to which he has added his many personal recollections. Among the greatest pleasures of writing this book has been talking with him about her gardens. The best praise I can imagine is Florence Yoch's sentence beginning a letter about her Carmel home in January 1971: "Dear Tom, I am trying to catch up with your suggestions re this garden."

Landscaping the American Dream

I

Country Life in California

In a career that began in 1915 and continued for more than fifty years, Florence Yoch created gardens for large Pasadena estates and modest Carmel backyards; for the magnificent villas of Hollywood producers and for public courtyards and parks; and for the sets of some of the most celebrated movies of the 1930s, including her landscaping of Tara in *Gone With the Wind*. With her partner, Lucile Council, Yoch visited and studied the great gardens of Europe, but her own designs have an independent character that is vigorously American. "Genuine design springs from significant needs," she wrote. "When we learn to analyze our own needs and carry out solutions in terms of Californian conditions, we will build a tradition of landscape gardening as genuine as any."[1] Yoch was boldly utilitarian in analyzing the actual needs of her clients, emphasizing comfort and practicality in the gardens of even her wealthiest employers. She discarded the ideal of a lazy country house, maintained by a vast gardening staff. Instead she assumed that busy owners wanted their gardens to be easy to keep and to enjoy.

Florence Yoch, second from the right, posing in 1908 with her five sisters and her mother, Catherine Isch Yoch, in black.
(Courtesy of Ms. Elizabeth Lewton)

Adapting European formal garden designs to the California land-scape, Yoch created gardens rich in architectural detail and in varieties of plants, yet intimate and casual in style. Among landscape designers of the early and mid twentieth century, she is unique in the major role she gave to eccentric or irregular garden features—leaning trees, angled walks or stairs, unexpected variations on geometrical patterns. These elements produce a feeling of tranquillity, of ease with the effects of time, that gives age to New World landscapes. Her plans avoid perfect geometries and bend, as ancient villages did, to existing conditions in the real world. She thus connected California sites to the most primitive and simplest archi-tectural traditions at the same time that she appealed to the most sophisti-cated clients. In their successful accommodation to severe limits on space, maintenance, and water, Yoch's gardens are especially useful models for the late twentieth century.

Early Life

California has always been a place of dreams closely connected to the landscape. The early Spanish explorers named the state after an island in a pastoral romance, and later settlers had extravagant hopes of finding a land without the restricting limits of seasons. Agriculture as practiced on the heroic scale at the missions and haciendas revealed the extraordinary abundance that could be raised from the sprawling plains. Drawing on these California traditions of Arcadian dreams and agricultural enter-prise, Florence Yoch designed gardens that were both imaginative and practical.

Family traditions supported this combination. Florence's father, Joseph Yoch, was three years old when he came with his family from Berlin to the United States in 1847. His father, who had been a stone-mason, worked first in this country as a contractor and farmer, then turned to coal mining, eventually owning some of the largest fields in Illinois. At nineteen, Joseph took over the family mines, and the company became Joseph Yoch and Brothers. After Jay Gould purchased the firm in the late 1880s, Joseph Yoch took his $60,000 share from the sale and moved his family to Santa Ana in Orange County, California. At 1012 North Main Street he built a spacious house in the Italian villa style, with orange groves on one side and a grape arbor and fish pond on the other.

Joseph Yoch successfully engaged in a variety of endeavors in Cali-fornia. He became a partner in the Black Star Coal Mine of Santiago Canyon in 1887, ranched at El Monte in Los Angeles County, and served for twenty years as a director of the First National Bank of Santa Ana. A quiet man, fond of nature, "a farmer at heart," as his granddaughter Elizabeth Lewton remembered him, he influenced Florence in her passion for the California countryside.

Joseph Yoch, from Samuel B. Armor, History of Orange County, California, with Biographical Sketches *(Los Angeles: Historic Record Co., 1921). (Courtesy of the Henry E. Huntington Library)*

Catherine Isch Yoch, Florence's mother, was an intelligent and educated woman, active in political and social affairs in spite of poor health. She had been a schoolteacher before her marriage, and she succeeded in persuading all but one of her daughters to graduate from college. The death of her first child, a son, was a devastating loss. She always described the six children who followed as "another of Joe Yoch's girls."

Florence, the last of the six daughters, was born on July 15, 1890. A picture of her as a young girl shows her looking shyly downward, a characteristic pose, her niece Elizabeth Lewton suspected, and one that was partly the result of being told by so many older sisters to "Shut up, Nuisance." In explaining how she emerged from this childhood reserve Florence Yoch told her friend Thomas Moore the story of a woman who worked with her mute chauffeur to gradually build him up and enable him to talk. She concluded by saying, "Lucile did that for me."

Much of Yoch's childhood was spent outdoors. On long drives by horse and buggy from Santa Ana to Laguna Beach, she would insist that her father stop and let her pick armloads of wildflowers, her niece recalled. Early inspiration for her gardens that achieved an atmosphere of refinement in a country setting came from the two distinctive cultural enclaves in which her family participated: the salons of the hotel the Yochs owned and managed during the summer in Laguna, and the exemplary life of drama and music that the great Polish actress Helena Modjeska arranged at her country place. In these stimulating circles, Yoch as a young girl met talented men and women who were deeply interested both in the arts and in horticulture.

The Yochs helped establish Laguna Beach as a cultural resort for Orange County. There, in the 1890s, Joseph Yoch bought beachfront land and built the Laguna Hotel. In those early years, Laguna was several days' travel away from Los Angeles and was a place of notable freedom and informality. The Laguna Hotel, under Catherine Yoch's direction and with the cooperation of the rest of the family, became a center of cultured summer life, particularly for guests escaping the heat in Riverside and Pasadena. These early associations with her family's guests may have provided Florence Yoch with her first important connections to the Pasadena community, where she lived and where her landscape practice flourished in the 1920s and 1930s.

The appeal of the Laguna Hotel was specifically to cultural interests. At the evening entertainments, "presided over by Mrs. Yoch and her talented daughters," Madame Modjeska performed scenes from Shakespeare, and there was often music. Laguna was also developing as an artists' community. The painter Gardner Symonds stayed with Florence Yoch's uncle, and her father allowed artists to exhibit their work in the hotel's dancing pavilion.[2]

Catherine Yoch, from Samuel B. Armor, History of Orange County, California, with Biographical Sketches (Los Angeles: Historic Record Co., 1921). (Courtesy of the Henry E. Huntington Library)

Madame Modjeska and her husband, Count Karol Bozenta Chlapowski, were among the most influential visitors to Laguna and were good friends of the Yochs. In Poland, Count Chlapowski's family had long been involved in agricultural projects and innovations. The count's father introduced the latest farming methods from England, and in 1848 the Prussian government used his plan for land reform in its emancipation of the peasants. Madame Modjeska later recalled the dreams she shared with friends in Warsaw of California as an agricultural paradise. "Fancy, coffee grows wild there! All you have to do is to pick it; also pepper and the castor-oil bean, and ever so many useful plants!"[3] After she and her husband emigrated from Poland, they created a large estate in Modjeska Canyon. In their forest of Arden they combined their horticultural activities with their intellectual and cultural pursuits. In 1893 they hired Theodore Payne as gardener. Payne directed extensive horticultural experiments for his employers and later became well-known as a specialist in native California plants.

Madame Modjeska invited to her home many of the most famous men and women of her day, particularly actors and musicians. Gardening was a major topic of interest in this life of elegant outdoor leisure. "In the afternoons Madame and her friends would generally occupy chairs or hammocks on the lawn under the oak trees and read and chat or do fancy work," Payne recalled. "Later in the afternoon they would go horseback

The Yoch beach house at Laguna Beach about 1910. (Courtesy of Ms. Elizabeth Lewton)

riding." Among the guests, Payne remembered the Yochs of Santa Ana and the Langenbergers of Anaheim. Mrs. Langenberger had many rare and unusual plants, and her daughter, Mrs. Bullard, was the first to hybridize watsonia and had more than fifty named varieties to her credit. Payne also remembered Florence Yoch, then a little girl, who participated in this society devoted to drama, art, and gardening.[4] Many years later director George Cukor recalled that Count Chlapowski and Madame Modjeska encouraged the young Florence Yoch's interest in landscaping.

Stanford White designed the house at Arden, a rambling bungalow that combined disparate elements, including a Palladian window alongside an English cottage dormer. On the garden façade, broad stairs led to a balustraded terrace and arched entry, whose elegance of design contrasted with the casually curved stone wall leading to the rustic wishing well. The ranch's shaded walks, lined with great old trees and blooming vines, including many roses, were set along strongly axial lines. The garden contained informal plantings, comfortable benches, and a hammock. This was a garden well adapted to the demands of the Southern California climate. Useful features like wells and rustic arbors from a Mediterranean vocabulary for gracious country living answered realistic needs here as they did later in the work of Florence Yoch. But it was also a garden that supported the imaginative life of these new Californians, who enjoyed discussions of literature and presentations of music, drama, and

The Laguna Hotel, about 1915. This part of the building was once the Arch Beach Hotel, which Joseph Yoch cut into sections, moved, and joined to his Laguna building in 1896. (Courtesy of Ms. Elizabeth Lewton)

Madam Modjeska at the Well   Copyrighted By Graham 1902   MDHS

painting in an outdoor setting recalling classical forms that linked California scenes to Renaissance villas. Arden's inspiring blend of nature and art profoundly influenced Florence Yoch, who was to design gardens for hardworking owners with similar hopes of escape to idyllic landscapes on estates, ranches, backyards, or in movies.

Study and Books

Florence Yoch began her study of the new field of landscape architecture at the University of California at Berkeley in 1910, and then in 1912 traveled east to Cornell to spend a year in its College of Agriculture. But neither of these programs pleased her. With the spirit of wandering and independence that characterized her entire life, she changed schools again in 1914 and finally completed her education in 1915 at the University of Illinois at Urbana-Champaign, where she graduated with a Bachelor of Science in Landscape Gardening. Yoch continually emphasized the importance of study in her work. About a decade after her graduation, when a young neighbor, Ruth Shellhorn, who went on to become a well-known landscape architect, asked her what was necessary to prepare for a career in the field, Yoch replied with a list that began with four years of Latin and chemistry.

Florence Yoch's extensive library included the major works on garden design as well as on horticulture. By far the largest number of her books belonged to the field of architecture, for she believed that coherent gardens were best based on a rational consideration of underlying design principles. When she came in the late 1950s to jot down notes for a book on landscaping, she quoted extensively from writers as diverse as Horace, John Addington Symonds, and Charles W. Eliot. She weighted her buying particularly to books on the pure new style that Gertrude Jekyll and artists in the Arts and Crafts movement developed around the turn of the century in England. Colleagues and clients noted that she collected books and often carried such texts as Jekyll and Lawrence Weaver's *Gardens for Small Country Houses* around with her on jobs. With these books as helpful companions she worked to adapt European gardens to California. Yet, while Jekyll used color as a principal force to organize the landscape, Yoch relied on design. Daring breaks with convention in architectural structure gave freshness to her gardens and brought them in touch with the unpredictable outside world.

Two books were especially influential in helping Yoch make the leap from the grand scale of Italian villas and from the moist air and soil of English estates to the more domestic settings and the smaller, drier sites that were available to most of her California clients. In *The Story of San Michele* (1929), the Swedish physician Axel Munthe described building a villa in Capri. In *Viva Mexico!* (1908), the Yankee traveler Charles Macomb Flandrau—the author of *Harvard Episodes*—wrote joyfully of

Florence Yoch in her graduation picture, 1915. (Courtesy of Mrs. Robert E. Ward)

Madame Modjeska at her well in Arden, 1902. Cascading vines, an off-center tree, and freely growing colorful flowers became important devices in Florence Yoch's practice. (Courtesy of the Henry E. Huntington Library)

his experiences in Mexico. Yoch came to both books in the late 1920s (her copy of *Viva Mexico!* was from 1928), and she remained fond of them throughout her career.

Both Munthe and Flandrau were passionate individualists resolved to newly interpret their landscapes and to discover classical values as a bedrock beneath the superficialities of modern life. Both were attracted to rustic simplicity and practicality. Munthe began constructing his villa with only "a rough sort of sketch drawn by myself with a piece of charcoal on the white garden wall." He relied on the workmen's skills, not obtained through education or training in the usual sense, but instead inherited as a craft from father and "grandfather from untold generations, the Romans had been their masters."[5] Munthe's villa deeply interested Florence Yoch, who underlined the reference to it in her 1938 American Academy *Guide to Villas and Gardens in Italy,* gave it her highest rating of two checks, and added, "Don't miss, remember?"

Munthe advocated the simple ranchero life that was so often played at in the subdivisions of California. His writing on architecture paid attention to the small, personal scene, centered on a loved memento—a portion of an antique wall, a gift from a friend. His method became a model Yoch used to transform the heroic designs of great European gardens into the small scale of American suburban lots. As he did in his novel, she most often invented intimate places for reflection and conversation rather than grand parterres for admiration and parties. In her practice prior to the Second World War, she used small statues, pebble paving, pieces of columns, and other fragments from the past to add the dimension of time to the modern gardens.

Like Munthe, Flandrau admired the unpretentious. He praised the simple, playful style of Mexican peasant life, which made the ordinary magical. Freed by travel and observation from the prevailing cultural values of his class, Flandrau came to wry and independent conclusions. He mocked those gardens in the United States where the "prevailing color is wealth," and he mused that the only way to rescue their brashness of marble and riot of flowers was to wait a century for time's mellowing effects.[6]

Florence Yoch's landscapes from their first moments seem to have endured the effects of age: an angled walk, an off-center or leaning tree, paths interrupted by seemingly necessary turns or overgrown with plants, all express the softness that Yoch saw in Europe and that Flandrau had recognized as much of the storybook appeal of memorable gardens. Continually selecting from her education and from her reading for her ideal of "the supreme excellence of simplicity," Yoch found in the work of Munthe and Flandrau elegant forms inspired by observing primitive ways of life. With a similar disregard for the conventional and obvious, her own designs are refreshingly individual in their interpretation of landscape patterns. Through her studies, Yoch gained the discipline that would organize her designs and the range of associations that would enrich them. To achieve a confident ease in interpreting inherited forms, she began in her youth and continued into the last years of her life a series of voyages.

Travel

When her colleague Thomas Moore asked her why the work of Yoch and Council seemed so recognizable, so clearly signed by them that he could identify their gardens at first sight, Florence Yoch replied, "We attribute that to all the time we spent in Europe studying." She referred to the Villa Doria Pamphili in Rome as "my villa in college," and throughout her life she made many trips, often for months at a time, to Italy, Spain, France, and England. On these excursions, she and her partner visited gardens and discussed plants with horticulturalists, selected sculpture for clients' gardens, and browsed in bookstores. Both women kept albums of photographs, and Yoch filled several sketchbooks with notes and drawings, and then adapted ideas for work at home in California.

Yoch's four surviving sketchbooks indicate the remarkable thoughtfulness and visual awareness that she brought to her study of gardens. She listed plants, measured details, and drew plans and elevations ranging from very small elements, such as the fold of a wall, to large schemes, such as the layout of the many garden rooms at the Generalife in Granada. Besides close observation, these drawings suggest leisured en-

Florence Yoch's sketch for a corner of the Patio at the Wilshire Country Club. (Published in California Southland *17 [March–April, 1921], p. 15.) (Photograph courtesy of the Henry E. Huntington Library)*

JOUTH·WEJT·CORNER·OF·THE·PATIO

Yoch's bravura sketch of the Villa Aldobrandini at Frascati suggests its boisterousness.

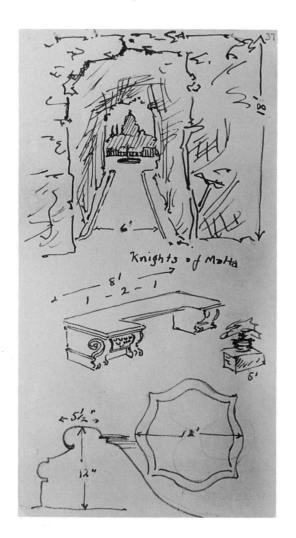

Yoch's drawing of a baroque Italian stair and fountain.

Left, Yoch's sketch of the main axis in the Roman garden of the Knights of Malta.

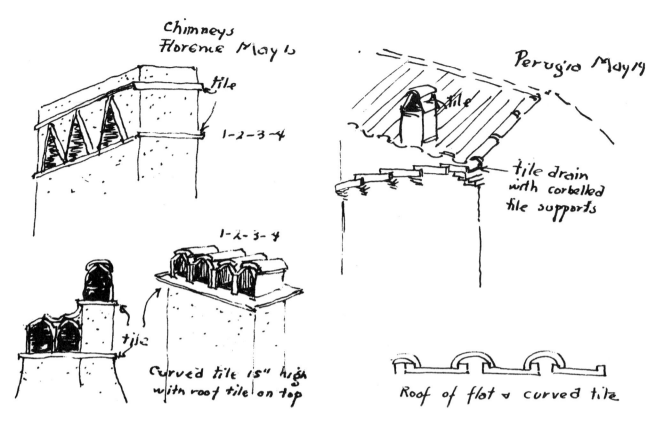

Florence Yoch's sketches of details in Tuscany and Umbria.

joyment. Florence Yoch took the time—often several days—to be in the gardens long enough to feel the walks, see the changes of light, hear the sounds of fountains and birds. The selection of subjects favors idiosyncrasy: for example, she observed in the front garden of an old house on Salem Common, that the beds seem regular but actually are not. The sketchbooks show a discerning eye for detailing that subtly jars expectation. The quality of eluding the conventional became a mark of Yoch's own designs.

Most important, and a unifying theme in all of Yoch's sketches and recollections, was her penchant for the notable feature that gives a garden its special character: the worn stone, the shadowed fountain, the venerable tree. Her drawings illuminate the distinctive details in every scene. Thus she turned her focus from grandeur and expansiveness, so fashionable in contemporary landscaping, to intimate scenes and personal scale more fitting to a democratic land.

Partnership and Working Methods

After her graduation from the University of Illinois in 1915, Florence Yoch began designing gardens for clients in Orange County and in Pasadena. Lucile Council, who had studied at the Cambridge School of

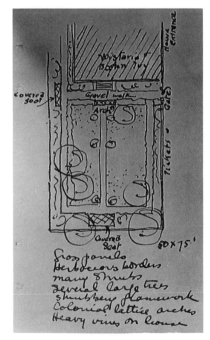

Florence Yoch's sketch and plant list, an old house in Salem, Massachusetts. (All sketches from Yoch's travel notebooks, courtesy of Mr. Thomas C. Moore)

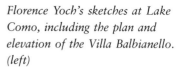

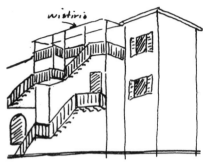

Florence Yoch's sketches at Lake Como, including the plan and elevation of the Villa Balbianello. (left)

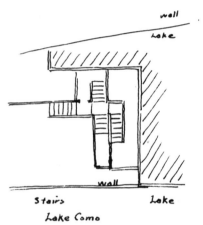

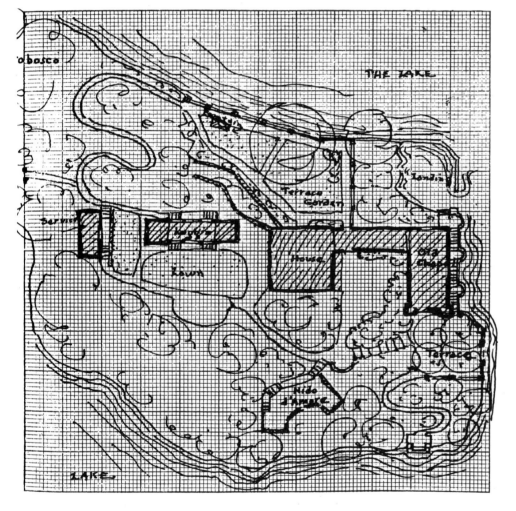

Florence Yoch's drawing of service
buildings at the Villa Cicogna
Mozzoni at Bisuschio. (left)

Villa Cicogna
Service house

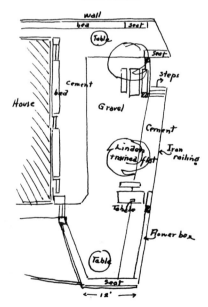

May 18-22
Lake Como

Plan of Tea Terrace
San Martino

wall
bed   Seat
Table
                    Seat
                    Steps
House   Cement
        bed   Gravel
                    Cement
                        Iron
        Linden   railing
        trained flat
                Table
                        Flower box
        Table
                Seat
        12'

Yoch's view and plan of the tea
terrace at San Martino on Lake
Como.

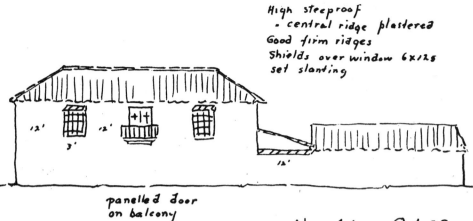

High steeproof
- central ridge plastered
Good firm ridges
Shields over window 6x125
set slanting

Cordova to Almodóvar
Oct 23-24

Farm houses

Iron gate to
steps to ter-
race

panelled door
on balcony

Almodóvar Oct 23

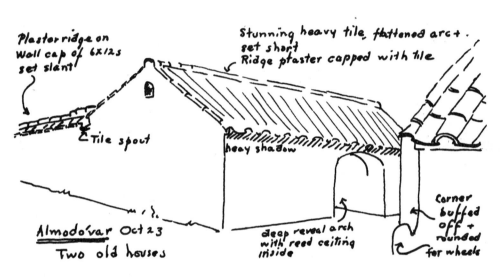

Plaster ridge on
Wall cap of 6x125
set slant

Tile spout

Stunning heavy tile, flattened arc+.
set short
Ridge plaster capped with tile

heavy shadow

deep reveal arch
with reed ceiling
inside

Corner
buffed
off +
rounded
for wheels

Almodóvar Oct 23
Two old houses

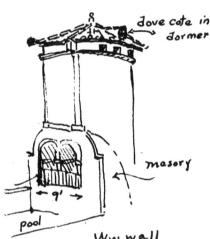

dove cote in
dormer

masonry

pool

Ww wall
Old pink tile roof
Heavy shadow at eaves
Arches of grey stone
Fe grill overlooking
pool

Slender window

slight reveal

Junction of 2 w

Very heavy tiles on roof   Almodóvar
Under eave lg. bl.
Door dk. br., brass knocker, jamb chamois.

grill to shed H₂O
first two, roofs tile, others 6x12.

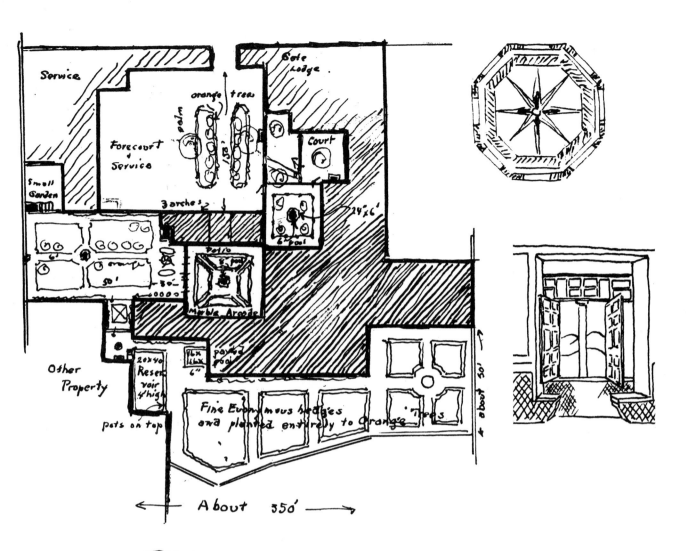

Labels within sketch (top plan):
Service
Gale Lodge
orange trees
palm
Forecourt & Service
Court
Small Garden
3 arches
24'x6'
6' pool
Patio
Marble Arcade
Other Property
Reservoir 4' high
20x40
pots on top
16'x 16'x 6'
paved pool
about 50'

Fine Euonymous hedges
and planted entirely to Orange Trees

← About 350' →

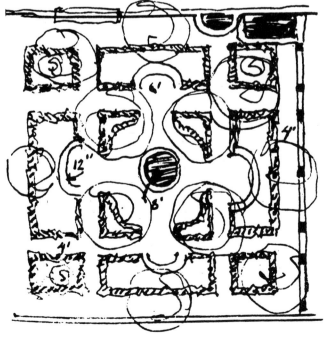

Labels within lower sketch:
5
5
4'
12"
6'
4'
S

*Florence Yoch's sketches in Andalusia
and Old Castile.*

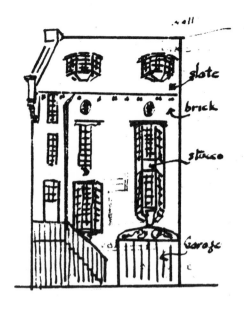

slate

brick

stucco

Garage

Door

Garage

Houses in
old Chelsea

Milmead
Bramley

Planting Plan

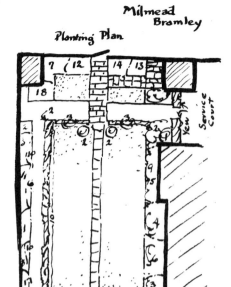

Service Court

Yew

Key to Planting Plan

1 Bay
2 Box
3 Mahonia
4 Cistus lad.
5 Rose
6 Acanthus
7 Laurustinus
8 Ferns
9 Rosemary
10 Megasea
11 Sorbus
12 Choisya
13 Red Fuchsia
14 Roses
15 Polyanthus primrose
16 Aucuba
17 Eglosa
18 Violets & Iris

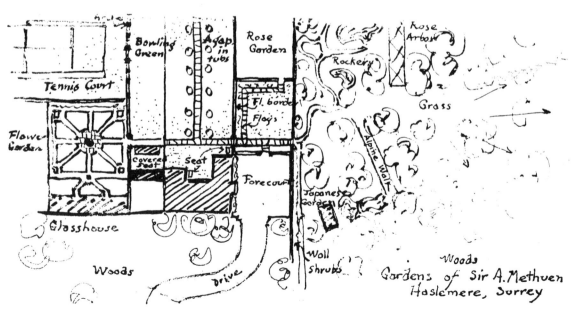

Bowling Green

Agap. in tubs

Rose Garden

Rose Arbour

Rockery

Tennis Court

Fl. border

Flags

Grass

Flower Garden

Covered Seat

Seat

Alpine Walk

Forecourt

Japanese Garden

Glasshouse

Woods

Drive

Wall Shrubs

Woods

Gardens of Sir A. Methuen
Haslemere, Surrey

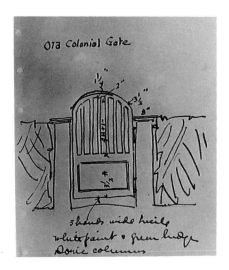

Old Colonial gate in Plymouth.
*Yoch's sketch records the width of the
gate as "5 hands wide Lucile." (left)*

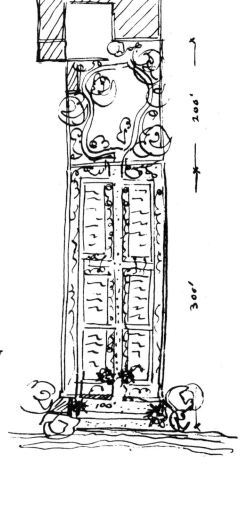

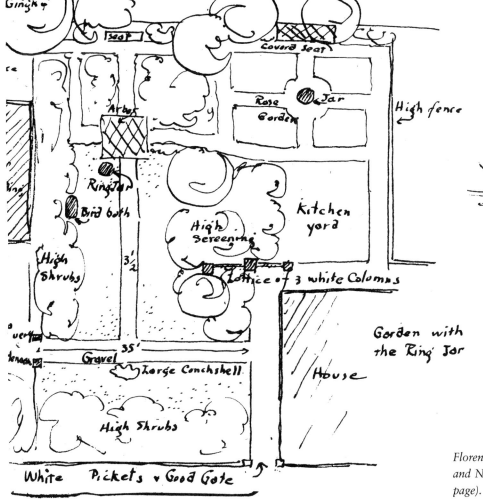

*Florence Yoch's sketches in England
and New England (upper left, this
page).*

Domestic and Landscape Architecture in Massachusetts and also at Oxford, joined her as an apprentice in 1921. In 1925 the two women formed a partnership and established their office in the garden studio of the Council home in South Pasadena; by 1932 they had achieved "an enviable reputation."[7]

Florence Yoch and Lucile Council worked, traveled, and lived together from 1921 until Council's death in 1964. Their partnership was notably absorbing and enduring, each woman finding sustaining powers in the other. As in all successful partnerships, their talents seem to have been separately weighted. Florence Yoch was the principal designer, and Lucile Council was in charge of the office. Margaret Pashgian, who worked in their office from 1929 to 1933 during some of their most important commissions, reported that Council was also the "plant orderer and finder" as well as supervisor on many jobs. After Council's death, Yoch recalled in a letter to Thomas Moore the "good olive trees . . . Lucile knew how to find."[8]

It is likely that from 1922 to 1940 Council prepared the office account book, with its elaborate breakdowns of all expenses, including figures for the costs per square foot of lawn, shrubs, trees, and even perennials. In the late 1930s, Yoch and Council employed five or six people in the office and about fifty men in the outside crews. In 1936 wages ranged from the young workman Alex Salcido's starting rate of thirty-five cents an hour to the experienced workman's $4.50 a day, the stonemason's $5.50, and the foreman's $8 a day. The figures in the account book show that the cost of design and supervision remained roughly the same proportion of total garden costs. In the Sturgises' moderate garden (1926–34) the landscape architects' fees for plan and supervision were about 20 percent and labor 40 percent of the expenditure. A breakdown of figures in the accounts for this garden indicate that in 1929, the rate charged for Yoch's hours was $5, for Council's, $3. On the 6.3-acre, labor-intensive project for Mr. and Mrs. Jack Warner in 1935, Yoch and Council's charges of $17,000 were 20 percent of the job's cost and labor about 30 percent. In 1939 their 20-percent fees (about $4,000) for the West Los Angeles garden of Henry F. Haldeman were almost equal to the labor costs.

When Florence Yoch wrote down the steps in landscape design in her notes, she started with "paced & measured survey," then "elevation sketches of site [including] extent, exposures, soils, existing features—natural, permanent, temporary, plants—number, habit, usefulness, color, class, condition." Then, "plant catalog, drafting & plan." These were followed by what seems to have been a schooling of the clients: "plant lesson theory and plant lesson field trip," and finally by "estimating construction—prices, catalogs, architectural rendering."

The amount of participation by the clients seemed to differ from one side of Los Angeles to the other during the 1930s. Yoch and Council worked on the selection of individual plants with Pasadena clients who wanted to be involved in developing and sustaining the horticultural variety of the garden. In contrast, less of this thoughtful interplay occurred with clients in West Los Angeles, where busy schedules and bold spending habits led to demands for instant effects. Mrs. Jack Warner was one of the few clients there who cared deeply enough about particular trees to go searching for her cypresses and yews. More typical is George Cukor, who, after an afternoon spent selecting a tree, said to the designer about choosing the rest, "Florence, you do it."

Yoch's method began with a great respect for the site, particularly for any existing trees. Cukor described her visit to his hillside estate, where she sat and mused until, suddenly rising, she declared a walk here, the pool there, and the lookout on the southern edge. From the beginning she was intuitive and authoritative in her approach. After the initial surveying and thinking about the site, she drew a very simple sketch that showed the basic configuration of the garden. In later drawings and in her decisions in the field, a garden went through several adjustments, as seen also in the plans for the Warner and the Banning gardens. Depending on Yoch's familiarity with the client and on whether she were using her own crews, the drawings might develop beyond the sketch into several drafts.

A few detailed plans survive—for planting, furniture, and pools. But rather than relying on construction drawings or on planting plans, Florence Yoch preferred to work at the site and make decisions on the spot. Throughout a project, spontaneous responses to the actual scene were more important to her. She never placed her confidence in drawings, for she was convinced that "you can't do a decent job just on paper," as Thomas Moore recalled. Drawings were primarily rough guidelines in achieving the final product on site; she simplified greatly the walls for the Parley Johnson house in Downey, for example, from the baroque curves of the original drawings in 1926. Construction documents, like those for the Warners' elliptical pool, sometimes said explicitly what she commanded throughout the project: "Consult Miss Yoch."

Even in an era prized for its careful workmanship, Yoch and Council were noted for the personal supervision they gave each job, regardless of the remoteness of its location or its size. Many of these jobs took six months to a year to complete. Yoch spent two weeks to find a single cypress for the Cukor estate, engaged in long and complex negotiations to buy the eight large yews for the Warners, and searched patiently for cuttings from rogue crape myrtles to suit her special color requirements at the Banning garden. Her involvement did not end with installation. Her surviving files include folders and booklets of recommendations to clients for watering systems, methods of trimming trees, and for the long-range care of particular plants. She individualized these instructions: twenty-three pages to Mrs. Preston Hotchkis in the 1930s, an entirely different set to Mrs. Albert Doerr in 1941.

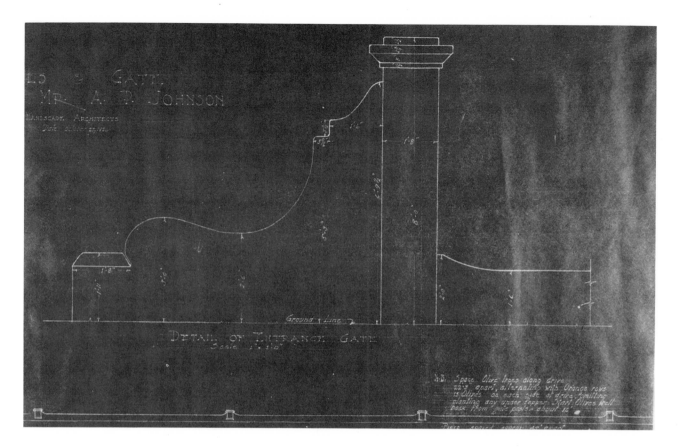

Clients in Pasadena remember her many kind gestures, particularly her willingness to take on small projects and execute them lovingly. Her surviving correspondence with friends in New Zealand, in Mexico, and in California is primarily about the exchange and acknowledgment of plants as affectionate remembrances. Affection even linked her jobs together, for she only accepted clients recommended by previous ones. This policy, consistent with her natural shyness in personal relations, ensured that she would spend her extravagant care on garden projects for clients who would appreciate it. Loyal to commitments once made, she gave generous attention to business and to friendship inextricably uniting these primary pursuits of her life.

To support the demands of creative planning on the site, Yoch and Council had at their command a group of remarkably skillful people, from foremen like Joseph Benoit and James Ross to craftsmen for individual items such as furniture and the ornamental terra cotta edgings that were a signature of their gardens. Besides the experienced workmen of her own crews, Yoch also relied on professional tree men to take care of other tasks; one was Frank Manning, who spent two weeks trimming major jobs like the Selznicks' garden, and another was Robert Hamsher, who did much of the tree moving from one site to another.

Yoch and Council trained their workmen well. Although both clients and workmen remember the partners' scrupulous attention to every detail

Yoch's original wall design, greatly simplified in the field, the A. Parley Johnson Garden. (Courtesy of Mrs. A Parley Johnson)

Yoch designed and had manufactured tiles to edge beds. The rounded tile (upper right) is her first, created for the Frank A. Bovey Garden 1921); the rope design (lower left) was made especially for the octagon tree beds on the main terrace of the Warner house. (Drawings by Mr. Timothy G. Scott)

*A Sampler of Benches.
For many jobs, Florence Yoch
designed benches, which she devised
in shapes from baroque
ornamentation to Shaker simplicity.
Each variation suits the taste of the
owner and the character and space of
the site.*

*(Photographs courtesy of Mr. Thomas
C. Moore)*

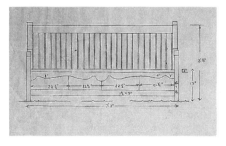

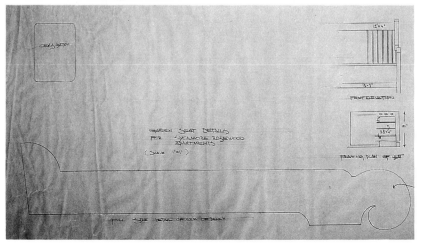

of a garden during the busy days of the 1930s, when Yoch was designing gardens for Hollywood movies as well as for wealthy Los Angeles clients, their time must have been stretched thin with so many projects. In interviews James Ross recalled that on a major job Florence Yoch might not be on the site for as long as three days at a time, and he was left with much of the responsibility for the installation. Alex Salcido said that on most jobs the partners did not appear every day because the "men knew how to follow the plan." Yoch and Council used only the best workers. "When contractors got a job from Miss Yoch, they felt good," noted Ross. "She had a great reputation." From employees they required unswerving loyalty and made rigid demands on the field and office staff.

Both women had exacting standards. James Ross remembered Yoch as someone who "just had that way—[she said] this ought to be so and so, and that was it. No one could change her mind." Council is similarly recalled, as illustrated by George Cukor's story of how she walked down a freshly planted border at his estate, pulled up the plants and tossed them onto the walk, and turned around at the end of the border to look the workmen in the eye and snap, "Now do it right." When Cukor summarized his recollections of the partners he characterized them in Damon Runyan style, as "a couple of tough customers."

One example of the partners' determination to arrive at the best solutions was Yoch's daring innovation in moving large trees, such as the tall cypresses that cranes lifted four stories in the air for the rooftop courtyard of the Women's Athletic Club and the thirty-foot-tall cypress trees that she planted at the California Institute of Technology. She also moved large specimens of Catalina cherries, Carolina laurel cherries, oaks, and other trees already on the site of some of the firm's residential jobs. In a typical process for preparing trees on the site, four or five of Yoch's men would first dig around a large tree and prepare it for boxing, usually in a six to eight-foot square container. After they had put on the sides, they would excavate below the tree, jack it up, cut the roots, and then build the bottom of the box. Using large rollers the men would then transport the tree along runways that would take it either to its new site or to a holding area away from the house construction. The crew would spend three days per tree in executing this painstaking method.

When the building was finished, several of the large trees would be rolled back in to frame the house, and the process would be reversed: the men would jack up the tree, remove the bottom of the box, lower it, and then remove the sides. Florence Yoch and Lucile Council determined the exact placing of the major trees, adjusting them until they achieved the right effect. The effort and expense generally paid off. Most of the trees lived and gave a pleasing sense of maturity to the gardens.

World War II took away many of the men who were able to perform such work. Without these knowledgeable crews, the meticulous garden installations Yoch and Council demanded in the 1920s and 1930s were

Florence Yoch (unknown newspaper, April 1925). (Courtesy of Mrs. Robert E. Ward)

Lucile Council (Pasadena Post, 29 May 1932, p. 5). (Courtesy of Mrs. Robert E. Ward)

impossible to achieve. This drastic change in the availability of skilled labor sharply restricted their practice both during and after the war.

The stringent demands she made on workmen and office help were consistent with Yoch's own devotion to work. Traveling to visit gardens, designing and installing gardens, writing about gardens, and collecting books about gardens seem to have almost totally absorbed her. She was always willing to expend time and money to achieve the high level of results she required. James Ross noted with Scottish acumen that Lucile Council was "a good deal closer" about money on a job than was Florence Yoch, "who wanted to get it done right and have it look good." In her eighty-first year, just days before she died on January 31, 1972, Yoch was out raking the walks and planting the garden of the Doud house in Carmel to be sure the job was done according to her standards.

Workmen moving trees on the site of the Selznick job. (Photograph by Florence Yoch, courtesy of Mr. Thomas C. Moore)

II

Patrician Gardens

One of the main goals of Florence Yoch's earliest gardens was to bring admired pieces of Europe home to America for wealthy clients who wanted to recollect scenes from their travels. Sometimes, as for Mary Stewart, Yoch did this in a set of views based on a single type, such as the Italian villa; at other times, as for the Parley Johnsons, she designed a garden around a set of mementos from different countries. In the first decades of this century there were several respected methods for satisfying the requests of clients for imported gardens: splendid display in the parks and parterres of Northeastern American gardens, particularly in Newport and on Long Island; subtle elaboration and smaller scale, best illustrated in Beatrix Farrand's stone-work, arbors, fountains, and parterres for the Bliss garden at Dumbarton Oaks in Washington, D.C.; and precise reproductions, such as those which Paul Thiene and A. E. Hanson provided for California clients.

Independent in working out her own understanding of what was needed and innovative in developing skills to meet these requirements, Florence Yoch introduced major changes in adapting European garden conventions to the native American scene. In particular, for clients

Pergola and bench, the Mrs. Richard Fudger Garden. The pergola looked over beds where "every shade of iris blossoms profusely." (Helen Wren, "Informal Charm," Arts and Decoration, *29 [October 1928], p. 46.) (Courtesy of Mr. Thomas C. Moore)*

whose background was business, whose fortunes were limited, and whose lots were small, she developed a style that gave good value: most efficient use, most economical detailing, and maximum effect with the least number of flowers and major trees. By late-twentieth-century standards, her gardens prior to the Depression may seem luxurious, especially in the schemes she and Lucile Council worked out for seasonal changes of flowers and in the labor-intensive technology they developed for moving great trees to achieve instant effect. By the standards of other notable designers of the period, however, her work was particularly frugal. A major portion of its cost was in things unseen: thoughtful planning, careful supervision, extraordinary preparation of the soil, and loving selection of each plant.

Yoch made comfort and ease of access the defining principles of her garden designs. For conservative clients in Pasadena and Santa Barbara, her gardens tended to be reserved and formal, unlike her more theatrical landscapes in West Los Angeles and her wilder, asymmetrical Monterey gardens of the 1950s and 1960s. The early gardens display her recognition of the ways busy Americans actually use their gardens and provide a refreshing sense of purposefulness in the arrangements of walks and garden rooms for entertaining and for work. Adorned with architectural features that pleased sophisticated clients by suggesting European scenes, these gardens are as elegant as they are practical.

Yoch's skill in appealing to members of the important gardening

Katherine Bashford's vignette of the pool garden, the Mrs. Howard Huntington Garden. (Courtesy of Mr. Thomas C. Moore)

POOL GARDEN for Mrs HOWARD HUNTINGTON
Florence Yoch landscape architect Pasadena

communities in Southern California brought her early success. She received a flush of commissions during the 1920s and even during the Depression years of the 1930s. By the time of her last gardens in Pasadena during the 1960s, she had designed more than 125 projects there, about one half of her work.

Yoch's first garden (1918) in Pasadena illustrates the innovations of her style. The much-photographed pool garden for Mrs. Howard Huntington (later Mrs. James R. Brehm) transforms the architecturally refined and elegantly bordered canals of English estates into a forest scene focused on a shaded spring. The freedom and openness of the finished garden avoid the tight channeling of the models, Edwin Lutyens's watercourses and arched springs at the Deanery (1901) and Abbotswood (1913), as well as the tidy limitations of the drawing Yoch's artist did for the project. The individualism of Yoch's interpretation here shows in the adaptation of a spacious English design suiting lavish country-house weekends into an intimate, informal garden fitting a simpler American life-style. The patrician gardens that follow Mrs. Huntington's share in its surprisingly unaffected qualities.

Il Brolino

For a spectacular hillside site, between mountains and ocean, Florence Yoch created in 1922 the varied garden rooms of Mary Stewart's Mon-

The pool garden, the Mrs. Howard Huntington Garden. The beshrubbed borders and mix of large trees dissolve the edges of the formal geometry. From Florence Yoch's Album of Gardens. For this portfolio of her work, Yoch insisted on soft-focus photographs, which added romance to the scenes. (Courtesy of Mrs. Robert E. Ward)

Forecourt, Il Brolino. Within a forest setting, the stair, walls, and arrangement of Italian vases set a formal basis for the whimsy of the topiary garden. Florence Yoch's Album of Gardens. (Courtesy of Mrs. Robert E. Ward)

Stair leading to pool and herm, Il Brolino. Florence Yoch's Album of Gardens. (Courtesy of Mrs. Robert E. Ward)

tecito home, Il Brolino, "the little garden." The understated name belies the noble plan, which originally proposed a rose garden, parterre, *bosco,* guest garden, sunken garden, paved terrace, lemon house, pergola, orchard, and cut flower garden. As the garden developed, Florence Yoch added formal elements (the precisely cut figures of the topiary garden), as well as informal ones (a terrace that sways around the grove of existing oaks). In what became a habit in her later work, the planting plan (August 1923) adjusted the right-angled shapes of the draft plan (November 1922) to take advantage of the site's most interesting features, including an existing small building, which became the Lemon House. The walled and gated Orange Terrace beside it runs obliquely into the edge of the wellhead garden on one side; on the other, a sunken walk (a pergola on the original plan) angles even more radically down to the cut flower garden.

Following her designs, tall gates surmounted with urns (rather than the balls of the original sketches) open into the stone-edged forecourt, which lies between the house and the mighty rampart wall and broad stairs leading to the formal parterre. The first, low bank of steps gives a gracious transition from the drive up to the raised garden. In startling contrast to the sternness of the high wall, which recalls the stony faces of Florentine hillside gardens, the scene at the top of the steps reveals multicolored topiary figures, the only such exhibit of sculpted plants that Yoch made.

In the early days of the garden, a set of large Italian vases sat on top of the wall and emphasized its height. They also gave a sense of enclosure to the raised parterre; this narrowing of vision made more dramatic the openness of the clear vista to the sea from the upper terrace. Two modern adjustments in the landscape have diminished the power of this wall and suggest how delicately Yoch coordinated all the elements of her gardens. Early photographs show ivy scrambling over the rampart, as though natural growth were assaulting a ducal outpost; later, when the ivy was allowed to completely wash over the wall and steps, the tension was lost. Moreover, the vases have now been moved from their position on top of the wall. With this change, the opening impression of the place is gentler than in the earlier version and the contrast between the severity of the public entrance and the friendliness of the intimate gardens is less extreme.

Yoch planned the architectural features of the upper terrace to frame the splendid views. Her original sketches show five different versions of the Water Gate, as she names it on the planting plan. She experimented with heights and masses in order to arrive at the lofty arched exedra that stands in the company of several upright eucalyptus trees. Her sketches all include a rendering of an off-center tree, an integral part of the design. Both garden architecture and landscape establish a strong vertical foreground to contrast with the lazy roll of the mountains in the distance.

Yoch's sketch for the Exedra, Il Berlino. (Courtesy of Mr. Bob Easton)

Yoch's sketches for the exedra and a vase, Il Brolino. (Courtesy of Mr. Bob Easton)

Similarly, in the opposite direction, the great bowl, the balustrade, the topiary figures, the Italian vases, and the villa itself lead in carefully designated stages to the spacious seascape. The route up the steps thus offers a series of varied perspectives and moods, culminating in a paradise with an inviting bench for viewing and a shaded nook for shelter.

Yoch established the formality of this scene with sculpted Italianate elements, including a broad wall of *Pittosporum tobira,* "cut flat." She regarded pittosporum as "the spaniel of plants" and, in another jotting, as a "faithful workhorse." Escaping the precision of these forms to give the illusion of an aged country retreat, cedars and vines overflow the rule of the balanced hedges, and eucalyptus trees gather into loose groves.

These Montecito terraces summarize on a smaller scale the principal elements of Italian villas. For the viewer sitting on one of the stone benches or looking from within the exedra toward the Pacific, the nearby central basin and fountain bowl serve as historical markers that make the distant sea seem even farther away. The composition also contains explicit quotations from European gardens. Yoch specified on the planting plan, "arch. Vicobello," and the exedra brings to mind the finale of the limonaia at that Sienese villa. In 1925, after visiting the Villa Medici in Rome, Mary Stewart sent her landscape architect an appreciative card: "We are enjoying 'our fountain.' Yours is wonderfully good and does you great credit."

View to the mountains, Il Brolino. Florence Yoch decided on the monumental size of the exedra after building several smaller mock ups and discovering that they looked insignificant against the natural scenery. (Courtesy of Mrs. Robert E. Ward)

Villa Medici fountain, Rome. Mary Stewart's postcard shows the raked gravel, holly oak, and masonry walls that suggest urban reserve in the Renaissance composition. (Courtesy of Mr. Thomas C. Moore)

Fountain and upper terrace, Il Brolino. Yoch's more joyful and open composition turned the walls of the Roman model into hedges and balustrade, scattered trees of several varieties and sizes, and framed the fountain with flowers. Florence Yoch's Album of Gardens. (Courtesy of Mrs. Robert E. Ward)

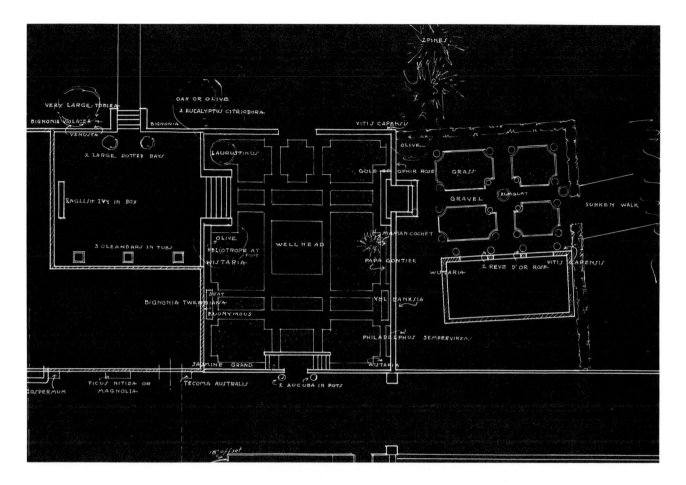

Alongside the house are several other garden rooms, less formal than the entry. From the driveway a gate opens through columns topped with carved baskets of fruit, which announce a relaxed theme for the grassy courtyard adjoining the house. The first view of this lawn, and of the oak-shaded terrace beyond, comes from the small platform just inside the gates. Stairs descend on both sides in a formal arrangement; but rather than promoting a sense of parade, Yoch used them to modulate to personal scale and gentler moods. The treads are narrow and short, their very low side walls curl up into a volute at the bottom of the steps. The walls of a wider set of stairs lazily curve down to the patio in a variation on the theme of leisurely movement.

The complex geometry in this sunken garden is radically different from the simplicity of line in the forecourt and the direct march of the stairway to the upper terrace lookout. A maze of stone walks, changing in width and in direction, invites varied routes of exploration, while a single, ancient wellhead suggests a possible focus to these amblings. Time has worn away the detail on the wellhead, and carved flowers remain on only two faces. In contrast with the antique elegance of the well, an informal group of unmatched pots suggests a humble use for its waters.

Detail of the planting plan (August 1923), Il Brolino. Left to right: the paved terrace (with small stairs and walk leading to the area that later became the Oak Tree Terrace), sunken garden with wellhead, Lemon House, sunken walk descending to the cut flower beds. (Courtesy of Mr. Bob Easton)

Gates designed by Florence Yoch at Il Brolino. Stone baskets replace the original urns. (Photography by Mr. George Waters)

Sunken courtyard, Il Brolino. Yoch penciled onto this picture changes in the stair wall and in the column. She replaced the plain top of the stair wall with a cap and volute in gray cement. Florence Yoch's Album of Gardens. (Courtesy of Mrs. Robert E. Ward) (right)

Antique wellhead, Il Brolino (Photograph by Mr. George Waters) (left)

Simpler enclaves lie on the edges of the property. Beyond the well-head and its lawn is another terrace, where sheltering oaks canopy a balustrade in an arc overlooking the lower woods. An early photograph shows a lone reader, who looks comfortable in this terrace, which Yoch scaled down from the exuberant landscaping of an Italian villa forecourt to fit a more reserved, private world. Farther on in what seems a secret walk, shaded stairs ascend through close hedges to a head of Hermes atop a stone pillar, recalling the statues that marked boundaries in the villas of the ancients and in Renaissance revivals: several herms look out from the hedges of the Villa Medici in Rome.

Borrowing wholeheartedly from Italian gardens, Yoch established at Il Brolino a civilized outpost in the sprawling wilderness. The amplification of choices for enjoying the landscape condensed on a relatively small American estate the range of opportunity available in Europe only to the most leisured aristocrats.

Oak Tree Terrace, Il Brolino. Symmetrical columns and furniture contrast with the off-center tree and unmatched urn and vase. Florence Yoch's Album of Gardens. (Courtesy of Mrs. Robert E. Ward)

The C. W. Gates Residence

Among Florence Yoch's earliest and largest Pasadena commissions, the Gates house was a showplace of flowers each growing season. The scale of the property was large, and thousands of bulbs and plants went in every year to refresh a formal garden of tree roses, a sunken pool garden with herbaceous flowers tumbling over stones, and whole meadows abloom across the front and sides of the property. Mr. John Peirce remembers looking forward to these dazzling shows amidst the then open fields on Arden Road south of the California Institute of Technology.

Front garden, Fair Oaks, C. W. Gates Garden. A walk sweeps out of sight in what seems an endless meadow of flowers. Florence Yoch's Album of Gardens. (Courtesy of Mrs. Robert E. Ward)

Rancho San Carlos

Within the orange and lemon orchards of his Santa Barbara estate, C. H. Jackson, Jr., built a rambling house around a central patio in a Spanish mode. Florence Yoch's photographs and records from this job (1931–33) show that she and the owners concentrated the new landscaping close to the main house. In her plan, the entrance, the patio, and the east garden offer shaded and decorated areas for the pleasures of outdoor life. Perhaps because of the enormous size of the ranch, she went out of her way to focus attention on the immediate scene. This she did primarily by defining the plant spaces. Ornamented pots and plant boxes abound, and more than 1,500 tiles in various figures (leaf, double arch, shell, and single arch) edge the plantings. The elaborate decoration in the garden—which includes Florence Yoch's own endearing pebbled picture of two terriers—matches that of the house, with its coffered columns, elongated dentils, classical door frames, and complex ornamental railings.

This assignment marked one of Florence Yoch's rare concessions to a client's desire for instant effect throughout the entire plan rather than in a few major elements. The importation of large trees and shrubs, including an aged camellia, brought the owners the rewards of an established garden.

In the long, enclosed patio at the center of the house Yoch mixed formal and informal patterns. Three palms suggest harmony, yet each is a different species. Random-sized pots in large and small clusters define three sides of a small pool, and plants overgrow one of its edges. With a prospect onto this pool, a small sitting area nestles safely in a boxwood-edged retreat off the main paths. A large orange tree leans over the parterre hedges to shade the bench. Walks lead sensibly but not always straightforwardly to the doors, the open gallery, and stairs along the patio. The largest and most important set of steps ascends to the bedrooms; it first breaks casually through a low wall, turns, and then rises in a long run beside Italian vases filled with flowers. More sensuously appealing than the stone and grass geometry in the sunken terrace at Il Brolino, all walks in the Jackson patio have the entertaining movement and color of flower or shrub borders.

The A. Parley Johnson House

The simplicity of smaller sites may have appealed to Yoch more readily than the sprawling ranches of her wealthiest clients, for she continually defined intimate spaces in even the grandest schemes. At many of the largest gardens she worked on, she did only individual areas. Smaller gardens, like the one she designed for the Parley Johnsons, required more ingenuity on the part of the designer and more imagination from the

Pool, Rancho San Carlos. Boxwood hedges, pots and clusters of herbs, geraniums, and fortnight lilies imply a line beneath the overstory of olive, orange and palm trees. The garden has just been planted, and wires stabilize the two citrus trees. (Courtesy of Mr. Thomas C. Moore)

View south from house, the A. Parley Johnson Garden. This lightly colored sketch suggests Moorish simplicity, an Arab outpost of strict discipline and economy softened by vines on the walls, bent trees, and balanced but unmatched plantings. The drawing lists the plants, left to right: *crape myrtle tree,* Eucalyptus citriodora, *Italian cypress;* Phoenix reclinata, *scarlet eucalyptus, large round boxwood, hedge of euonymus; existing pepper tree. (Courtesy of Mrs. A. Parley Johnson)*

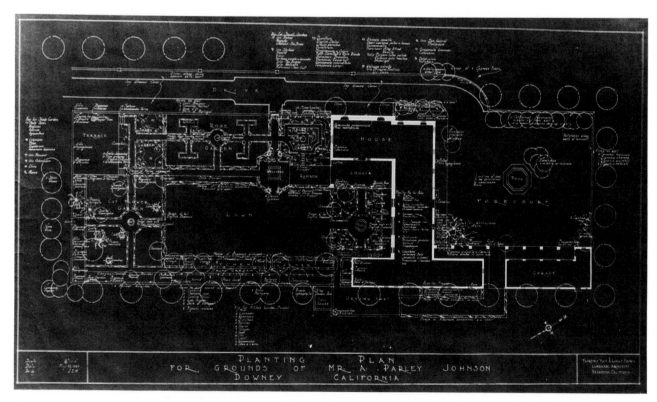

Plan, the A. Parley Johnson Garden. Unexpected turns in the walks, breaks in the line of the drive and the edge of the lawn, eucalyptus and hollyhocks in the forecourt animate the plan. Alongside the open spaces of the long drive, the square forecourt, and the rectangular lawn, the garden has such complex plantings that the smallest area, the Secret Garden, requires a key, given at the top of the plan. (Courtesy of Mrs. A. Parley Johnson)

viewer. This is especially true when the site has little dramatic character. Escaping limitations of size and topography with methods perhaps most familiar in Japanese landscaping practice, Florence Yoch borrowed views, created suggestive networks of paths, and established unpredictable rhythms contrasting closed and open spaces.

In 1925 the Parley Johnsons, working on their house with architect Roland E. Coate, commissioned Florence Yoch and Lucile Council to design a garden on a flat site in Downey. The lot, including the house, was a little less than an acre, set within a seventy-acre orange grove. A pretty drawing of the view from the dining room showed the principal space, which was to become, as Mrs. Johnson specified it, "a Spanish garden with an English accent." Yoch designed a walled garden where occasional cypresses accent parterres of flowers, and a large pepper tree shades a raised terrace. Yoch emboldened the effect of masonry during construction on this job by increasing the height of the garden wall and by simplifying the original drawings of driveway columns. This plan of small rooms for sitting and wandering suited people who had traveled widely and liked the simple, casual gardens they had seen in Europe.

As at a small Tuscan farmhouse, gnarled olive trees edge and shade the drive, which widens to form a passing place, then arrives at the focal point where the wall curves in front of a grove of Italian cypresses. Gently swelling, the drive turns into the forecourt, where manna gum trees break through the pavement, hollyhocks cluster in the drive, and vines clamber over the walls and balconies.

The house opens onto the large rectangular walled garden, which contains five parterres with flowers as well as two fountains, an orchard, and a kitchen garden. Beyond the walls, the main axis of the garden leads to a Mediterranean scene of stone pines and Italian cypresses on the southwest. Cypresses, Yoch later wrote, are "one of the most dramatically beautiful trees on earth," and were useful on this featureless site.

Like the curio cabinets Mrs. Johnson had in the house, Yoch's plan exhibits many gardens of varying size, level, and character. Arranged around the edge of the lawn, the five different parterres of flowers resemble the designs in Moorish gardens with their ingenious variations in the shape and placement of their beds and paths and of their architectural elements. The secret garden is a square with two corners rounded, the walks in the rose garden go to the centers of the beds, and paths in the cut flower garden go around its periphery. Repetitions connect these pictures. The three gates into the main garden are all arched, although each one is different; stucco columns in the arbor lead to wood posts in the ramada.

Major walks and steps link the garden rooms and offer unpredictable views through the spaces. Some paths move directly to a goal and others, teasingly, require a turn in order to progress farther. The entry from the drive into the walled garden leads past the rose parterre and the secret garden to an antique wellhead, from which there is a view over the lawn.

Gate from the drive, the A. Parley Johnson Garden. The elegant ironwork and the proportions of the panels and frames, which are narrow on the sides, wider at top and widest at the bottom, show the care and calculation that went into every detail. (Author's photograph)

The route to the house turns left, beneath the rustic arbor combining jasmine, 'Silver Moon' rose, and clematis, then moves under the full shade of the loggia. From here the visitor enters the patio, centered on a Moorish basin. On the windward side of the patio the path runs among fragrant plants like choisya and lemon verbena, and then continues on to the kitchen garden.

Supporting the complex rhythms of geometrical patterns in the design, Yoch's planting mixes hedges and orchard rows with seemingly random flowering trees and cypresses. Oleanders line the steps from the patio to the lawn; a single large pink crape myrtle by the loggia gives a colorful foreground for views into the garden. Closing the vista at the end of the lawn, a mixed collection of Mediterranean trees suggests a curved alcove behind the cut flower parterre. As a counterpart to the density of pattern and planting in most of the garden, Yoch and Council worked out a simple raised terrace for the existing single large pepper tree; nothing competes with its heroic individualism, emphasized by its location on the far edge of the scene.

In contrast to the diverse patterns around it, the central lawn panel seems serenely simple. Yet even here Yoch introduced irregularity. She carefully measured and noted in red the final shape on the construction plan: 93 feet six inches by 34 feet. The proportion is almost a three to one, but not quite; the inexactness suits the slightly awry and personal proportions throughout the garden and the house.

During construction, Florence Yoch added the wall fountain that concludes the vista from the loggia across the patio. She used a small rill to connect the fountain to the pool. Further increasing the Moorish feeling in this area, she introduced another major change from the single potted vine in an early plan. She planted a large palm on one side and a rambling vine on the other. These create a large foreground frame for the friendly picture of the font and its randomly sized pots.

The rich carpet of these scenes, which give scents, flowers, food, and the recollection of past gardens to the owners, has lasted well. Fifty-five years after it was planted Mrs. Johnson said, "The garden has always been a pleasure." The structure has proved so satisfactory that she found no need to change it; gardening, as she observed, "was just a matter of putting the right things in it."

The Douglas Smith Estate

For Douglas Smith's large lot on a slope high in Altadena, Florence Yoch created in 1925 a garden notable for its variations on classical forms. Instead of displaying the intricate texture of the flat Johnson garden, here the design has a formal simplicity to contrast with the opulent view of the San Gabriel Mountains. The straightforward structure of walks and avenues is softened by ivy-covered columns lining the walks, by grass-

View from loggia across the patio, the A. Parley Johnson Garden. (Courtesy of Mrs. A. Parley Johnson)

filled borders of stones, by loosely branching fruit trees, and by gaily colored herbaceous borders.

Tile fountain, the Douglas Smith Garden. (Courtesy of Mr. Thomas C. Moore)

Rather than merely imitating European gardens for Douglas Smith, Yoch drew on their conventions to create simpler designs in modest scale; this original approach intensifies the dramatic contrasts. The spring walk, a flowered border in the fashionable English style, runs along the boundary wall of the property. Yet, in the manner of Italian peasant enclosures, poles raised above the wall open the space up by offering framed views of the San Gabriel Mountains. The walk concludes with a tile-backed fountain, where a lead dolphin spouts water into a scallop shell basin. Just beyond this refined, eclectic composition is the much more relaxed lookout, small and vine-covered. Within this place on the edge of the garden, formal and informal elements mix. The symmetry of the matched Italian vases and boxes of ferns at the entrance contrasts with the irregularity of the crooked tree to the left and the climbing rose to the right. Broad steps give an elegant stone base to the rustic, arbored retreat.

Similar contrasts animate the center of the garden. An oversized pool interrupts a flower parterre. Beyond the pool, symmetrical columns offer one conclusion to the view at ground level. Above them loose groves of trees suggest a more whimsical alternative. A large palm by the pool seems a surprising ingredient in the orderly beds; the large fronds make the views into the further reaches of the garden seem farther away. A curved seat surrounding the palm brings its grandeur into human scale

Pool and parterre, the Douglas Smith Garden. (Courtesy of Mr. Thomas C. Moore)

and offers a place for contemplation. The unusual proportioning of enormous trees to small beds and the unmatched sides of the walks show Yoch's willingness to take chances with design formulas. Never capricious, these playful inventions always serve basic human desires for shade, water, and spaciousness.

Lookout, the Douglas Smith Garden. (Courtesy of Mr. Thomas C. Moore)

The Mrs. Richard Fudger Garden

Among Yoch's most successful and acclaimed works, the small garden (16,000 square feet) in 1926 for Mrs. Richard B. Fudger in the Los Angeles enclave of Hancock Park has the variety of a country hacienda within a cramped urban setting. The American Institute of Architects gave the design its 1930 Honor Award for "skill and interest of design in a peculiarly shaped lot." Yoch chose it to illustrate the publication of her talk "Fitting the Land for Human Use," which she gave at a meeting of the Southern California chapter of the American Institute of Architects in 1930.

Simplicity and informality give this garden a natural poise in its eight outdoor rooms, which include an enclosed patio, a terrace with a view over a shaded lawn, a rose garden, a raised garden, and a pergola. The subtle abbreviation of these traditional garden forms matches the combination of imported Spanish motifs that Roland Coate employed in

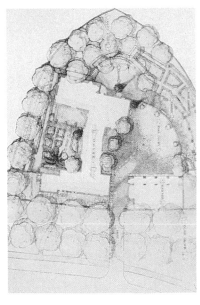

Plan, the Mrs. Richard Fudger Garden. (California Arts and Architecture 38 [July 1930], p. 19.)

creating the gentle curves of walls and stairways in the house, which succeeds admirably in reconciling colonial Monterey with original Spanish architectural styles. Drawing on Iberian conventions, Yoch's garden plan uses bold walls, hidden courts, and stucco steps that carefully respond to the varied levels of the house. On the dining side, the enclosed patio offers a generally rectangular parterre and fountain; the motor court ends in a curved pergola; and in the third main section, the back garden, a serpentine path winds through a complex parterre and a mock forest.

Asymmetry and curves in the landscaping suggest country ease. The double bands of trees, which give privacy across the front of the house, are bowed slightly in a subtle response to the opposite bend in the street. Several trees lean into the entry garden, freed from the rigid constraints of a formal plan. The patio fountain sits off-center in an irregular shape. The parterre behind the house has unmatched sections. The stairway to the upper garden on the south does not lead directly to the walk into the parterre, as the broad path past the patio garden does not lead precisely to the gate in the front wall. Groupings of unmatched pots on top of the walls, around the fountain, and along the balcony further emphasize the informality of these arrangements. These seeming imperfections in balance correspond with the many curves of a house where the entire center section of the architecture bends.

These disruptions of symmetry often have the additional function of expanding the feeling of distance. Like the noble palm that dominates the small fountain in the Moorish garden of the Johnson house, a large palm bends forward boldly into the view from the loggia to the south garden; beyond it a smaller tree looks even farther away. From the large, lazy bend of the pergola, the tighter and smaller half circle of the west terrace seems more remote.

The garden has varied walks of hand-laid stone and decomposed granite that travel through lawn, flowers, stone courts, and woods. In contrast to these invitations to exploration and to mystery, other places in the garden establish charming resting spots, where the lines of pots, finesse of detail, and variety of plants entertain the eye and obscure the lack of space.

Legend has it that while this garden was under way, a red sports car sped down the short drive and crashed into the heavy wooden gates that closed the entry courtyard of the house from the street. The driver leaped out, rushed to the door, and demanded to buy the house "at any price." After agreeing to sell the house (for $65,000), the Fudgers had Roland Coate design a house in the French country style and built it in Beverly Hills. Florence Yoch designed the new garden, which was calmer in plan, to suit the mood of the client after her surprising encounter with Howard Hughes.

Entry, the Mrs. Richard B. Fudger Garden. One of Florence Yoch's favorite pictures. (Courtesy of Mr. Thomas C. Moore)

The Ira Bryner/Albert Doerr Garden

In 1929, Florence Yoch and Lucile Council prepared a garden for Mr. Ira
L. Bryner on a sloping lot with a view to the hills above the arroyo in
Pasadena. The drive divides the space in two: an upper level with the
house and its terraces perched obliquely to catch the view, and a lower
area where paths entwine through green and flowered garden rooms. This
landscape, in a suburban lot of less than two-fifths of an acre, combines
the sweeping drive, arbor, parterre, and citrus grove of an Italian villa
with an English manor's rose garden, orchard, lawn, and summerhouse.

For the steep hillside site, Yoch greatly increased the variety of walks
from her narrower repertoire at Il Brolino. As she noted, the root of
"meaningful, useful" designs is in "traffic carrying the bonework." In the
theater of the Bryner garden, movement finds many different rhythms.
The entry drive curves dramatically up past the foundations of the villa to
a small parking area. A flat, lazily bent walk in the lower garden recalls on
a smaller scale this opening theme. Axial paths rise from the terrace south
of the house up to the rose arbor, from the terrace up into the orchard, and
from the English lawn up to the summerhouse. Eleven flights of stairs
accelerate progress through the garden in steps that are straight or bent,
narrow or wide, single or double. Like the delicate calibrations of level in
the paths of the water parterre at the Villa Gamberaia in Florence, which

Entry drive along the orange grove,
the Ira Bryner/Albert Doerr Garden.
(Photograph by Mr. George Waters)

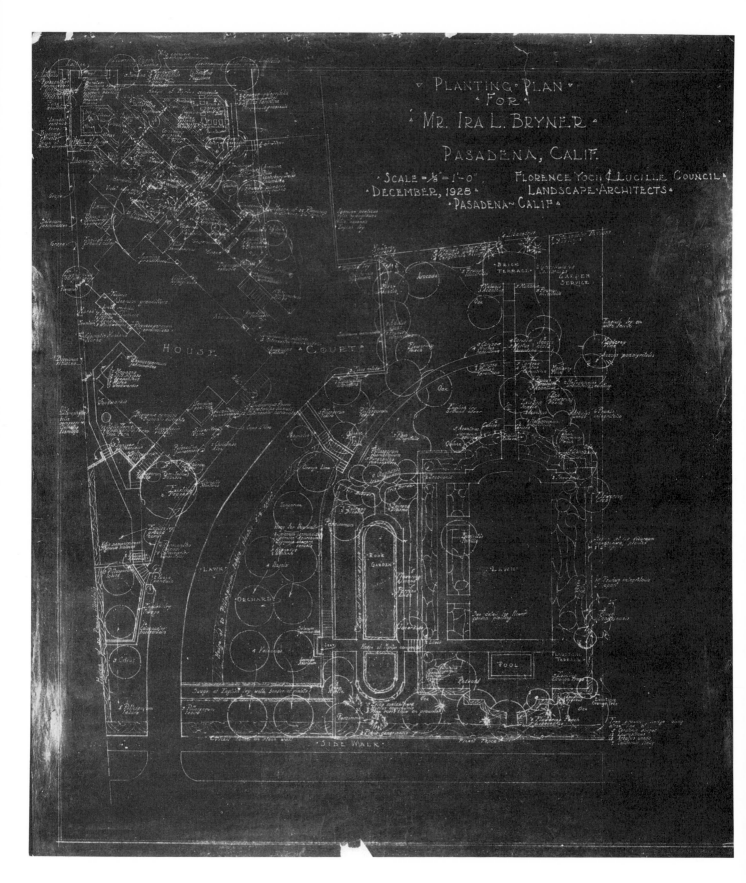

Covered terrace, the Ira Bryner/Albert Doerr Garden. (Photograph by Mr. George Waters)

Planting plan, the Ira Bryner/Albert Doerr Garden. (Courtesy of Mrs. Harriet Doerr)

Open terrace, kumquat tree and pipe arbor, the Ira Bryner/Albert Doerr Garden. (Photograph by Mr. George Waters)

Florence Yoch admired, sets of two or three steps announce transitions from one area to the next and dramatize the sense of new perspectives in the scene. Yoch lovingly detailed and individualized these steps. For one pair she drew back the corner of the adjoining bed. The treads and risers of another set of steps were roughened by twigs and rags set in the molds. These many steps and paths conclude in sitting places and garden rooms: a wisteria-covered wooden arbor that shades the south façade of the house, a small rose arbor, a shaded court garden off the study, a summerhouse, a rose garden, and a quiet pool.

Stairway angling to the lower garden, the Ira Bryner/Albert Doerr Garden. (Author's photograph)

Yoch used perspective devices to make this garden seem larger than it is in fact. The long terrace behind the house is widest at its center: one end draws in to a stair down to the drive, the other end narrows to pass a boxed kumquat tree and then narrows farther to a small arbor, which frames a smaller sculpture in a sequence of diminishing forms.

Yoch adapted conventional garden designs to this particular site by allowing natural features to intrude into the regular patterns. An old stump blocks an orchard walk and justifies a turn. The Roman circus of the rose garden breaks unexpectedly for a cross walk, which moves on to similarly disrupt the formal pattern of the lawn. The Lutyens-esque green panel, surveyed by the hillside summerhouse and neatly edged in white azaleas, invited a central canal or basin. Instead, the expected pool is wedged against the walk at the far end, and the lawn is dichondra, a plant not used as lawn in England. A squirrel planted the acorn for what became a large tree alongside the pool, and his contribution is consistent with the eccentricity in this part of the garden. Besides these variations within classic figures, the orchard and the citrus grove form irregular shapes to fit the local geography. Similarly, the hillside groves display the original wildness of the place in easy harmony with the gently curving walk and the simple pavilion.

White azaleas line the lawn leading to the summerhouse, the Ira Bryner/ Albert Doerr Garden. (Photograph by Mr. George Waters)

In the efficient system of this plan, each area is responsible for multiple functions. At the end of a route up steps and past the large kumquat tree, the rose arbor beckons with flowers and friendly shade, and increases the vision of distance in the compact space. The orchard produces fruit and gives a block of foliage in sensible order to the oddly shaped area between the terrace and the garage. The citrus grove recalls the old traditions of Pasadena, and its useful tile runnel revives Moorish practice.

In 1941, Albert and Harriet Doerr bought the Bryner house and commissioned Yoch and Council to help simplify garden maintenance in keeping with wartime reductions in staff. With the revisions, including the suggestion to pave an area previously devoted to tulips, came a nineteen-page set of instructions, "Garden Directions, October 16, 1941." The education of her clients was an important part of Yoch's practice. Mrs. Doerr remembered that Florence Yoch wanted those who owned her gardens to learn and use the best horticultural methods.[1]

The Mrs. Irving Sturgis Garden

In 1926, Yoch and Council began a garden for Mrs. Irving J. Sturgis on a small corner lot in Pasadena. Their work continued over the next eight years. The plan unified a series of elements from varied landscaping traditions in a setting about one third the size of the Johnsons' walled garden acre. Against the simple mass of the Sturgises' front lawn, whose right-angled walk contrasted with the elegant curve of the hedge and the loose overstory of trees, Yoch played the different themes of the rear garden's five rooms: a lawn, a Spanish patio with fountain, English borders, a parterre and pool, and a cutting garden. Yoch's deft handling of these spaces, which she linked with an intriguing pattern of walks, combines the imaginative complexity of an English wilderness with the discipline of a French parterre.

More important here than in the larger gardens for the Johnsons, the Fudgers, and the Bryners, Yoch's tricks in geometry—large elements in the foreground, smaller ones in the distance—increase the feeling of space. From the house, for example, the lawn is the largest element; beyond it the first flower border is broad, the next thin. Old orange trees in a seemingly relaxed arrangement support the precise channeling of

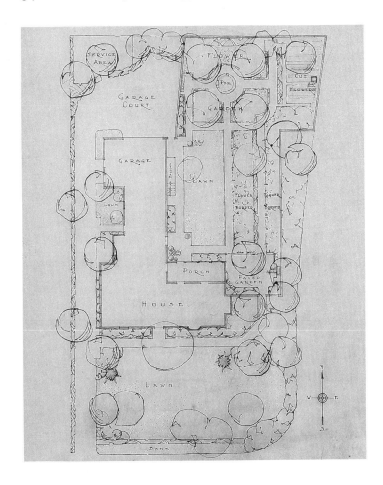

*Plan, the Mrs. Irving Sturgis Garden.
(Courtesy of Mr. Thomas C. Moore)*

vision, which culminates in the palm-framed view to the mountains. One gnarled orange tree divides the lawn into a large foreground section and a smaller background area; oranges similarly divide the flower borders and the cut flower garden. A tightly planted band of trees between the wall and the property line suggests enclosing woods where there is in fact a busy corner.

The notably lush display of flowers in a central position created the dominant effect of this garden, which was a pretty place, much photographed and published in its day. Besides the abundance of flowers, which give a sensual balance to the intellectual richness of this design, garden furnishings add a decorative dimension, particularly at the pool. A reproduction of Verrocchio's small angel stands in the center of the little pool, and asymmetrical rushes keep him company. Varied collections of ornaments edge the pool: glazed pots, old tile pots, a watering can, an old rocking chair, and even a set of three small ceramic elephants. The feeling of intimacy so integral to this garden suggests an especially close relationship with the client and an easy familiarity with the demands of so small a site.

Orange tree and parterre, the Mrs. Irving Sturgis Garden. (Courtesy of the Henry E. Huntington Library)

The Florence Banning Garden

Yoch's plans and drawings in 1948 for the garden of her friend Florence Banning reveal the arduous process of thought and study required in creating a landscape just right for the place and for a client resolved to be economical. Working on the Bannings' half-acre Pasadena lot, Yoch made many changes on site to produce a more relaxed landscape than the kind with specific European associations that had been central to her practice in the 1920s and 1930s. Her new landscape style suited the decline in availability of skilled workmen and much tighter budgets. It also fit the American self-confidence of the postwar era, in which Europeans had less influence as arbiters of taste.

In this job Yoch did not use a skilled foreman and large crew to handle the installation. The plans therefore carry the kinds of informal directions that Yoch previously gave in person on the site. The illusion of ease in the garden required many calculations. The first draft of the plan put formal beds on the northeast slope of the garden, lawns on the lower level. The next stage articulated the walks and spaces more carefully: the curve that enclosed the top of the garden, the small court under the two oaks, and the walk along the woods on the southeastern edge of the site.

Then, showing that eccentricities in the plan were the result of careful deliberations after the basic design was in place, Yoch penciled in adjustments to provide variation in pattern. She extended a flower border right over a path to block the vista up the steps from the lawn, thus making access to the upper garden more mysterious than the simple beeline of the early axial walk through the center. Many changes concern

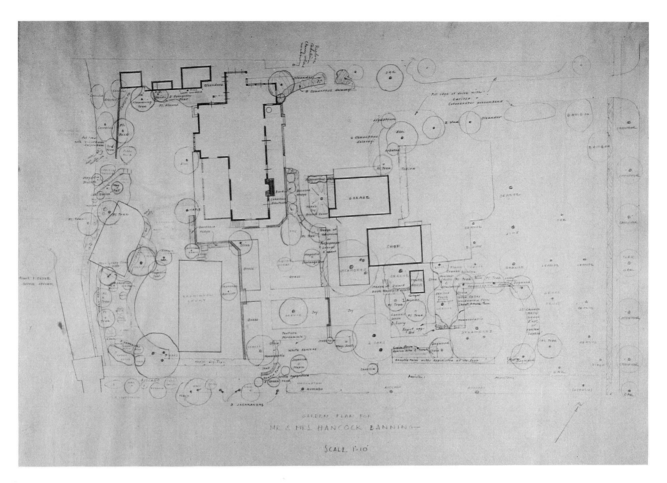

Revised plan, the Florence Banning Garden. Lawn becomes a major feature. (Courtesy of Mrs. Florence Banning)

the width of the passageways, which on the first plan were uniformly 6 feet wide. These ranged eventually from broad foreground walks of 6 feet 4 inches near the house to smaller paths 4 and even 3 feet wide in locations farther away.

The clear architectural lines and the emphatic, dignified entrances near the house convey an air of serenity. Higher than the lawn, the processional walks and spacious terrace suggest a lofty overview, like that available from the raised walks of an Elizabethan garden. Below this platform, the open lawn washes in a lazy roll along the side terraces and across the entire length of the back façade of the house.

The Moorish scenes, English borders, and formal European sources of earlier gardens are less important here. The practical, simple moments of her earlier work and of the peasant gardens she admired emerge more obviously as signs of an important shift in Yoch's thinking about what was essential. Always attempting to economize in gardens and get the most for the least money, she here settled on a terrace close to the house with a clear view over the lawn, a badminton court, herbaceous beds, and a cut flower garden. A very few elements furnish the garden. Yoch designed a curved teak bench for the shaded barbecue terrace, from which, as on an English estate, there was a good view back to the house.

The density of plantings in her earlier gardens rarely permitted this opportunity for admiring the house from a distance.

Yoch placed a second bench at the end of the main walk connecting the house with the southern edge of the property. In the original plan, this bench was also curved and thus softened the corner of the path. As the plans progressed, the space at this corner expanded (as it did even more so in construction), for the walk widened to form a small Mediterranean court beneath an aged olive tree, which protected the very simple country seat. This rustic scene establishes an alternative pole to the refinement of the curved teak bench. Yoch's earlier gardens were filled with a richly sensual array of plants and with intellectually subtle geometries. In this efficient garden the range of moods is contained between two comfortable sitting areas.

Details of Gardens

Perhaps because of her natural inclination to restraint and to abstraction, Florence Yoch was notably successful even during the 1920s in designing compact, low-maintenance gardens for forward-thinking Californians who wanted charming outdoor rooms. Her creation of landscapes requir-

Corner with simple bench, the Florence Banning Garden. (Author's photograph)

Bench at the Florence Banning Garden. (Photograph by Mr. George Waters)

ing minimum space and care became the model for later gardening developments, which spread from California to the rest of America in the 1930s and 1940s as space became precious and skilled labor rare.

The challenge of narrowly bound spaces must have appealed to her, for she chose many commissions for them even at the height of her career. Most of the published pictures of her work, especially in Winifred Dobyns's *California Gardens,* are of intimate areas. Within walled and hedged retreats, pleasing displays of flowers were possible with easily maintained vines, shrubs, and potted plants. The scale was humane and unassertive, the effect concentrated colorful, and subtle.

The Misses Elizabeth and Hallie Davenport   Early in her career, Florence Yoch designed a courtyard garden for the Misses Davenport (1922). It illustrates her basic principles: complex walks to create unexpected routes through the garden and leading beyond it; an architectural element as focus but not neatly centered; a formal parterre with sections that only seem to match; and mixed plantings that include diverse flowers in the parterre, a flowering peach tree, occasional vines, and scattered pots.

The success of this garden earned Yoch considerable recognition. In 1927, Rex Newcomb included two pictures of it in his book, *The Spanish House for America,* and credited Yoch with the design; she is the only landscape architect he listed in the book's two hundred illustrations. *California Arts and Architecture* (October 1931) published a later pic-

Patio, the Misses Davenport Garden. (Courtesy of Mr. Thomas C. Moore)

ture of the garden in fuller growth. Yoch typed a proud message on the back of her photograph: the garden "illustrates what may be accomplished on a narrow city lot. The house and garden are on a lot only 60' wide."

Mrs. Frank W. Emery/Mrs. Ruth von Platen   In the late 1920s, Yoch and Council worked as consultants with architect Myron Hunt on the entrance court and pool terrace for the Emery house in San Marino. The rose-swagged, curving balustrade of the forecourt welcomes guests to the house and establishes a boundary from which to view the spacious lawns. The task here was to control the space rather than to expand it.

Along the side axis from the main house is a sunken pool garden, resonant with associations from the designs Lutyens used for Tudor manses. Greatly reducing the scale and using an alcove of native oaks to conclude the scene, Yoch produced a peaceful native bower, an escape from the California sun rather than a direct copy of the broad stonework, bare center, and busy topiary of English models. The stair that divides and then descends in narrow flights to the stone edge of the pool, the simple urn beneath the oaks that conclude the vista, and the low herbaceous borders create an intimate room for outdoor meditation. The retreat provides an important alternative to the richness of the rose garden, the vastness of the oak-forested hillside, and the sprawl of the lawns elsewhere on the estate.

Forecourt, the Mrs. Frank Emery/Mrs. Ruth von Platen Garden. (Author's photograph)

Mr. and Mrs. Preston Hotchkis To suit Roland Coate's informal architecture and Mrs. Hotchkis's pleasant recollection of her childhood in the country setting of Rancho Los Alamitos, Yoch created in 1929 a rustic feeling in this San Marino garden. Within the regular hedges of the parterre are diverse flowers in a colorful mix that Mrs. Hotchkis constantly changed. Crape myrtles in balanced but unmatched places mark the opposite ends of the entry garden, and a splendid crab apple tree partially screens the view to the road and gives a dramatic show in the spring. A single oak, seemingly a volunteer, closes one end of the space. This simple, comfortable arrangement illustrates Yoch's description of a successful garden—one "in which every plant is significant and happily used."

Mr. Sherman Asche In 1937 Florence Yoch and Lucile Council designed two contrasting areas in a Pasadena garden. In front, a broad path extends the view across the façade of the house. On a small scale and with the simplest of materials—a broad band of ivy, a center of decomposed granite, a concluding apse of oaks—the serene design suggests a classical amphitheater and also gives convenient access to the side porch.

Colorfully contrasting with the cool shade of this reserved composition on the north side, the sunny south garden suggests an Italian terraced hillside with two stairways, one ascending through an allée of apricot trees, the other through flowers. The geometry of the plan's rectangular beds disappears beneath the abundance of English herbaceous plants, including roses and gelsemium, which cascade over the stone walls and along the edges of the walks.

Mr. Emerson Spear/Mr. and Mrs. Herbert Van de Kamp In 1937–38 Yoch and Council created a garden that resembled their design for the Council house in which they lived for so many years in South Pasadena. Yoch set a herbaceous border on the west side of a long lawn stretching between the oak-shaded atrium of the house and a wisteria-covered arbor in a seeming woods. On the east is a cluster of trees, which shade a camellia walk. Within these informal frames, the elegant arbor against a forest backdrop seems like a temple in a grove as well as a good spot for barbecues.

The relaxation of classical forms is the theme throughout this garden. At the street, an arched gate, covered in vines, announces the cottage charm of the place and welcomes visitors into an entry parterre. Walkways offer a rich variety of choices: to the front door, to the lawn, to the woods, to the studio. The simplicity of the gate contrasts with the subtlety and complexity beyond it; the structure and its vines connect the opening of the garden with the wooden arbor that closes the main scene.

The newly planted entry garden, the Mr. and Mrs. Preston Hotchkis Garden. (Courtesy of Mr. Thomas C. Moore)

Stair amidst flowered banks, the Sherman Asche Garden. (Author's photograph)

Arched gate, the Emerson Spear/ Herbert Van de Kamp Garden. (Author's photograph)

Mr. Edward R. Valentine Among Yoch's most inspired undertakings was the arbor of pleached gingko trees, designed to form diamonds, golden yellow in the fall, over the smaller diamonds in the paving of the walk in this 1946 San Marino garden. White azaleas give a lush edge of foliage to the parade. Her invention adapted plants from Oriental habitats to a traditional Italian architectural scheme and took practical advantage of the slow-growing and easy-to-maintain gingko.

For her widely traveled clients, Yoch drew on European landscape designs to give her gardens the serenity and comfort of well-remembered places. A sense of absolute rightness makes even her most subtle compositions accessible so that a visitor readily feels at home. The first visit to one of her gardens gives the pleasure of recognizing in a new place familiar patterns, yet never in totally expected arrangements. She wrote an inspiring paragraph that attributed this satisfaction to the conquistadors, who, when they arrived in California, "believed that Heaven had sent them to take possession of a new land that they understood at first sight."[2]

Diamonded arbor with gingko trees and white azaleas, the Edward R. Valentine Garden. (Photograph by Mr. William Aplin)

III

Gardens for Movie Moguls:
The Roman Style

Florence Yoch's practice included substantial commissions for clients in West Los Angeles during the 1920s, and her work greatly expanded there during the 1930s. Among her more important jobs were the Bishop estate for a family at the top of traditional Los Angeles society and the villas of great movie producers and directors, among them Dorothy Arzner, David O. Selznick, George Cukor, and Jack Warner.

The demands of the movie moguls differed radically from those of Yoch's Pasadena clients. Rather than preferring understatement and a natural look, Hollywood called for stunning scenery. An immediate dramatic impact on arrival mattered more than the pleasing surprises of a thoughtful walk. Accordingly, Yoch made her gardens more obviously theatrical, spacious, and expensive. Grand perspectives replaced subtle pictorial effects, and unlike the rustic ornaments that decorated her Pasadena gardens, here valuable statues, baroque columns, and figured urns were prominently displayed.

The West Los Angeles commissions allowed Yoch to make lavish gestures in space and architecture. For these new people, building on raw, treeless sites, she provided monumental

Stair from the pool, the Jack Warner Garden. (Courtesy of Mr. Thomas C. Moore)

plantings that immediately gave them visible credentials. Contemporary writers on the new Los Angeles places emphasized landscape connections to the antique world. In *Designs for Outdoor Living*, Margaret Goldsmith noted that the Cukor estate suggested "in spirit and classic refinement of detail a Greco-Roman country home . . . freely interpreted in the modern American spirit." The outdoor life of the Romans and the forms they developed for it were models that Californians might find suitably presented in this villa, Goldsmith observed. "Cicero had his bathing pools out-of-doors. The younger Pliny had his pergola and tennis court. The Romans were the first people to make the transition between house and garden in the form of terraces. They had sanded walks up to their favorite lookouts, summer-houses and dining pavilions, many fountains and pools around which to plant water-loving flowers."[1]

Yoch accomplished the change to more ostentatious classical forms without sacrificing the moments of intimacy and personal scale that controlled her more eclectic style elsewhere. She softened Roman motifs with ramps, curving walks, pebble work under arbors, and stairs turning to descend along the face of a terrace wall. To these familiar features, Yoch added more explicitly theatrical ones suiting the film industry's dreams of life in a grand mansion. At George Cukor's, large statues accompany the guest up a ramped walk to the lookout; at the Warners', a curved, divided stair dramatically concludes the pool terrace; a villa portal, seeming to invite Renaissance processions, opens into the Bishop estate.

Yoch and Council's initial approach to their West Los Angeles clients, too, was theatrical. The colored mounted presentation drawings for most of these gardens differ significantly from the simple blueprints that sufficed in Pasadena. The 1939 plan for the estate of Henry F. Haldeman shows a parterre, a long allée, an English lawn (which offered views of the Los Angeles Country Club and made it seem part of the garden), and a tropical woods. Palms planted in pairs, clumps, and groves unified the project as well as giving a range of sultry and stately effects.

Il Vescovo

In 1927, Yoch worked with the architect Gordon Kaufmann on a magnificently scaled project, Il Vescovo, for W. T. Bishop. Seen from the neighboring hillsides, the estate strikes a monumental posture. A grand villa gate welcomes visitors at the bottom of the long drive, mighty walls support a terrace that seems suspended over the view, and the mansion sprawls in isolated splendor along the slope of its hill. To achieve the effect of a princely retreat, Yoch moved in a forest of trees, including forty oaks and eighty-seven Italian cypresses.

House and garden bring stately elements into personal scale in

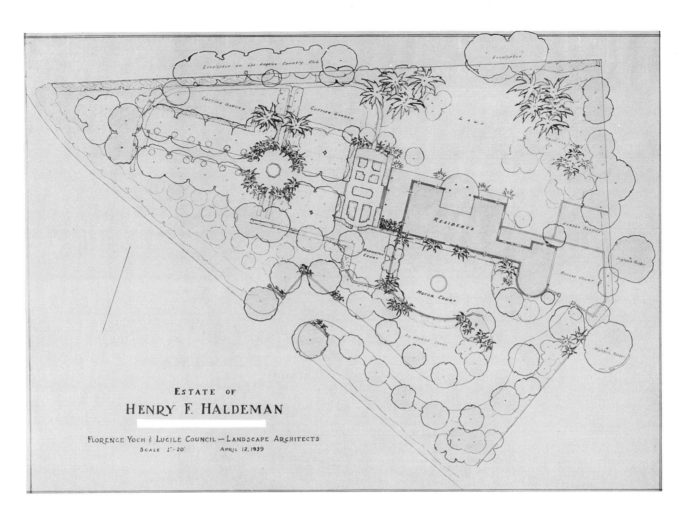

ESTATE OF

HENRY F. HALDEMAN

FLORENCE YOCH & LUCILE COUNCIL — LANDSCAPE ARCHITECTS
SCALE 1"-20'   APRIL 12, 1939

*Plan, the Henry F. Haldeman Garden.
(Courtesy of Mr. Thomas C. Moore)*

*Garden façade for Il Vescovo.
(Courtesy of the Henry E.
Huntington Library)*

Viewing terrace, overlooking the city of Los Angeles, Il Vescovo. (Courtesy of the Henry E. Huntington Library)

Entry, Il Vescovo. Vines in trellis pattern cover drive wall and new trees frame the upper gate leading from the forecourt to the house. (Courtesy of the Henry E. Huntington Library)

asymmetrical arrangements. A tympanum surmounts in classical style the central block of the house, but the façade below has only one large window, deliberately off-center. The garden gate, which seems so grand from a distance, is much smaller close-up and sits within boundary walls that do not match in height. The entrance court is an ellipse, as in an Italian villa, but the stucco borders are very low and suit the surprisingly narrow, enclosed stair that leads to the main door.

The landscaping supports this architecture of contrasting proportions. Yoch planted trees to form balanced but unmatched groups along the hillside. She also transposed villa motifs into human scale by creating intimate scenes. A stairway descends into a shaded patio by the house; a parterre opens at a corner for a welcoming bench, where three different walks come together. In her photographs of so vast and expensive a project, Winifred Dobyns in *California Gardens* focused on this side angle to summarize the achievement in the landscaping. Here Yoch created a tranquil picture that also suggests a range of choices: resting in a sunny nook, climbing stairs, parading down the broad walk, taking the narrow side path, or enjoying the spacious view.

In contrast to the protected, comfortable enclosure of the patio and other secluded nooks, the parterre offers a splendid view of the lower-lying properties. This design, which draws the lavish natural scenery into the garden, closely resembles the Villa Rufolo's flowered terrace at Ravello. Florence Yoch knew this garden well, and she ranked it among the best in Italy. In her interpretation of it for the Bishops, she aimed for a more unified effect by replacing the distracting carpet-bedding of the Italian terrace with a boxwood parterre centered on a fountain. The forthright basin and its green garden establish a serene foreground for the vast panorama, as the Villa Medici bowl and a complex topiary garden had done for the Santa Barbara seascape at Il Brolino a few years earlier. The greater simplicity of Yoch's later work has the aesthetic advantage of a stronger, more immediate effect.

Throughout the Bishop garden, Yoch worked out solutions that avoided pretentiousness yet kept to the grand spirit of the project. She used low, friendly walls along the drive and walks, uncentered gates and unmatched trees, and charmingly unpredictable routes along flowered paths. After this late 1920s garden, her work for leading Hollywood figures showed further refinements in her style, combining the wit of her Pasadena mode with the swagger appealing to Hollywood.

The Dorothy Arzner Garden

A highly inventive director, Dorothy Arzner was working with Katharine Hepburn, Colin Clive, and Billie Burke on *Christopher Strong*, the tale of a daring aviatrix who challenged convention, when her garden was

Terrace corner, Il Vescovo. (Courtesy of the Henry E. Huntington Library)

Terrace, Villa Rufolo, Ravello. (Author's photograph)

finished in 1933. Suiting Arzner's own expressive and independent role as the rare woman in a masculine field, her site was a rocky acropolis high in the Hollywood hills.

Any garden here would be difficult. Yoch developed a radical plan for the steeply sloping hillside that required vast excavations and walls, costing five times those at the Bishop estate, to create a series of terraces. Connected by more than seventy steps, these levels display herbaceous borders amid vine-clad walls, a corner for sunning and another for reading in the shade, a secret gate, and a small arbor for enjoying the breathtaking views. At the very top of the garden stands a rustic pergola, made of simple Doric columns supporting rough wooden beams. It looks like the remains of some primitive shrine.

This garden celebrates extremes by mixing the savage and the comfortable. On what seems a dangerous roost, a pergola stands. Vines and trees break into the straight walks and geometrical shapes of the beds. Yoch moved and brought up many large trees: an orange in a six-foot-six-inch-square box, three oaks in five- and six-foot-square boxes, a cypress, three Monterey pines, a guava, a kumquat, a carob, and an English laurel. These mature trees with gnarled trunks give shade and fruit as well as make the garden seem to be in the midst of an ancient grove.

A 1932 construction photo of the Dorothy Arzner site with garden wall heights mocked up with wood. (Courtesy of Mr. Thomas C. Moore)

Achieving the right balance in this garden was a painstaking task. The many steps required delicate calibrations to fit them in, and each flight has a different width. Jobs were done and then redone. Walks were relaid, timbers restained, areas expanded, and steps added. The skilled work of training vines and espaliering trees cost more than moving the trees from the street up onto the property.

The unaffected architecture of the garden includes a random-sized flagstone terrace, stucco steps, decomposed granite walks, and a pierced wall made of roof tiles in the manner used by peasants throughout the Mediterranean world. Within the severity of Yoch's stripped down, ruthlessly economical design, small statues, like household gods or models of the spirits of the place, add surprisingly witty and sentimental notes. These figures are so important to the garden that Florence Yoch even loaned Arzner a sarcophagus and mask for a fountain. Yoch's special understanding with this client enabled her to express new dimensions of daring primitivism with the same vocabulary of elements that she had used earlier to create the more sedate and intellectual garden for the Parley Johnsons. Her success with the Arzner project led to other commissions from major directors and producers in the film industry, where a more sybaritic style prevailed.

View of Los Angeles from the Dorothy Arzner Garden. The small figure offering a tray adds a friendly and gracious note in the foreground of the vast scene. (Courtesy of Mr. Thomas C. Moore)

Stair, atumble with vines and flowers leading to the pergola, the Dorothy Arzner Garden. (Courtesy of Mr. Thomas C. Moore)

The David Selznick Garden

Florence Yoch's project in 1934 for Mr. and Mrs. David O. Selznick had tentative beginnings. Irene Selznick originally walked through the site specifying design elements to Yoch and Council. When they told her that "we don't know how to do what you want" and that they preferred to work with the landscape vocabulary they had found successful, they presumed they would not get the commission. After the Selznick contractor called to ask them about the placing of some trees, however, they got in touch with Mrs. Selznick, who summoned them back with the observation that since she kept finding their gardens were the ones she liked best, she wanted them to get right to work.

The house was already under construction, leaving little time to prepare plans, so Yoch sketched trees directly on photographs to determine their locations. These charcoal drawings show how theatrical her ideas were for landscaping the house. Trees form a graceful proscenium arch across the front façade, leaving the center open for the view. Except for the big trees in this composition, Yoch made no concessions to the desire for immediate effect. As she later wrote, "The man in a hurry is not a good gardener." Irene Selznick observed that "Miss Yoch didn't stint there [on topsoil] or on any of the sensible priorities. Money was sunk where it didn't show, so we had a grand new house, a splendid tennis court, a few nice trees, and many tiny plants. Miss Yoch said we were to practice patience and let them grow—a big order in that overnight town."[2]

Comfortable family life is the theme of the Selznick garden, and Yoch and Council recognized that this required a major shift in their style. As in earlier jobs, the landscaping brought textural interest and romantic suggestion to the house. Vines on large trellises stretching from the ground to the eaves soften the rectangular forms; leaning old trees suggest venerable age. But many familiar elements become less important. A parterre is incidental and occupies a small place to the side of the house. Instead, in what must have seemed a novel arrangement, the principal feature is the open, uncluttered lawn, which occupies almost a quarter of the lot and is readily accessible from the south façade of the house for viewing and for play. On one edge a walk lazily bends along a border of multi-trunked crape myrtles, underplanted with alyssum and iris. Along the side of the property lie the accoutrements of suburban life at its best: a tennis court, a playhouse, and a tree-enclosed playground.

This garden marks a shift of emphasis in Yoch's practice. In front of the house, the unusually large motor court has a formal shape, but the rest of the garden is deliberately ahistorical. There is no statuary. Stages for cars and games dominate this unabashedly American plan. In this commission for the first time Florence Yoch acknowledged the needs of

Entry, the David Selznick Garden. (Courtesy of Mr. Thomas C. Moore)

Florence Yoch's sketch of trees on her snapshot of the front façade, the David Selznick Garden. (Courtesy of Mr. Thomas C. Moore)

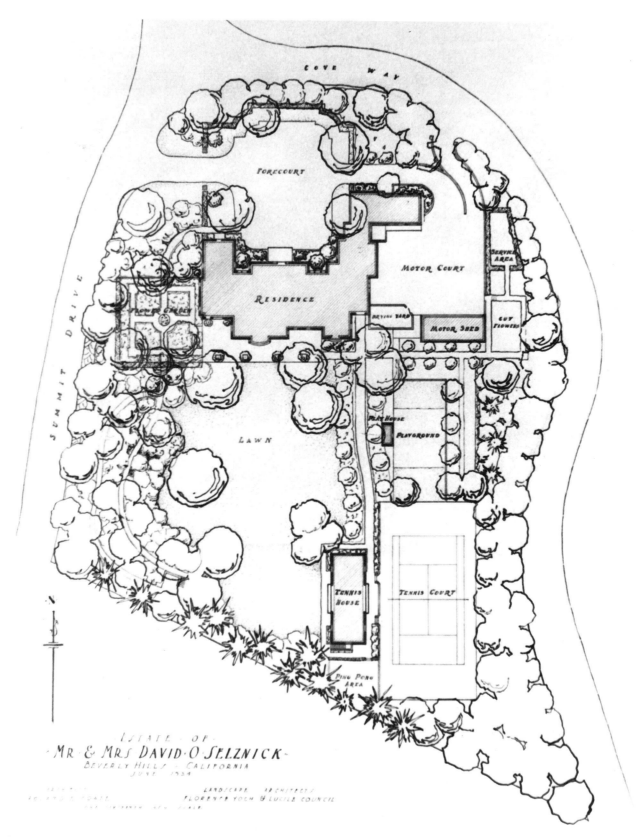

COVE WAY

FORECOURT

SERVICE AREA

MOTOR COURT

RESIDENCE

DRYING YARD

CUT FLOWERS

MOTOR SHED

SUMMIT DRIVE

PLAY HOUSE

PLAYGROUND

LAWN

TENNIS HOUSE

TENNIS COURT

PING PONG AREA

ESTATE OF
MR. & MRS DAVID O. SELZNICK
BEVERLY HILLS · CALIFORNIA
JUNE 1934

LANDSCAPE ARCHITECTS
FLORENCE YOCH & LUCILE COUNCIL

Plan, the David Selznick Garden. (Courtesy of Mr. Thomas C. Moore)

The gently curving walk from sports areas to main house, the David Selznick Garden. (Courtesy of Mr. Thomas C. Moore)

Yoch's sketch on her snapshot of the garden façade, the David Selznick Garden. (Courtesy of Mr. Thomas C. Moore)

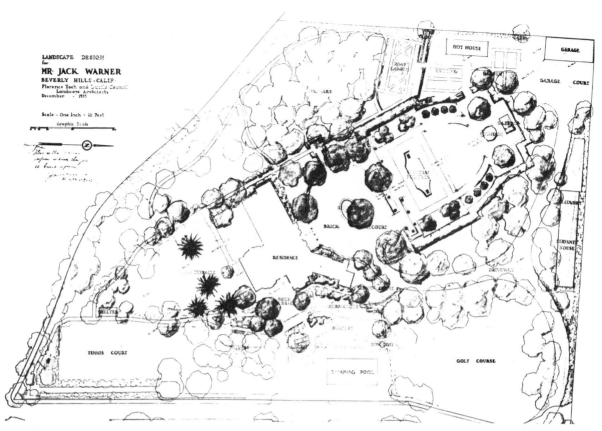

children. Sizable areas for play respond to the changes, more obvious and universal after the war, in the ways Americans wanted to use the outdoors.

Plan, the Jack Warner Garden. Jack Warner has written on the plan, "This is the plan on which this job is based." (Courtesy of Mr. Thomas C. Moore)

The Jack Warner Garden

Much grander than the Selznicks' estate was the project for a garden of 6.3 acres (within a property almost three times that size) that Jack Warner commissioned from Yoch and Council in 1935. The producer had divorced his first wife and married Ann Boyer, a Southerner. She turned the existing Spanish house in which Warner had lived into a columned plantation. Between December 1935 and June 1937, Yoch and Council worked on the gardens, their most extensive residential project.

Yoch transformed the site into the magnificent grounds of a baroque villa. Formal terraces and fountains rise in front of the house, and the back lawn is shaped like a robust Roman arch. Neoclassical pavilions at the tennis court and at the pool offer shaded seats for the audiences of the good American life, in which sports provide the drama that plays did in the theaters of the Arcadian Academy in Rome.

Yoch made the house the greatest performer in the first act of the garden spectacle. From the entry gates of the estate, the long drive turns, turns again, and then again to expand the impression of space on the property. Aged sycamores lean out over the road to create a languorous

The forecourt, with elliptical pool, off-center oak tree, and playful cupid, riding a seahorse, the Jack Warner Garden. (Courtesy of Mr. Thomas C. Moore)

avenue. From its shade, the visitor catches different views of the golden hilltop villa, a brilliant contrast to the dark forest that surrounds it. From the first day of their planting, these trees made the drive seem a venerable road into the past. Although Florence Yoch had used drives lined with trees on other jobs, the daring angles of the almost horizontal sycamores and the extraordinary length of the winding road are much more audacious than the upright, short rows of trees she used along the driveways at the Athenaeum at the California Institute of Technology and at the W. S. Charnley estate in San Marino.

Sycamores leaning over the drive, the Jack Warner Garden. (Author's photograph)

The Warners built for crowds and called for bold effects. The view into the garden from the elliptical, ivy-covered forecourt dazzled guests as they emerged from their cars. Echoing the grandeur of the main façade of the house, with its monumental, deeply-fluted columns and massive tympanum, the focus in the foreground is the noble stairway, an *escalier* suitable for the parades of courtiers. Behind it rise the carefully graduated walls of the seahorse terrace and the small fountain terrace. The visual sequence ends farthest from the mighty house in a curve of undulating pillars and rough-hewn beams that suggest a rustic country arbor from the hills near Rome.

Forecourt, the Jack Warden Garden. (Author's photograph)

On these terraces between the villa and its arbor, Yoch staged several garden entertainments. The opening events are formal. From the forecourt, side banks of steps, announced with classical urns, curve up to a broad walk defined with splendid eighteenth-century lead planting boxes. From here the wide, main stair rises to the next level, where lead *putti* welcome the visitor and more Cupids tame spouting seahorses in the long,

North Garden walls during construction, the Jack Warner Garden. Florence Yoch wrote on the plan of the North Garden (5 March 1936), "Note different sizes of all piers and walls." (Courtesy of Mr. Thomas C. Moore)

View of the grand stairway into the North Garden, the Jack Warner Garden. Vines and shrubs green the walls. (Author's photograph)

The Seahorse Fountain, the Jack Warner Garden. (Author's photograph)

Curved ramp to the highest terrace, the Jack Warner Garden. (Author's photograph)

rectangular pool. Small statues, urns, and vases below eye level make the visitor seem important. The route draws in along a gently curving ramp that leads to the uppermost level. The reward for those with the energy to walk so far is the beauty of a small pool, which has a simple design of square and circular forms that summarize the more complex shapes of the lower garden. A bench and accompanying statues set in the shrubbery create a friendly nook in this rich mogul theater.

Principles of theatrical scenery organize the great spaces of this garden. High hedges frame the front terraces and draw closer to each other to force the perspective and make the space seem larger. The brick used in the paving of the forecourt repeats in the cap of the foreground wall and in the edges of stairs and ramps as they climb into the distance. Along the sides of the terraces, major trees play dramatic and individual roles. A single sycamore seems to have strayed in centuries ago alongside the main stair. Recalling the trees that line the drive, trios of great sycamores lean over the walks that edge the seahorse terrace. To support the illusion of distance as the garden recedes away from the viewer, these sycamores give way on the next level to smaller trees, four noble yews on each side that close in the focus along the ramped walks. These yews were so important that Mrs. Warner and Florence Yoch spent weeks negotiating for them with an eccentric widow, who survived by occasionally selling one of the items in her tree collection. Warner and Yoch had to assure the woman that they would take good care of the plants, which each had a pet name. Impressed by their choices, the widow set aside her rule to part

Leaning sycamores on the edge of the Seahorse Fountain Terrace, the Jack Warner Garden. (Author's photograph)

Newly planted yews, the Jack Warner Garden. (Courtesy of Mr. Thomas C. Moore)

with only one at a time and let them have the eight they needed, Mrs. Warner remembers, for $1,000 a piece.

The geometry of the walks is complex and appeals to the Hollywood taste for the unexpected. The wide steps to the upper garden are clearly visible from the forecourt, but the route to them is not, and access requires several turns along curves and straight lines. Farther on, Yoch continued this pattern of seeming indirection by reversing curves in the ramps and stairs. The plan is consistent yet is not readily intelligible; it takes to a larger scale and to lazier arcs the designs Yoch first worked out in patrician gardens.

Beyond the Italianate bravado of the central spaces, Yoch added elements from English gardens. She made the herbaceous borders extraordinarily wide to fill an awkward space between the house and the existing pool. Farther on, stone arches support bridges on the face of a forested hillside below the house. Along the shaded, misty paths water cascades. Ferns grow readily despite the dry California climate.

In many places, Yoch herself contributed special decorative effects. In the center of the brick forecourt, the most public area of the garden, she put her signature in the composition of the reflecting pool. She specified that leaves should be cut in the stone cap and that she was to participate personally in their design. The plans directed the workmen to "Consult

Stone bridges over waterfalls, the Jack Warner Garden. Yoch adapted William Kent's design for the Venus Vale at Rousham. (Author's photograph)

Leaf pattern on forecourt pool coping, the Jack Warner Garden. (Author's photograph)

Miss Yoch for leaf ornament." Under the protection of a single tree, which she sited informally to one side of the basin, the delicate carving creates a note of intimacy. As another personal touch, in an arbor where two walks meet south of the house, Yoch laid a pebble floor, which seems like a fragment of an ancient villa.

Among the designs Yoch photographed was her transformation of the existing stairway rising from the pool to the house. New, simple steps, freed of their original Spanish lanterns and tiles, ascend from the pool deck between low walls that change from relaxed stucco curves to more formal brick and then to the refined columns and urns announcing arrival at the entry to the private movie theater. The symmetry of the classical architectural elements contrasts with the romance of the tumbling flowers and the caprice of the leaning tree. In the plantings along this stairway Yoch achieved the illusion of time's effects on a long-established garden. Yoch yielded at the Warner estate to the Hollywood demand for instant landscaping. To make the barren Beverly Hills site immediately verdant, more than $13,000 worth of specimen trees and shrubs were moved in at a time when 6-foot boxed trees cost only $125.

On this project, with a budget of about $100,000, Yoch worked on a scale and with a lavishness that carried her far beyond the requirements of more frugal clients. Rather than condensing variety into a small space as she did in Pasadena, here she bowled over guests with grand effects through large-scale planning and earthworks. She combined the example

Pebble paving, the Jack Warner Garden. (Author's photograph)

Stair, intimidatingly direct, from the pool to the main house, before Yoch and Council began work. The Jack Warner Garden. (Courtesy of Mr. Thomas C. Moore)

Stair from the pool, the Jack Warner Garden. Curved masonry, opulent plantings, and an overhanging tree now make the walk an amiable experience. (Courtesy of Mr. Thomas C. Moore)

of French models, which she admired for their graceful handling of crowds, with less severe, earlier sources like the Italian party villas of Frascati, Lucca, and the Veneto. With wide steps, languorous walks, leaning trees, and low walls she emphasized the horizontal spaces, gently accented with upright urns and plants. On the narrow verges of the large public scenes were shaded benches and secret doorways, giving opportunities for quiet interludes. The Warner garden was primarily for fêtes, and through its design Florence Yoch solved on a heroic scale the new requirements of wealthy Americans who wanted to play and entertain in outdoor spaces.

The George Cukor Garden

In contrast to the public display of the spacious Warner estate, the villa garden Yoch produced in 1936 for director George Cukor is on a smaller, more intimate scale. The main lot is long and narrow, and Richard Dolena, Cukor's architect, pushed the one-room-deep house against the slope of the hillside. Unifying the thin, level areas that remained for the garden, Yoch strung together the green garden rooms of the upper entry terraces, the open lawn and pool areas, and the gradually rising borders of flowers. At the highest point of the garden a graceful arbor offers a view over Beverly Hills.

The simplicity of the overall design provides a controlling structure for individual areas of varied size and character. Inside the principal garden door a Cupid on a pedestal welcomes visitors beneath an overhanging oak. A large jacaranda near the entrance to the house and a smaller Chinese magnolia by the bedroom porch give seasonal color. In contrast to this welcoming enclosure, the lawn offers the freedom of open space. Past the lawn, the pool deck establishes a minor axis across the main line of the garden and focuses on a small temple-like structure built for dressing rooms. The flagstone deck joins the pool and a shady barbecue terrace, which helps shift the line of the garden in a new direction. Gently nudged by a flowering crabapple, the walk past the pool bends through spring flower borders that lead up to the arbor.

These borders were profuse in their day, for Cukor was said to have spent $1,000 for new plantings each year. He seems to have left these decisions to his own gardener, and in her notes on a plan Yoch tried to insist on a series of revisions: "*Please* take out Cistus, Yellow Flax, and other shrubs that have been added to this border [by the pool]," "*Please* replace Sutera & Ivy Geranium from Evans Nursery here . . . take out Convolvulus now planted here [at the entrance to the loggia]," and "Do not plant flowers along this walk [in the orchard] any more."

The atmosphere of this garden is relaxed and unpretentious. Both entrances to the grounds are simple, at one a peasant fountain, at the other

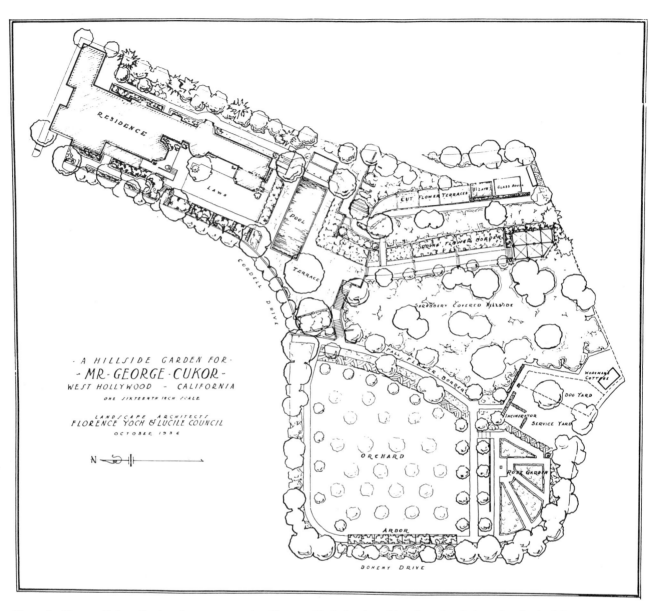

Plan, the George Cukor Garden. In seven months, Florence Yoch developed her first sketch into this finished design. (Courtesy of Mrs. Robert E. Ward)

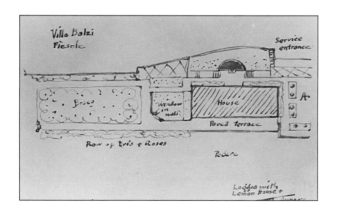
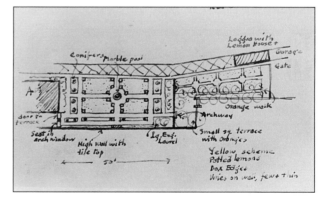

Florence Yoch's sketches of Villa Le Balze, Fiesole. (Courtesy of Mr. Thomas C. Moore)

View of pool, the George Cukor Garden. (Courtesy of Mrs. Robert E. Ward)

The ramped walk to the arbor, the George Cukor Garden. (Courtesy of Mrs. Robert E. Ward)

a Cupid. Jacarandas seem casually placed, yet they mark corners and hide buildings from view on the slopes around the house. The surviving sketch plans reveal the gradual progression by which Yoch arrived at the natural arrangement that makes the garden seem to belong rightly to the hillside; Cukor described her sitting on the ground working out the plan in her mind and then giving him the first design, which he saved. It shows the basic scheme, which changed as she made it simpler in outline and subtler in detail. The garden and its furnishings, like the Italian vase used as a fountain, echo the Villa Le Balze in Fiesole, where the English landscape gardener Cecil Pinsent formed a series of outdoor rooms that file along the edge of a slope. Florence Yoch had seen this uninhabited villa and its garden, which she evaluated highly in her Italian guidebook, noting beside the printed phrase "Modern garden," her comment "but good." Yoch's sketches of Le Balze show its primarily rectangular patterns, which contrast with her creation of more organic shapes for Cukor's garden, which seems to recline comfortably above the hillside.

The prevailing naturalness of Cukor's garden, its holiday ease, reveals Yoch's ability to vary her treatment of a steep site. At Dorothy Arzner's she aimed for Attic sternness, at Cukor's for Pompeian softness. In creating images of luxury and leisure in West Los Angeles, she usually avoided the austere model of Tuscan villas in favor of the richer Italian designs of the seventeenth century. Scale and expense increased to dramatize effects: driveways bent through forests (Haldeman, Warner); large parterres divided into radically different sections (Haldeman, Bishop); vast lawns rolled through the center of the scene (Selznick, Warner). She introduced new features to accommodate popular sports: tennis or badminton courts and swimming pools.

Besides benefiting from the economic advantage of working with those who had money to spend during the 1930s, Yoch seemed also to welcome the opportunities in West Los Angeles for carrying her work into fresh, even extravagant dimensions. She created an explicitly theatrical style to match a different set of conditions from those of the patrician world with which she began. The shift to new kinds of scenery for movie-oriented clients suited her own restlessness, for Yoch was constantly changing houses, traveling to new places, and studying new plants. Innovation was as central to her private life as it was to her garden designs.

View back down walk from the arbor, the George Cukor Garden. The large statues were originally intended for the rose garden. (Courtesy of Mrs. Robert E. Ward)

Florence Yoch and Lucile Council surveying the lower garden stair location during construction. The George Cukor Garden. (Courtesy of Mr. Thomas C. Moore)

Stone stair to lower garden, the George Cukor Garden. The finished plan shows a stair with two straight flights, which Yoch changed on the site to this curve. (Courtesy of Mrs. Robert E. Ward)

The pool terrace, the George Cukor Garden. A pair of classical statues survey the best of outdoor American living: a pool, a barbecue, and cushioned seats beneath the shade of an oak. (Courtesy of Mrs. Robert E. Ward)

10

IV

Illusory Landscapes:
Movie Sets

In her movie work Florence Yoch created romantic scenery. These projects expanded her skills in flamboyant directions that drew strength both from the simplicity, economy, and permanence she insisted on in her Pasadena practice and from the neo-Roman extravagance of the mogul villas in West Los Angeles. In accordance with producers' demands for splendor and sentimentality, she stretched her landscape techniques to achieve the lush effects required for five Hollywood scripts: *The Garden of Allah* (1936), *Romeo and Juliet* (1936), *The Good Earth* (1937), *Gone With the Wind* (1939), and *How Green Was My Valley* (1941). Yoch's sets played major parts in these movies. All the screenplays were based on books, and the literary descriptions provided her with important directions for designing the Capulet garden, a North African villa, a Chinese courtyard and fields, Tara's oaks and lawns, and a Welsh meadow of daffodils.

Yoch eagerly accepted these commissions. When David Selznick suggested the possibility of working on sets for *The Garden of Allah*, he found that Florence Yoch "is so anxious to do the garden . . . regardless of when we make the picture, that she states if there is any chance of our

Tara, Gone With the Wind. *In the finished set, grand trees (the tall central trunk is visible rising out of the foliage mass on the right) frame the house. Peacocks and flowers (tied onto the branches and planted in pots on the hill) decorate the scene. The lawn, to a line short of the bottom of the picture, adds a suburban touch close to the hearts of most viewers. (Photograph courtesy of the Academy of Motion Picture Arts and Sciences. Copyright© 1939 Selznick International Pictures, Inc. Ren. 1967 Metro-Goldwyn-Mayer Inc.)*

getting together with her, she will, on her trip to Europe which she is about to take, hop over to Africa and do some study on this matter."[1] Movies gave Yoch the chance to develop aspects of her work in new ways. She created sets for immediate dramatic effect, and this bolder style dominated her work in the late 1930s.

Fabricating Hollywood scenery also challenged Yoch to find new ways of working. The institutional nature of movies required her to participate as a partner in a team effort rather than to exercise absolute authority as she did on her residential projects. She was by nature thrifty and therefore concerned with permanence but learned to build film sets that were ephemeral, used for a few days or even a few moments, and then cast aside, like the sad relic of Tara that sat on a back lot years after the production of *Gone With the Wind*. In a business where getting the job done fast was important and where women rarely had authority, Yoch was notable for succeeding with unusually difficult and delicately timed assignments. She produced 10,000 daffodils in bloom at once for *How Green Was My Valley* and performed other feats to accord with shooting schedules that did not allow the leisurely six months or so that she customarily spent on even the smallest private garden.

Yoch's movie landscapes, made during the late 1930s, illustrated fantasy alternatives to the Depression: the exoticism of North Africa, the elegance of Tara, the flourishing Chinese rice fields, and the primal beauty of flowers in a Welsh field. These movies touched her heart, for they illustrated her own enterprise. In these, characters triumph over adversity through the redemptive power of the landscape.

The Garden of Allah

The Garden of Allah, the first film on which Yoch worked, carried the audience off to Algiers with Marlene Dietrich, Charles Boyer, and Basil Rathbone in an opulent version of Robert Hichens's novel. Producer David Selznick knew that scenery had been a crucial element contributing to the success of the first (1927) movie version of the story, and he chose to employ a major landscape architect, well known for her use of traditional Mediterranean forms, in order to compete with the earlier movie's highly praised sets. "One of the most important things in the picture . . . is the Garden itself," he noted. "In my opinion, work on the planting of this should be started at once, possibly at Palm Springs. *I would urge we engage Florence Yoch for the job,* even though she would cost us a good deal of extra money. The landscaping must be simply magnificent, as so much of the story depends upon the beauty of this garden."[2]

As part of Selznick's scrupulous preparation for the movie, he sent Florence Yoch to North Africa in May 1935 to research actual desert and oasis locations. She was to stop off in Algeria to photograph the original garden, find a painter of African desert scenes, and see a garden at Biskra.

The burst of daffodils that carpet the meadow in How Green Was My Valley. *(Museum of Modern Art/Film Stills Archive; courtesy of 20th Century-Fox)*

Selznick also wanted her to record the costumes, architecture, and customs of a Trappist monastery and to see a former monastery at Staouelli, about twenty miles from Algiers. Yoch would receive up to $400 for the excursion from Rome, where she would be staying in any case as part of her annual European trip, and $1,000 for work on the movie, should Selznick take his option. When he sent his best wishes on her departure, he cleverly added his hope that "this arrangement will work out so satisfactorily that it will be the beginning of a new and interesting phase of your career."[3] He was right.

Yoch took on each of the tasks for this trip and in her own enthusiasm added more. On May 3, she wrote the film's first director, George Cukor, that she was taking many pictures, had seen and photographed a fire dancer, and was planning to take a car out into the dunes on a six-hour trip that previously had required ten days by camel. She also expressed affectionate concern about Cukor's Hollywood estate. "I do hope your own garden is coming along nicely—I yearn to get home and pat it into shape." The following week, on May 10, Yoch wrote Selznick a more formal letter from the Grand Hotel Flora in Rome. Reviewing the information she had already sent to Cukor, she reported that she had taken about 200 pictures. "The Garden is lovely for living purposes here, but I think you will have to take a good deal of license for photographic purposes," she realistically advised.

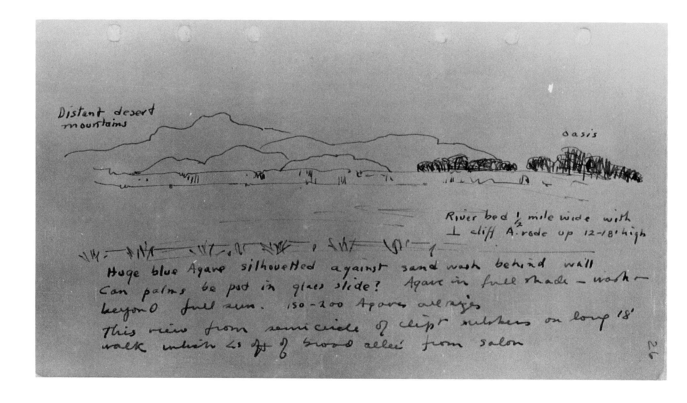

Distant desert mountains

oasis

River bed ½ mile wide with ⊥ cliff A rode up 12-18' high

Huge blue Agave silhouetted against sand wash behind wall. Can palms be put in glass slide? Agave in full shade — wash beyond full sun. 150-200 Agave all sizes. This view from semicircle of clipt rubbers on long 18' walk which 4 ft of broad allee from salon

Yoch treated this research trip with the thoroughness with which she dealt with all projects. In her travel notebook, she recorded plants, garden designs, and buildings. She catalogued plants according to their location: mountains, desert, oasis. Under trees, she listed ficus, olive, Brazilian and Mexican peppers, carob, ash, umbrella pine, date palm; under shrubs: pomegranate, rosemary, cistus (pink and white), oleander, Spanish broom, lavender. Another list included flowers: scarlet poppy, thistle, red clover, amaryllis, daisy, helianthus, dwarf iris, statice, cassia, pink convolvulus, white tree mallow, pink scabiosa, thyme, oleander, and genista. She could readily find all these plants or their close relatives in California, and her notes would help in reproducing the illusion of the North African scene for Selznick.

Her most extensive notes were on the Villa Landon, the model for the garden in the story. She drew a plan showing the layout of the grounds: the avenue of clipped rubber trees, the wall with seats set into it, the road to the desert with a viewpoint just prior to the gate. The scattered pavilions and relaxed plantings of philodendron, bamboo, palms, and ficus were in a more tropical vocabulary than she was accustomed to using in California. Yoch's notes on the plantings at the Villa Landon were precise, and she included a list of the plants by height: bamboos at three feet, hibiscus at eight, lantana at twelve, and date palms at fifty. A publicity still shows Dietrich standing in front of a mix of these plants within a frame of large date palms.

Florence Yoch's sketch of a desert view including oasis and distant mountains, "huge blue agave silhouetted against sand wash." (Courtesy of Mr. Thomas C. Moore)

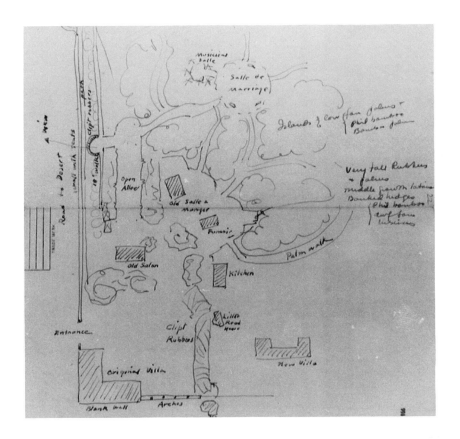

Florence Yoch's travel notebook sketch of the Villa Landon's garden. She used a double-sized sheet to record the fragments of avenues, the "islands of low fan palms," and the desert views. (Courtesy of Mr. Thomas C. Moore)

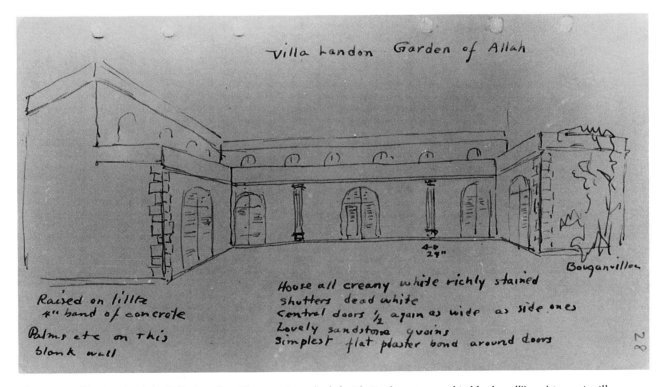

Florence Yoch's sketch of the Villa Landon. She noted on the left side "palms etc. on this blank wall" and bougainvillea on the right. (Courtesy of Mr. Thomas C. Moore)

Yoch also described the semicircular lookout at the Villa Landon and observed that it came off the central allée at a slight angle. This easing of geometrical regularity resembled her own designs. Such subtle details were central to her manner of defining a place as special and suggesting time's effects on its appearance.

During the spring and summer of 1936, after Cukor left the project, Selznick and his new director, Richard Boleslawski, filmed the movie, their first in the splendors of technicolor. It is hard to say precisely how much effect Yoch's research had on the sets, but her observations on the restrained character of the actual locations of the story supported the overall tone in the finished movie, in which Selznick strived for understated effects. When the movie was released, the critic for *The New York Times* praised *The Garden of Allah* as "a distinguished motion picture, rich in pictorial splendor yet unobtrusive." Yoch copied into her own notes a phrase from the *New York Times* review, which admired the authors of the screenplay for their ability to "state their case succinctly."[4]

Romeo and Juliet

In 1936 Yoch designed the landscape scenes for a serious film version of Shakespeare's *Romeo and Juliet*. George Cukor directed the movie, which starred Norma Shearer (Juliet), Leslie Howard (Romeo), John Barrymore

The set of the villa entrance court, The Garden of Allah, with Charles Boyer, Marlene Dietrich, and David O. Selznick. (Courtesy of the Academy of Motion Picture Arts and Sciences)

(Mercutio), Basil Rathbone (Tybalt), and Andy Devine (Peter). The producer, Irving Thalberg, chose the play to connect the rowdy young art form of the movie with the central traditions of Western culture. Shakespeare's play possessed both a fashionable Italian location and the impeccable credentials of the most venerated writer in English. Thalberg was so concerned with authenticity that he hired Yoch, noted for her inventive translations of Italian garden motifs to America, to design the principal landscapes. Such scrupulous attention to detail was expensive, and Thalberg admitted during the filming that the movie was likely to fail to make a profit. He had decided that the gain in prestige was worth it.[5] Personally and passionately involved with *Romeo and Juliet,* Thalberg claimed, "I've never had any picture closer to my heart." He spent the summer supervising the movie he deemed a "monument to his career" and allowed a budget so luxurious that Cukor had Yoch build a lavish garden and spent four days' shooting time for the few film moments of the balcony scene.[6]

In contrast to the movie's primarily architectural sets, including the arched loggias of the opening and closing scenes as well as the central square of Verona, Florence Yoch produced three notable landscapes. She created images of an open countryside and olive grove near Verona, the enclosed garden of the Capulet palazzo, and the cemetery where the play ends. When asked if he gave her directions for the designs, Cukor replied, "Of course not."

In Yoch's first scene, Romeo leans pensively against the column of a ruined temple in a sunny, flowered meadow. The contrast between archi-

Meadow scene, Romeo and Juliet. *Romeo musing amid Italianate ruins. (Copyright © 1936 Metro-Goldwyn-Mayer Corporation. Ren. 1963 Metro-Goldwyn-Mayer Inc.)*

tectural decay and cheerful nature mirrors the tension between Romeo's despair and his youth.

Similar conflicts between opposing elements enrich the landscaping of the lavish set Yoch developed for the Capulet garden, which "occupied all of the huge Stage 15" and required thirty arc lamps for light.[7] The plan of the many-leveled garden, like the intrigue of the plot, is not readily comprehensible. Rather than the parterres and formal lines of trees that might be expected in a historical design, disparate elements, including a single urn, a statue, and a freestanding column, suggest the singularity of the lovers.

Two unmatched canals are the most surprising features of the set. Cypresses closely line one of these pools, which Romeo walks along when he enters for the balcony scene. The second pool rests between formal rows of Italian vases with lemon trees. This open, regular composition appears in the bright morning scenes, including when Paris tries to awaken his would-be bride with musicians. These mirror canals, rarely found in the confined atrium of an actual Italian townhouse, expand the space by adding the moody drama of reflecting water. The spacious scene the camera views from Juliet's balcony is ambiguous and shifts from a cold stone court to a flowering tree, from the dark canal to the sunny one.

The most traditional motifs become unstable in this strange world. The single, gnarled tree where Romeo gives his opening lines, the pots of flowers that line the stairs, the deeply incised paving (modeled on the court of the Villa Pia behind the Vatican), the vine-covered walls are familiar elements in Yoch's repertoire. Yet their effect, like that inspired by the eclecticism of architectural elements in which windows, balcony, columns, and corbelled arches come from several periods, is unsure and discomforting. The movie stills emphasize the insecurity the landscaping conveys with its displacements: blossoms support the balcony, vines replace solid walls, and a dark recess eats out the supports of the terrace on which Romeo stands to speak with Juliet.

Yoch tampered with recognizable Italian sources to make their effects more disturbing. Her photograph album contains shots of the cypress-edged pool at the Villa Falconieri and the open fish ponds of the Cardinal d'Este's villa at Tivoli. Transported to the film, the uneven masses of the cypresses, further interrupted by fruit trees, appear to be the fragments of what was once an ancient plan, now lost and difficult to recover. The orderly *limonaia* has an even more untrustworthy role, suggesting clarity just before chaos erupts at the discovery of Juliet's seeming death. Wandering vines and foreboding shadows obscure the edges of the Capulet garden and threaten it with gloom. The garden's many lovely flowering trees, in single pots or hovering between cypresses, resemble the young heroine and hero, poignantly disassociated from a unifying pattern. Yoch had only to shift slightly her customary emphasis

Capulet Garden, Romeo and Juliet. *Florence Yoch's snapshot of the cross axis of the set focused on a herm. (Courtesy of Mr. Thomas C. Moore)*

Capulet Garden, Romeo and Juliet. *Cypresses and fruit trees line the moody canal. (Copyright © 1936 Metro-Goldwyn-Mayer Corporation. Ren. 1963 Metro-Goldwyn-Mayer Inc.)*

on individual features, like a tree leaning nonchalantly out of line, to make them seem lonely.

Continuing the theme of isolation and narrowing the focus on death for the conclusion of the tragedy, randomly spaced cypresses dominate her third scene, where a road curves and descends through a graveyard to the Capulet tomb. The panorama of small temples, occasional pines, and bands of cypress looks like the background of a Renaissance Italian painting, here dressed in mourning. The large obelisk monument, suggesting both death and immortality, makes the smaller elements in the rest of the scene seem farther away. Suiting the frustrating incompleteness of the lovers' lives, a broken avenue of cypresses darkens the top of the road, which might have risen somewhere hopeful, but is here turned into a downward route for the dirge of a funeral procession. By making the patterns of the landscape express the struggles of the characters, Yoch ingeniously changed her practice to suit a powerful new medium.

The result was worth Yoch and Cukor's effort. Movie reviewers recognized the extraordinary quality of the landscapes in the production. Frank Nugent described the "jeweled setting. . . . Ornate but not garish, extravagant but in perfect taste, expensive but never overwhelming, the picture reflects great credit upon its producers and upon the screen as a whole." Nugent even suggested that the movie was superior to the stage version, and he particularly acclaimed the "balcony scene, no longer confined to a miniature window and painted garden." Thalberg must have been pleased with the honor the picture conferred on the movie industry, which could make "a dignified, sensitive and entirely admirable Shakespearean—not Hollywood—production."[8]

Cemetery in Verona, Romeo and Juliet, *showing the road taken by Juliet's funeral cortège. (Photograph by Florence Yoch, courtesy of Mr. Thomas C. Moore)*

The Good Earth

In 1937, Yoch worked again for Thalberg on the filming of Pearl S. Buck's novel, *The Good Earth.* Sidney Franklin directed the movie, which incorporated scenes that George Hill had shot in China years before. For new scenes, the producer commissioned Florence Yoch to design a Chinese farming countryside and an urban courtyard garden.

To create wheat and rice fields called for work on a vast scale, similar to Yoch's earlier projects for parks in Orange County, California, at Shoshone Falls in Idaho during the 1920s, and for B.F. Johnston's garden in Mexico in the early 1930s. At the MGM ranch near Chatsworth in the San Fernando Valley, she built and flooded a long, rippling terrace that converted the arid California scene into a shimmering rice paddy just outside the gates of the Chinese town. Her success in creating this large panorama showed her ability to work out technical problems in a major enterprise well beyond the proportions of most gardens.

Besides these field scenes, she helped design the courtyard of the Great House, the object of poor Wang Lung's hopes. Central to the movie's celebration of domestic harmony, the courtyard offers two contrasting aspects of the house. Yoch used devices from her residential practice to suggest both the formality of this forecourt and its pleasant intimacy. The script called for the outer court to be immense and imposing, but the finished scene has a great deal of charm. The monumental doors, the tower, the bronze lions, and the sculptured dragon create in a Chinese vocabulary the formality of the scene. The delicately carved wood gate (which borders several camera shots), the small ceramic pots, the low walls, and the randomly spaced trees offer more informal notes, softening the foreboding severity originally intended for the scene. The design, despite its Chinese pretensions, is in fact a simple parterre with four sections. The low walls and creeping vines play the parts of hedges, which focus on a large stone well, shaded by a crooked tree.

The view to the other side of the court shows a succession of frames that direct attention to the main door: first and largest, the pillars and carvings of the gate, then the trunks of the mighty trees, and finally the doors themselves. Other elements support this symmetrical arrangement and also increase the feeling of space in the scene. On either side in the foreground two large pots, one dark and the other light, lead to smaller ones in the distance. The wisteria vine blooming overhead and the natural effect of the trees seeming to rise spontaneously through the paving give a

Rice terraces, The Good Earth. *Yoch cut these peasant fields into the hillsides of the San Fernando Valley. (Photograph courtesy of the Academy of Motion Picture Arts and Sciences. Copyright© 1937 Metro-Goldwyn-Mayer Corporation Ren. 1964 Metro-Goldwyn-Mayer Inc.)*

The entrance gate of the Big House, The Good Earth. *(Photograph courtesy of the Academy of Motion Picture Arts and Sciences. Copyright© 1937 Metro-Goldwyn-Mayer Corporation. Ren. 1964 Metro-Goldwyn-Mayer Inc.)*

domestic informality to the scene as well as imitate the naturalism of historical Chinese gardens.

Yet the movie shows that the materialism embodied by the Great House, attractive as it seemed when viewed from Wang Lung's poor farmhouse, is precarious. Thalberg built the locust plague into a great sequence, in which only a violent solution—burning some of the farms—saves the land. For the finale, the film returns to the Great House, which has lost its symbolic power for Wang Lung. He is preparing to sell it and return to his roots on the land.

Gone With the Wind

Gone With the Wind grew in importance in David Selznick's thinking after he bought the rights from Margaret Mitchell in the summer of 1936. He recognized early that he found himself "charged with re-creating the best-beloved book of our time." The film became "the greatest work of my life."[9] Selznick chose to film Gone With the Wind as the romance of a family home, and so he asked Florence Yoch, who had designed the gardens for his own house, to landscape Tara. This was Yoch's most notable job in the film industry. The 1939 Souvenir Theatre Program recognized her achievement with the credit, "Tara Landscaped by Florence Yoch."

Selznick insisted on retaining in a central position the book's theme of Scarlett's triumph over despair when she returned to the ruined plantation. He decided to "stress the Tara thought, more even than Miss Mitchell did." Selznick "cooked up an ending of my own" to give an unconventional twist in which the heroine gets the plantation but neither her beloved nor her husband.[10] To bring to life his plan for making Tara the central image of a lost Eden, Selznick was willing to spend money generously. The Set Construction estimate, 17 October 1938, reveals his emphasis and his extraordinary support for Yoch's work. To landscape the gates, drive, garden, and verandah of Tara, the budget allowed $16,000, whereas the landscaping for Twelve Oaks and for Rhett's new Atlanta house together was to cost only $10,000.[11]

Yoch's role seems to have been primarily research and installation. She traveled to Georgia to study plants typical at a plantation like Tara, and then figured out how "to take California trees, shrubs and vines and do tricks with them so as to make passable likenesses to Georgia trees, shrubs and vines."[12]

Technological ingenuity and efficient production were requirements of the job, and consultants working with Yoch admired her success. She began work in January 1939, on location at Forty Acres, on the back lot of the studio. Wilbur Kurtz (the film's historical and technical adviser) described her on the job:

> She was superintending the planting of certain trees around Tara, which had been hauled—roots and all—on trucks. Two real magnolia trees had been secured, and some very creditable bushes and vines were being emplaced. As for dogwood, some sort of tree that had the right lines was set up, and for blossoms, the skillful fingers of the Property Department had fabricated hundreds of amazing replicas which they tie on greenery as shooting requirements demand. A gang of laborers and plaster artists were making oak trees, huge affairs built of wooden framing, chicken wire and plaster, all around tall telephone poles—the upper ends of which show as poles and serve as anchorage for guy wires running to the top of the house. On these guy wires will be tied green leaves in clusters, so that the proper shadows may be cast upon the front façade and on the foreground. . . . I've never seen such an amazing performance.[13]

Tara, Gone With the Wind. *Wilbur Kurtz's snapshot of the plantation set during landscape installation. (Courtesy of Mr. Herb Bridges)*

A primary concern was to have the landscaping resemble the location for the plantation in the novel. Susan Myrick, a technical consultant whom Margaret Mitchell had recommended to Selznick as knowledgeable about Georgia matters, at first worried about "Spanish moss somewhere or trees . . . like those of California." But after a few moments listening to director George Cukor talking with Yoch, Myrick decided that the landscape architect "knows her stuff" and was not going to settle for conventional landscaping formulas. Instead, Yoch listed "dogwood trees and boxwood and post oaks and mimosa and cape jessamine . . . the hospitable air of a Southern home." When Cukor asked what plants would show that Scarlett's mother was from a cultured family on the coast, Yoch's answer included 'Maréchal Niel' roses and cape jessamine.[14]

The finished product became photogenic through landscaping devices that Yoch had used throughout her work to dramatize the façades of houses. Huge trees frame Tara's porch. As she had arranged similar trees in Selznick's own garden, she did not make them simply symmetrical but balanced masses against each other. Continuing this informal poise in other parts of the composition, a crape myrtle on the right side of the porch answers the large vine clambering up a pillar on the left. Trees seem to flourish behind the house and shade its roof. The rough-edged drive rolls lazily up to the side of the house, and a low hill, rather than the smooth lawns of suburbia, lies in front. These relaxed shapes and plantings give Tara the grace of refined country life.

Indeed, the assured ease of Yoch's landscaping at Tara supports Selznick's message in the film, which contrasts the spiritual authenticity of the plantation's family life with the vulgar materialism that followed the Civil War. Throughout the picture the comfortable home of the O'Haras is a touchstone, and its landscaping suggests unpretentious integrity. Tara's venerable oaks, productive fields, and nostalgic plantings of roses and jasmine connect this house to Depression dreams of a lost paradise, which romantic hope and American resolve might revive.

Tara, Gone with the Wind. *The rambling house Miss Mitchell described seems to nestle into the top of the hill. (Rendering by Mr. Timothy G. Scott)*

Tara, Gone With the Wind. *Kodachrome version for* House and Garden, *November 1939. The photographer took an oblique shot that eliminates the hill (just out of sight on the right) and massive trees that added rustic character to the landscaping. But note the rough lawn that avoids suburban tidiness. (Photograph courtesy of* House and Garden. *Copyright© 1939 [renewed 1967] by Condé Nast Publications Inc.)*

Maker's Mark

SIV

KENTUCKY STRAIGHT BOURBON

WHISKY

Old Style Sour Mash

Distilled, aged and bottled by the
STAR HILL DISTILLING CO.,
on Star Hill Farm, Loretto, Kentucky

$7.00, including wax

It's not the distinctive sealing wax that costs more; it's what's inside the bottle. Maker's Mark is made expensively; by hand; in small amounts, and flavored with home-grown wheat to make it softer. Bill Samuels, a fourth generation distiller, makes it on his farm near Loretto, Kentucky—but not for everyman. People who don't really care how whisky tastes shouldn't pay the $7.00 (more or less) for a bourbon as good as Maker's Mark. Those who do care will get their money's worth.

V

Later Gardens, 1950–1971

In February 1958, Florence Yoch began work on a book about landscaping. In her initial outline, she planned a "theoretical" section of three chapters on aesthetics, garden history, and her axioms for American garden design, and a "horticultural" section of fourteen chapters on the combination and use of plants. For years she jotted down her opinions, on scratch paper, on old check forms, in the margins of ads torn from magazines, but she never developed these notes beyond a draft for the first chapter. Perhaps Yoch realized that the inspired surprises of her gardens could not be encompassed in any one set of formulas for landscape design.

Yoch attempted a summary of her views on "the basic secret for a successful garden" in one of her longer notes:

Only a flourishing garden is pleasing; therefore, choose plants that can grow happily in the spot you select for them, with the minimum of care, plants that will develop naturally into such shapes or heights as will best serve your needs with the minimum of pruning or tricky training, plants that have pleasant, restful appearance and whose fruit, flowers or leaf color come at a desired season.

Florence Yoch's notes for a book on landscaping. (Courtesy of Mr. Thomas C. Moore)

Among historical models, Yoch most admired the medieval garden, with its agricultural and culinary usefulness, and she hailed its survival in the "fields and orchards, orderly and green" of early California. In the suburbs of modern America, particularly in California, she wrote, "again, as in medieval times, gardens have come to explain the living habits of their owners. We now find increasing numbers of moderate homes with swimming pool, barbecue terrace, patio, shady corner, cutting garden." This attention to the needs of her clients distinguished all of her work. She wrote in a letter to Mrs. Lockwood de Forest in 1940:

> With the increasing improvements of our homes and the thoughtful attention given to materials, new, old, practical and attractive, we discern that a more orderly type of thinking is also showing its effect in the planning and planting of our gardens. While it has been the hope and intention of garden planners of all times to produce pleasing or even beautiful results, there has been for some generations a self-conscious and transparent effort at elegance. Nowadays, a more forthright recognition of utility affords a fresher type of satisfaction. Gardens are not regarded to exist exclusively for the benefit of plants; but, rather that plants exist for gardens. That is to say, plants are materials, of enormously diversified characteristics, and can be useful as a stone wall or as atmospheric as a cloud. It seems to me that plants lose none of their traditional romance if handled constructively, as well as pictorially. They attain to the position of very special friends, proven and dependable, when one has softened, blended, and shaded bleak and glaring places.

Beginning with the principle of utility, Yoch discovered an enormous range of possibilities in plants and designs. In her later gardens she moved away from her generally rectangular or curving designs of the 1920s and 1930s. She incorporated into several plans an emphasis on angularity by using 45-degree angles for abrupt and exciting rhythms in keeping with contemporary architectural shapes. Oblique pathways inviting movement gave energy to even the smallest sites. Reversing direction, Yoch also developed a style in which spaces and walks no longer take readily recognizable geometrical forms. Along with this manipulation of traditional designs, she introduced in her northern California projects a plant palette of native trees and shrubs, and in her own garden she let these dominate.

In marked contrast to the lush plantings that many designers used in the benign California climate, Yoch's emphasis on simplicity in the plantings of all these late gardens gives them a chaste appearance. "Too great variety is a disturbing element" in a garden, Yoch wrote. "The most difficult task in composition is elimination and discrimination, . . . and no phase of a carefully worked out plan is as exacting . . . as is producing a sound planting plan" because of the "effort to find things that will not overgrow." She pushed this severity to its limits in the bold abstractions of the Davis garden in Pasadena and the Doud house in Monterey to achieve starkly dramatic effects.

Angular Gardens

Rancho Los Cerritos

In 1946–47, Florence Yoch and Lucile Council created a courtyard garden at Rancho Los Cerritos, the R.B. Honeyman, Jr., ranch in San Juan Capistrano. Here they introduced notable variations into the conventional idea of a parterre by drawing on Moorish geometries. The design of the small entry area for this informal holiday retreat took such free forms, however, that no specific historical model can readily be found.

Lying between buildings of different heights, the court has an irregular architectural frame within which the garden introduces unexpected elements. A new wall connected the buildings and introduced a bend to the already asymmetrical area. In the enclosed space, Yoch and Council created a rill, a font, and a parterre of four beds. These standard ingredients of traditional Spanish and Moorish gardens appear in original ways to suit the configuration of the modern ranch building. No part of the garden exactly matches another. The main walkway is ten degrees askew of a right angle; only the minor axis is orthogonal. The large pool is

Courtyard wall, Rancho Los Cerritos. (Courtesy of Mr. Thomas C. Moore)

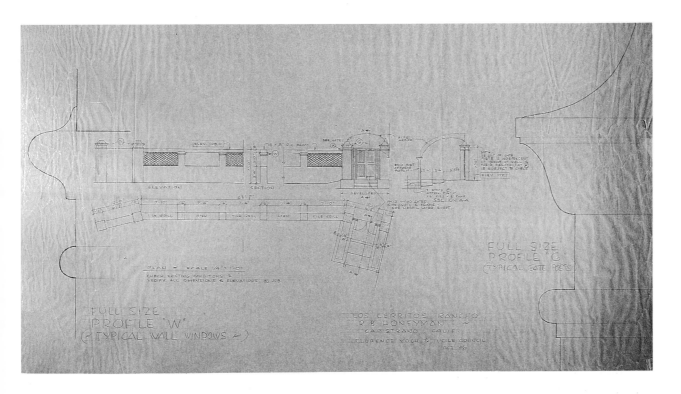

not in the center of the garden space yet is the focus of four different walks: one 17 feet wide, another 7 feet, and two 5 feet wide.

Throughout the composition, adjustments in line introduce variations in geometry. To form the central space around the pool, wide cuts on three sides of the parterre beds suggest an octagon, although the fourth angled side is missing and needs to be imagined. The rill does not run down the center of the broad walk but is pushed to one side, making access to the house easier and dividing the space into more interesting sections than exactly matching halves.

A similar formula, playing orderly rhythms against surprises, determined the plantings. Three sections of the parterre and one bed along the house have hedge borders; the fourth section of the parterre is a patch of open lawn. Four different trees—Southern magnolia, Arnold crabapple, white oleander, and coral—mark the parterre beds.

Repetitions link the extremely diverse collection of plants in the courtyard. Gardenias grow in three of the beds, as do cycads and the similarly tropical-looking Australian tree fern. Hibiscus, bouvardia, begonias, agapanthus, and camellias grow in two beds. Distinctive plants—

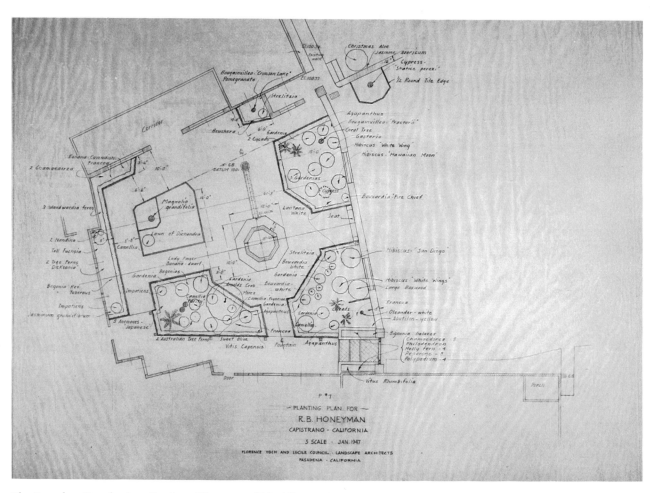

Planting plan, Rancho Los Cerritos. (Courtesy of Mr. Thomas C. Moore)

Summerhouse, the Mrs. G.P. Griffith Garden. Florence Yoch's 1931 slide shows the bronze faun rising from a frolic of flowers. The elliptical-shaped building conceals an awkward corner of the garden. (Courtesy of the Department of Special Collections, University Research Library, UCLA)

Orange flowers aglow in the Spanish Garden, the Bernard Hoffman Garden. Florence Yoch's slide aims at the tall, cobalt blue vase she set for bold contrast at the end of the path. (Courtesy of the Department of Special Collections, University Research Library, UCLA)

The sunken pool garden, the C.W. Gates Garden. Florence Yoch's slide (about 1925) shows within a classical design her dramatic contrasts between forthright and angled walks, formal and rustic planter boxes, violet and yellow flowers. (Courtesy of the Department of Special Collections, University Research Library, UCLA)

Pool, Mrs. Irving Sturgis Garden. Florence Yoch's 1929 slide shows Verrocchio's angel, ambling elephants, scattered pots, and an old watering can that form a foreground. The herbaceous border and lawn imply distance within the very small space. (Courtesy of the Department of Special Collections, University Research Library, UCLA)

Gala borders frame the serene lawn panel, the W.H. Council Garden. Yoch's slide shows how the bench nudges the viewer to the sunny walk and spaces beyond. (Courtesy of the Department of Special Collections, University Research Library, UCLA)

Right: Pool Garden, the Mrs. Frank Emery/Mrs. Ruth von Platen Garden. (Author's photograph)

Left: Pool, dichondra lawn and summerhouse nestled in the woods, the Ira Bryner/Albert Doerr Garden. (Photograph by Mr. George Waters)

Below: Arbor engulfed with Cècile Brunner rose, the Ira Bryner/Albert Doerr Garden. A pink azalea blooms in the pot. (Author's photograph)

Right: Terrace, the Ira Bryner/Albert Doerr Garden. The paving emerges from the rose-covered arbor, then widens and narrows as it flows past the white azaleas and kumquat tree. (Author's photograph)

Far left: View from the house to the mountains, Il Brolino. The walled topiary garden and exedra set a classical foreground for the forests and mountains of Santa Barbara. (Photograph by Mr. George Waters)

Left: Looking back to the villa from the topiary garden. Exotic birds and cheerful flowers are surprises amongst the austere gravel walks and precisely sculpted hedges. (Photograph by Mr. George Waters)

Below: A heart in the side garden devoted to the suits in a deck of cards, Il Brolino. The central tree is on its way to a cakestand, a traditional English figure. (Photograph by Mr. George Waters)

The sunken garden, viewed from the gates at the forecourt, Il Brolino. The monastic simplicity of the stone geometry contrasts with the luxurious rolls edging the steps on the left. (Photograph by Mr. George Waters)

The courtyard in 1948, Rancho Los Cerritos. (Photograph by Mr. M. Barnett; courtesy of Mr. Thomas C. Moore)

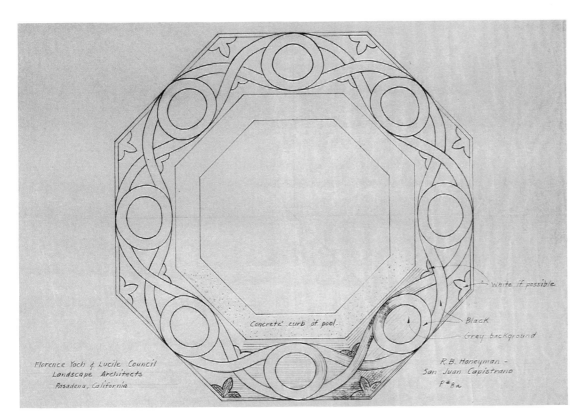

Pebble pattern for the pool, Rancho Los Cerritos. An entwined pattern, like a vine, gives whimsy and movement to the strict octagonal basin. (Courtesy of Mr. Thomas C. Moore)

PATTERN FOR DRAIN —
S. HONEYMAN · CAPISTRANO

Drain cover, in a design resembling chased Spanish silver, showing finesse of detail in even the smallest elements. Rancho Los Cerritos, (Courtesy of Mr. Thomas C. Moore)

including favorites from Yoch's repertoire, like Italian cypress and sweet olive, as well as ones she used more rarely, including banana and bird of paradise—accent each section and contribute to the Iberian effect of this garden.

The Hugo Oswald Garden

Carrying to an extreme her earlier experiments with angles in the Honeyman garden, Yoch designed a garden in 1965 for Mr. and Mrs. Hugo Oswald in Ukiah that relies almost exclusively on 90- or 45-degree angles. Only the curving drive on the edge of the landscaped scene shows natural bends in line. The resolutely angular plan was Yoch's first design after the death of Lucile Council.

In the awkward space framed by the house and the detached office, Yoch created a complex of corridors, levels, stairways, and rooms. Unlike the many gardens where she introduced an eccentric note into a regularly rectangular space, this garden has no ordinary spaces to disrupt. Instead, angles and imbalance have become a basic landscaping principle, relieving the tidily matching sections of the house and inventing garden rooms of strangely syncopated rhythms. Even with long acquaintance and study, the subtlety of these formulas remains fresh and unexpected.

Repetitions in the plants and trees, chosen to suit the skills of clients new to gardening, tie together the varied areas with flowers and foliage. Four large oaks provide shade over the central areas of the courtyard. Evergreen Southern magnolias wall one side of the pool; deciduous Yulan magnolias answer them on the other side near the house. Fruit trees between the courtyard and the tennis courts form one edge of a frame for a vista, while on the opposite side of the pool, more flowering fruit trees complete the border. A grove of sweet gum trees establishes the west edge of the garden to balance the office; corresponding to this grove on the east, a matching set of gingko trees forms a screening island in the drive. Yoch wrote many basic directions, such as specifications that the gingkos "need good soil, holes 3′ deep, plenty of water."

The quick-turning angles of this garden, as tightly planned as a ship's cabin, contribute to a range of adventures in a compact scene. Even the shortest walk through these landscapes of pool, lawn, and terrace requires at least one turn and offers several views ranging from formal allée to informal grove. The various moods produced by this garden are more romantic and ambiguous than the assertiveness of the angled lines suggests. On the principal terrace, a pair of boxed trees (Yoch suggested oleanders, Texas privet, or citrus) in parallel positions frame a wide stair to the lawn; two matching trees placed asymmetrically mark the walk to the pool. A magnolia and an oak form the sides to create the feeling of a narrow hall on the walk between the open terrace and the pool deck.

Plan, the Hugo Oswald Garden. (Courtesy of Mr. Thomas C. Moore)

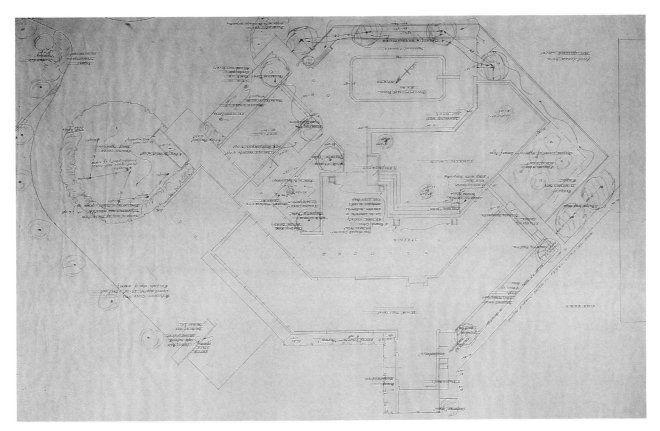

Wisteria, seasonal flowers, and fruit trees soften the rigid lines, and fragrance is an unusually important element in this garden, where magnolias, star jasmine, Burmese honeysuckle, Mexican orange, and citrus perfume the air.

The W. O. Minor Garden

Further experimenting with designs in which 45-degree angles play a principal part, Florence Yoch in 1968 prepared a plan for the main house of Mr. W. O. Minor's rural estate in Merced. She specified that the pool was to have its "long axis 45° to direction of house." This arrangement left a triangular-shaped space and angled walks between the pool and the house. On one side she put narrow steps and a walk, on the other a ramp leading down to the pool deck. The arbor over the kitchen entrance uses 45-degree angles overhead in diamond shapes.

This plan does not give 45-degree and 90-degree angles a dominant role, however, and nongeometrical shapes appear throughout the garden in greater proportion than in her earlier work. Straight lines prevent corners on two sides of the triangle between house and pool, and she directed that the owners should preserve the existing slope to further soften the geometry of the space: "Keep rise here." A detail sheet shows how the contractor was to bend the top of the arbor and to use curved roofing tiles to line planting spaces. Toward the garden edges, curves determine the shape of the lawn and of the drive. She wrote that flowers and vegetables should be planted on "shallow natural terraces" and specified paths to follow a "natural gentle slope."

Yoch's notes for this garden show the primacy of practical considerations in her work, which here includes a "4′ path for delivery of wood." An arrow indicates the "direction of the wind," and she planted a windbreak of Monterey cypresses and a tall hedge of *Magnolia grandiflora* to prevent northern gusts from disturbing the pool deck. Summer watering was a major concern at this site, which didn't have elaborate, piped irrigation. Instead Yoch called for a trench along the oleanders by the pool, a runnel for the oranges, a shallow ditch connecting the basins around the olives, and the planting of driveway trees to catch "gravity flow in summer" to make for easy provision of water. It seems Yoch did not supervise the installation of this job, since she pointed out on the plan that a "dry rock runnel must be traced on ground" and requested, "Mr. Minor note: please do not permit any substitution of plant varieties without consulting F. Yoch."

Careful calculations in the planting make it seem part of a natural pattern. A grove of tightly planted Canary Island pines establishes the junction of the main drive and the guest drive, and the roads here seem to

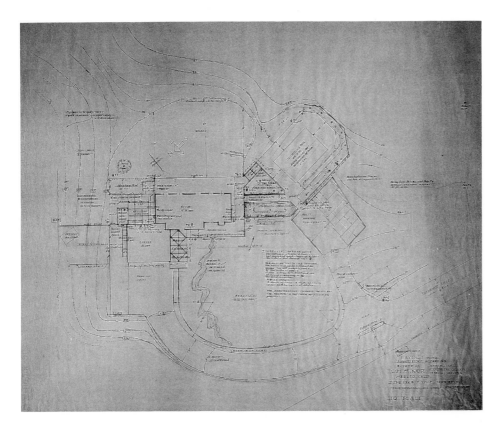

Plan, the W. O. Minor Garden. In this plan Yoch minimized the area of conventional grass, and she instead used the existing barley field and a meadow of African grass. (Courtesy of Mr. Thomas C. Moore)

Tree planting plan, W. O. Minor Garden. (Courtesy of Mr. Thomas C. Moore)

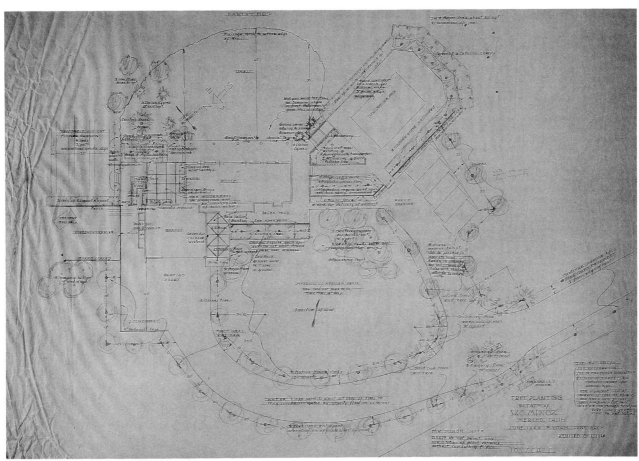

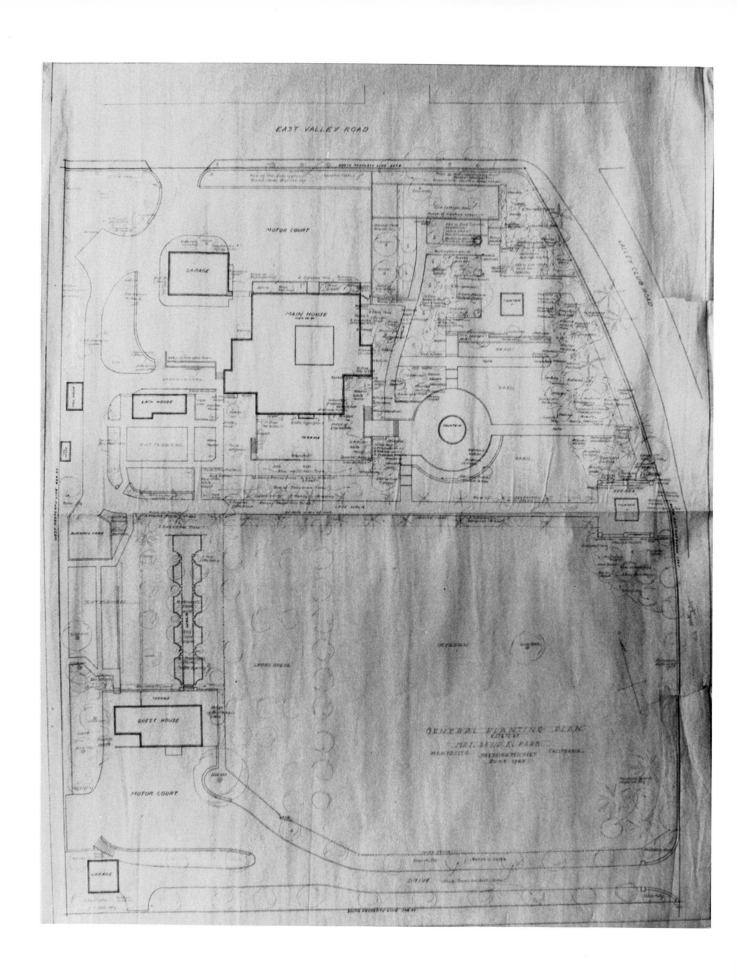

be going through a native forest. Near the house, smaller-scaled olives frame the parking area for guest cars and enclose the family parking court. By the pool, a grove including locusts, pomegranates, and a pistachio suggests a wilderness, contrasting with the formality of the pollarded magnolias and the hedges walling the deck. A similar balance of formal and informal elements frames the view southeast from the house over the barley field: a copse of stone pines and cypresses on the north matches a grouping of cypresses, oleanders, Catalina cherries, and magnolias around the pool on the south.

Plants provide the focus here that architecture accomplished more often in Yoch's earlier gardens. Rather than to statues or gates, walks lead to orange trees, cypresses, and crape myrtles. Pines and cypresses obscure and make more mysterious the view to the mountains. To part with a view even temporarily is a startling effect in a California garden. The contrivance of this plan, which defers views and involves the participant in ambiguous routes through the garden, gives drama to an American country farmhouse. Yoch's allowance for lack of expertise in installation and her concern for using the natural water supply make this design an especially useful model for late twentieth-century gardens.

Classic Gardens in Southern California
The Mrs. David E. Park Garden

A major commission from 1957 to 1961 was the development of the grounds of the Spanish colonial house owned by Mrs. David E. Park in Montecito. The main garden lies to the west of the house and mixes the precise geometrical shapes of pools, terraces, and a circular fountain with the casual lines of the sinuously bending jacaranda walk and the west boundary wall. Ignoring the usual Italian convention of relaxing geometric patterns as the garden moves away from the house, Yoch concentrated loose curves near the main house. Moreover, Yoch changed her practice of narrowing walks as they became more distant from the house, and instead mixed wide and narrow pathways throughout the garden. The dense texture of interlocking walks offers numerous routes for exploration. Like the Piet Mondrian painting *Broadway Boogie Woogie*, the Park garden suggests a restless energy; even the focal points of the rectangular terrace, the circle, and the exedra do not simply conclude an axis but have walks beckoning on to other areas.

Among this garden's most eccentric elements, a large stone blocks a walk, and an oak intrudes into a band of Seaforthia palms. These unexpected deviations from her own and Italian garden practice contrast with more regular, repeated elements of geometry, color, and plants. The garden rooms are in basic shapes: rectangle, circle, and square. Single jets play in three fountains of similar size; two square, one circular. Formal

General planting plan, Mrs. David E. Park Garden. (Courtesy of Mr. Thomas C. Moore)

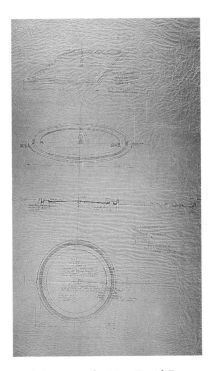

Pool drawings, the Mrs. David E. Park Garden. Yoch specified white terrazzo for the surrounds of the three pools, and black slate bottoms and channels. (Courtesy of Mr. Thomas C. Moore)

avenues of jacarandas, palms, crabapples, and olives mark principal walks. Yoch used single colors in bold patches. The plan calls for a "bright blue corner" in the shade of the palms, an "orange and flame corner" near the house, and a "scarlet and vermilion corner" by the exedra. This outdoor conversation room was planted almost entirely in white (white Chinese wisteria, white Lady Banks' rose, double white Cherokee rose, gardenia, white peach, and *Clematis armandii*). In the grove that marks the western edge of the property, palms, Monterey cypress, oleander, and flowering fruit trees recur throughout.

A major change between an early and a late plan for the walk to the guesthouse shows how Yoch worked to achieve both practicality and mystery in her design. The original plan for the walk carried it directly to the door of the guesthouse; the later version shows the walk arriving closer to the west side of the house. The change adds no actual distance to the walk from main house to guest quarters, but makes that progress less obvious and also gives readier access around the guesthouse itself. Moreover, in this late plan, the existing oak tree becomes a focus and an interesting diversion that further varies the guesthouse walk.

For Mrs. Park's garden, Yoch took the classical idea of an exedra well beyond the usual form of a retreat in a grove. Expected effects of dappled light, the softening of branches and entangling vines here are pushed to the side. The benches are hard and do not face each other, the scale is

Pool bottom slate patterns, the Mrs. David E. Park Garden. (Courtesy of Mr. Thomas C. Moore)

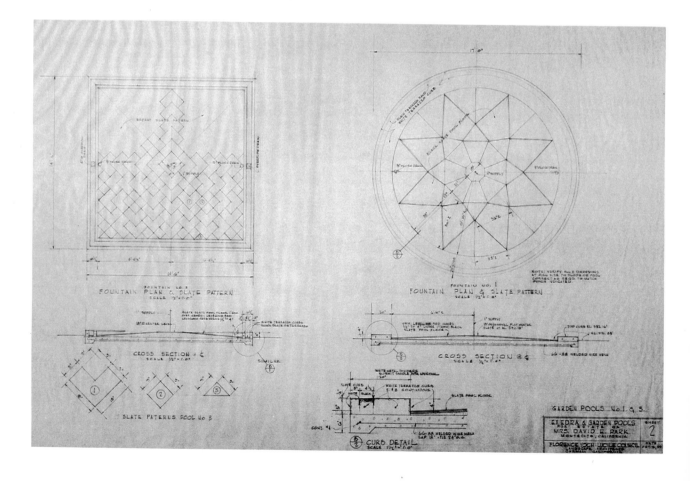

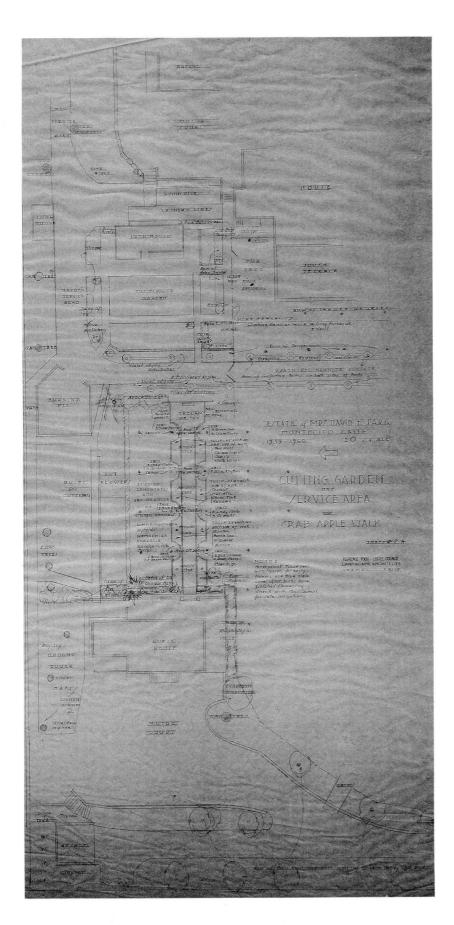

Planting plan for cut flower and service area, the Mrs. David E. Park Garden. (Courtesy of Mr. Thomas C. Moore)

unusually large, the vine cover only implied. Now in decay, the exedra is even more stark than Yoch originally intended. What survives are its minimalist elements: water and stucco in geometrical shapes.

Some visitors to this garden might recognize conventions like the olive-lined drive from an Italian villa, the small garden rooms from fashionable English country houses, and the white court from a palace in Granada. But Yoch reinterpreted these historical elements in a style that experimented with new combinations of plants and new variations on geometrical patterns.

The Charles Edwin Davis Garden

Blending traditional garden motifs in an elegant contemporary California landscape, Florence Yoch developed a garden for the modern villa of Mr. and Mrs. Charles Edwin Davis in Pasadena between 1965 and 1969. This was the fourth house she landscaped for these clients and the first without the help of Lucile Council. Nostalgia was an important part of the project. From the site it was possible to see the grounds of the Davises' first home, and they brought with them a white crape myrtle from their original garden.

The stark simplicity of abstract forms gives the new garden a notable purity of character. As in the Park garden, close to the house Yoch packed

Sketch of exedra, the Mrs. David E. Park Garden. (Courtesy of Mr. Thomas C. Moore)

Plan, the Charles Edwin Davis Garden. The many revisions developed individual areas: the cut flower garden, the crape myrtle walk, the iris walk, the magnolia walk, the rose garden. (Courtesy of Mr. Thomas C. Moore)

Planting plan for the crape myrtle walk, the Charles Edwin Davis Garden. Viburnum and "free growing yews" form a border contrasting with the trimmed hedge of Wilson's holly. Masses of agapanthus open and close the walk; between them stretch groups of spring bulbs. (Courtesy of Mr. Thomas C. Moore)

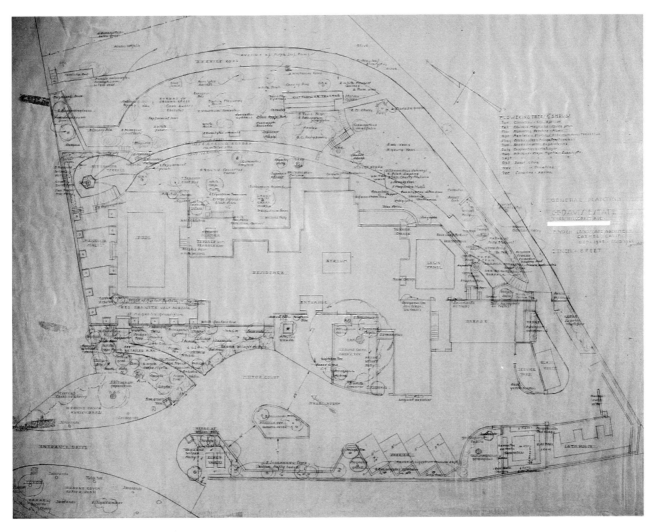

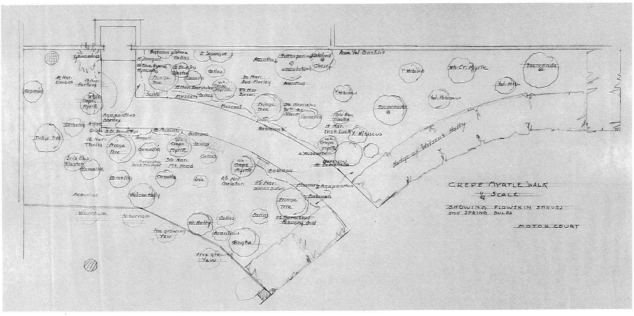

scenes tightly: the crape myrtle walk, the Moorish fountain on its pergola-covered formal terrace, the sunny white rectangular court for the pool, and the shaded magnolia allée. Below the house a single long walk bends lazily through woods and spring borders.

Rather than intricate walks and diverse plants, the repetition of a few elements creates the impression of dramatic change. The terraces that begin and end the long walk have common ingredients: large oaks with hexagonal screens over their feet to keep off summer watering, which would kill these native trees; lines of masonry drawn in the ground; and stairways to other parts of the garden. But the effects of the places vary widely. The walk begins in the artful fantasia on a villa stair at the red granite terrace and ends in the exotic wildness at the tree fern terrace. Along the walk, Yoch exhibited contrasting plants, including German iris and California violets. A loose grove of Yulan magnolias is an evocative variation on the neat line of evergreen magnolias along the sides of the pool.

Among the most startling features is the flight of stairs that floats down from the magnolia walk to the red granite terrace, where the woodland path begins. This stairway recalls in an unadorned form the stairs of the Villa Palmieri, which Yoch had photographed and studied fifty years earlier. Forming a shell pattern, masonry lines in the terrace draw together to focus on a large oak. The composition is baroque in its complexity of curves, modern in the simplicity with which it renders them.

The Davis garden seems especially good-spirited, even humorous,

Magnolia walk, the Charles Edwin Davis Garden. (Photograph by Mr. George Waters)

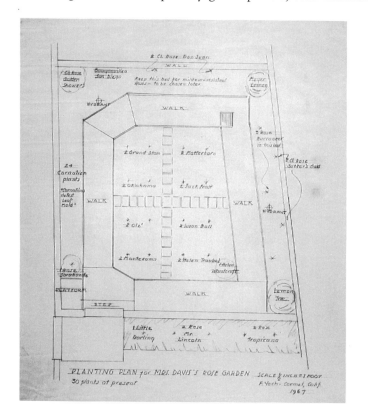

Plan, rose garden, the Charles Edwin Davis Garden. Yoch refined the simple square of the original plan into this more complex, naturalistic figure. (Courtesy of Mr. Thomas C. Moore)

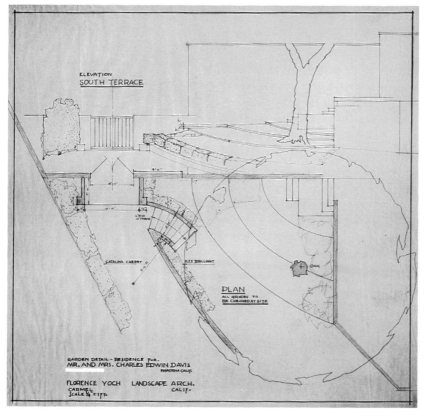

Red Granite Terrace, the Charles Edwin Davis Garden. (Photograph by Mr. George Waters)

Detail plan of the Tree Fern Terrace, the Charles Edwin Davis Garden. (Courtesy of Mr. Thomas C. Moore)

Curved walk through woods and flowers, the Charles Edwin Davis Garden. (Photograph by Mr. George Waters)

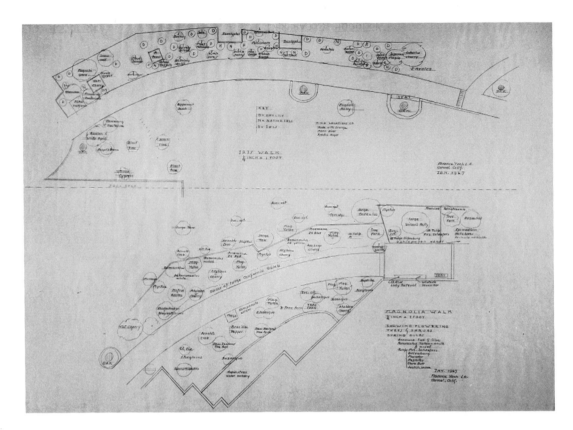

perhaps because of Yoch's ease with these friends who worked with her more as colleagues than as clients. Besides its audacious combinations and simplifications, this garden also expresses an unusual tenderness in the gentle curves of the front walk from the drive to the pool area and of the long walk through the woods. Both pathways respond sensitively to the natural scene.

Planting plans for the iris walk (using native California and German iris) and the magnolia walk (edged in California violets and campanula with background groups of anemone, ranunculus, and tulips), the Charles Edwin Davis Garden. (Courtesy of Mr. Thomas C. Moore)

The Mrs. Reese Taylor Garden

In 1969 Florence Yoch wrote to her friend Thomas Moore, "I have succumbed to pressure and flattery and am doing over a place in Pasadena for Mrs. Reese Taylor . . . an intelligent gardener and a friend." Instead of a large garden like the one that she and Lucile Council did earlier for the Taylors, the new project was for a series of courts around a house that almost filled its small lot. Avoiding the shipshape 45-degree angles of the Oswald garden and the complex choreography of paths in the Park garden, Yoch relied entirely on rectangular forms to create a green architecture of elegant equilibrium.

In several small areas, Yoch used a very few elements to suggest formal landscapes she had developed more richly in earlier projects. The garden axes are forthright. The front walk leads directly to the front door; the cross axis parallel to the front of the house moves straight to the

Plan, the Mrs. Reese Taylor Garden.
(Courtesy of Mr. Thomas C. Moore)

Entry walk and cross axis, the Mrs.
Reese Taylor Garden. (Author's
photograph)

drive; and central, broad stairs connect the two back terraces. Matched pairs of plants and architectural ornaments emphasize the bold simplicity of this design. Star jasmine frames the entrance walk; orange trees, yews, and beds of roses line the cross axis; and myrtle hedges form the long sides of the garden. Fountains, statues, and beds of Arizona cypress dramatize the steps to the pool. A centrally placed Chinese fringe tree concludes one end of the view across the front of the house; in back, the pool steps focus on a single oak.

Yet within these notably clear formal patterns, Yoch worked in eccentricities to give variety. From the entry, the view down the crosswalk to the drive begins in the court of orange trees, moves to the English garden room of yews, and finally to the beds of roses. Using a similar contrast of scale in the vertical plane of the back garden, Yoch put four magnolias against the north wall of the upper terrace to establish a large-leaved foreground, and behind them she espaliered the smaller-leaved *Camellia sasanqua* to suggest a distant background.

Minor discrepancies intriguingly disturb the balance of patterns throughout the project. One of the four beds of jasmine lining the front walk swells by the front door, narrowing the walk to make it seem longer from the street. A crape myrtle replaces the expected orange tree in the grouping of six trees on one side of the entry; the other side has only four trees. Asymmetry marks even the three-panelled trellis that faces the south end of the pool area, for a door cuts through its left side. The garden's edges, beyond its up-front formality, give way to loose plantings of vines and fruit trees along the north wall of the pool. In one corner of the upper terrace, a stone path meanders into a miniature wood. As abstract as a bonsai composition, the "woodsy planting" contains a sweet olive, an oak, and a small fountain.

Most unusual is the garden scene Yoch designed to expand the narrow strip of space outside the loggia. Here, as in a theatrical backdrop, she worked primarily in two rather than three dimensions. A sarcophagus fountain, like the one that ornamented Dorothy Arzner's garden more than a generation earlier, plays in front of a black mirror, which rises above a narrow passage paved in black slate. Yoch had long appreciated the capacity of black to extend space, and she frequently used it, as in the three pools of the Park garden, to enhance the reflective power of water.

In her seventy-ninth year, Yoch created this garden of remarkable ingenuity and promise, her last in Southern California. Its scenes collected some of her most beloved devices. She integrated into this composition Spanish moments (the orange courts), showy flowering trees (white fringe and plum), English topiary (yews), French elegance (the pool terrace, fountains, and statues), California informality (the upper terrace), quotations from her own designs (the line of magnolias), and even

Columnar yews corner an outdoor room, the Mrs. Reese Taylor Garden. (Author's photograph)

the stylishly avant-garde (the slate and mirror scene). Her long experience in developing courtyards, in which she used subtle geometries for intimate spaces, gave her the power to combine diverse gardening modes in the Taylor garden, which suggested worlds beyond its walls.

The Monterey Style

For the small lots of historical adobes in Old Monterey, Florence Yoch sculpted plants and spaces into freer forms and reduced structure to resting spots connected by short paths. She made in her last projects a virtue of informality, to which her designs had inclined from her earliest work for parks and historic adobes in Southern California. Adapting the courtyard formulas of her 1920s work to Northern California traditions, kinder sun, and different plants, she distilled in little garden rooms the vistas and variety of her beloved California. In these gardens, parterres become labyrinths and groves wildernesses. For some of America's oldest houses she produced her most contemporary landscapes.

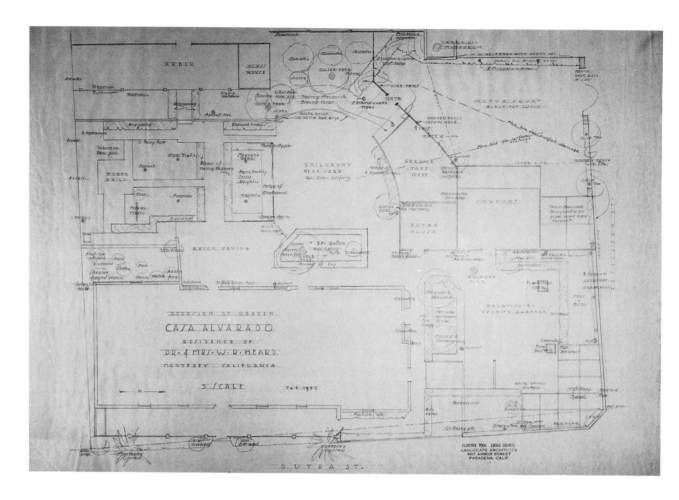

Casa Alvarado

In 1955, Florence Yoch and Lucile Council redesigned the garden of an 1830s adobe, Casa Alvarado, for Dr. and Mrs. W. R. Heard. In less than 10,000 square feet of outdoor space, the landscape architects made several garden rooms: the brick terrace, the fan-shaped children's grass play yard, the rectangular north garden, the east arbor and glasshouse, a parterre, mock groves of olives and camellias, and work and service areas.

The axial arrangement and central fountain of traditional courtyards are only a distant memory behind this design, which revels in displacement and diversity. Each area contains a remarkable variety of plants. North of the house, Yoch used perennials, boxwood, roses, and magnolias to frame a small rectangular space. The corner opens to a view of the Bay from an arbor planted with white Chinese wisteria, tree wisteria, clematis, and climbing roses ('Sombreuil', 'Violetta', 'Madame Alfred Carrière', and 'Irish Fireflame'). Peonies, hellebores, bulbs, climbing roses, espaliered loquats, apricots, and a cherry give further entertainment along the perimeter. There is a suggestion of pattern in this diversity. The arbor forms squares, which change to rectangles that widen and

Plan, Casa Alvarado, W. R. Heard Garden. (Courtesy of Mr. Thomas C. Moore)

narrow in keeping with the garden wall. A Monterey cypress grows right through the complicated geometry. Individual trees seem to drift casually across the space and teasingly screen the views. Behind their placement lies an old trick, for these trees emphasize the impression of distance for those entering from the back garden by diminishing in size: buckeye, apple, and tree wisteria.

Although balanced, the composition avoids matching sections. Boxwood encloses one area in what seems to be the beginning of a parterre; across from it, another boxwood hedge, around totally different plants, suggests the conclusion of the rectangle. But where closure should come, one boxwood hedge curves away, the other turns 90 degrees. In the center of the opening between the hedges, the buckeye seems a wild intruder, until the discovery of its interlocking arrangement with the surrounding magnolias and with the line of trees leading across the space to the Monterey cypress. A gathering of three magnolias both frames the buckeye at the exit and provides counterweight to the arbor in the opposite corner of the garden. The calculations that give each element several functions are complex; the resulting harmonies depend on an appreciation of syncopated rhythms and of suggested rather than explicit patterns. Displacements and interruption of visual lines prevent the garden from having many simple, photogenic views. Instead, awareness of total context is most important, and multiple perspectives are possible from every viewpoint. As Yoch wrote, "One of the most revealing, satisfying experiences in life is to come to a consciousness of design."

The children's play yard is the most informal area of the garden. It combines a straight line on the side near the house with a curved one on the far side, stretching the range from the architectural to the natural. Framed with strawberry trees, the garden gate is the principal focus, but it is not in the expected center of the arc. Three more walks lead out of the yard; for more sedentary visitors, two benches give choices for observing the garden. The possibilities for moving conceal the tight physical limitations of the space. A grove of olives and camellias edge this room.

Identical matches of plants are rare in this garden: the pair of arbutus, the trio of espaliered loquats, the four *Magnolia veitchii*. Yoch freely used escallonia, magnolias, olives, climbing roses, wisteria, boxwood, rosemary, viburnum, and watsonia. Even agricultural plants have escaped the tidiness of orchard planting and seem to have strewn themselves throughout the garden: loquats on a wall, a hedge of blueberries, apricots among the magnolias, a cherry tree by an arbor. Yoch combined here her taste for the practical, "fitting the land for human use," with a new desire to create the effect of scenes apparently untouched by people. Daringly, she sought to achieve this goal on a small site without character and with a considerable amount of construction.

The garden rewards explorations down walks that widen and narrow like a brook through varied scenes. In the distance, a viburnum beckons

Dining terrace at swelling of walk, Casa Alvarado. (Florence Yoch's photograph courtesy of Mr. Thomas C. Moore)

Path through flowers to raised arbor, Casa Alvarado. (Florence Yoch's photograph courtesy of Mr. Thomas C. Moore)

from the side rather than at the predicted end of the path, and suggests areas beyond reach of foot. On another walk, from the brick terrace to the side of the west arbor, the view concludes in a composition of mixed pots at a welcoming platform. Yet another walk, partly obscured by plants, crosses to a stone stair that rises to the arbor. The stair is visible from the first leg of the journey, but the route to it is not, for three rose bushes ('The Fairy') conceal the connecting crosswalk.

In this garden Yoch joined together the relaxed shapes of English parks and the taut networks of Italian avenues to disguise the congestion of the site. Loosening the geometry of her earlier courtyard designs, she involved the visitor's imagination in completing forms that earlier gardens would have made explicit.

Abrego Adobe

In the same year that she worked on the Heard garden, Florence Yoch also created a plan for the garden of the Abrego Adobe. Within the narrow channel of the available land, the design created a path that shifts from side to side, widening into rooms as it moves around two faces of the house in scenes from orderly to wild. To meet the requirements of the Casa Abrego Club, the garden establishes five outdoor gathering places. Existing trees and the configuration of the building gave individual character to the garden rooms. Instead of walls or hedges, Yoch successfully proposed to the early club members, short of money, a screening wire fence covered with ivy. As she observed, "There is no beauty without thriftiness."

At the south end of the site, a small gate opens into the first area, which has the most regular form. Four plants (sweet olive, yew, boxwood, and an old crabapple) mark the corners of an imaginary square. As an eccentric note the walk from the gate bends around an old boxwood. A long bench gives a unifying line beneath the disparate windows of the façade. The lines of escallonia and matching bed of rhododendron reinforce the implied square. The boxwood, the dogwood, and even the hedge of "Mrs. Heard's small green succulent" hint here at an English garden room and herbaceous border.

Looser in structure and more domestic in feeling, the next room is a peasant patio. Pots hold strawberries, thyme, and pelargonium; a temporary bed holds trailing rosemary. In the background, parsley panels diminish in size as they move away from the main vista.

The walk around the house contracts in the third room, which a pipe arbor overhead further encloses. This intimate outdoor hallway mixes a formal pattern (three pots in a row) with four different vines (two roses, clematis, and wisteria). Overhead, the arbor contains squares within a

Yoch's bench sets a stable base for the disparate windows, Abrego Adobe. (Author's photograph)

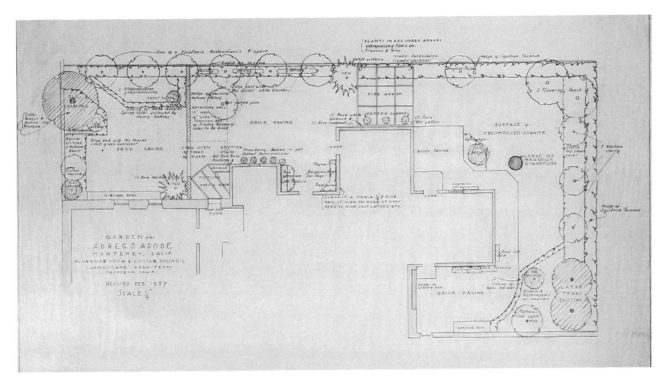

larger square; on the ground, a waxleaf privet hedge and a line of pots narrow the walk to create a small rectangle.

The next area is most informal and pastoral. Principally composed of green foliage, the magnolia-shaded court contains a spacious but unregimented area for open-air meetings, while the rambling brick paving offers a retreat for smaller gatherings. Repeating the opening line of the first garden, a final hedge of *Hebe menziesii* closes this large space, separates it from the adjoining grove, and curves on to conclude in a service box for the gardeners.

Plan, Abrego Adobe. (Courtesy of Mr. Thomas C. Moore)

The Francis Doud House

In 1970 Florence Yoch worked on a garden for another venerable building, the Francis Doud House, which overlooks Monterey Bay. The 1860s house is in the New England Colonial style, and Yoch included a considerable amount of wood fencing and arbor work to connect the garden to the vernacular architecture. The plan of this, her last garden, developed even further the naturalistic, sculptural style she had used for the nearby Heard and Abrego adobes.

Economy controls this design. In a small space and with her time short, Yoch gathered together elements that mattered most to her: vine-covered arbors, a bench set within a simple parterre of flowers, fruit trees, and a wild meadow. Each plays several roles in the design by creating varied paths and recalling larger landscape scenes. The walk through the parterre offers bits from the Mediterranean past: tile edging and an old olive jar from Italy, pomegranates and oranges from Spain. Three different arbors mark the principal sections of the garden. One is in the classical style with columns and capitals, a second is a composite of formal diamond shapes in a relaxed arc, a third is an unpretentious wood ladder so simple it seems to spring from the easygoing architecture of the house.

Natural and civilized forms intermingle freely in this garden. On the south side, regular shapes play the dominant role. The flower parterre includes orthogonal walks, a refined arbor with Ionic capitals, a comfortable bench, and wall trellises of squares. Yet the walks are all of different sizes and create four diverse beds. A bush orange and a pomegranate frame the house in a composition balanced by the single olive and arbor on the opposite side of the area. Making asymmetry even more dramatic, Yoch moved the tall yew from its planned location inside the parterre to an outside position marking the gate. In contrast to the isolation of this tree, which also conceals the connection of the back walk with the parterre, the olive melds into the arbor. More rambunctious, vines (including blue moonflower and Rose 'Austrian Copper') mix on the walls of the house, and others (Rose 'Belle of Portugal', lavender wisteria, two jasmine) engulf the arbor.

Flower parterre, the Francis Doud House. (Florence Yoch's photograph courtesy of Mr. Thomas C. Moore)

Plan, the Francis Doud House. This plan went through many drafts as Yoch and the women's committee considered alternatives. (Courtesy of Mr. Thomas C. Moore)

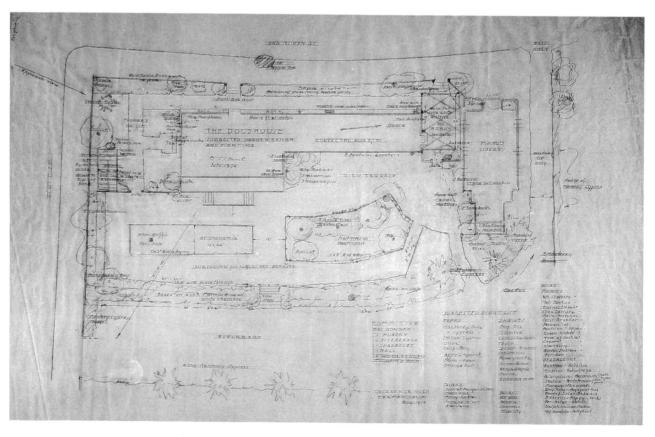

The esplanade side of the garden develops scenes of opposing elements and character. The symmetry of a divided stair disappears quickly at its base in a rough-hewn bed of ivy. A rectangular bed of shrubs occupies a seemingly central position in the area but lines up with only one end of the stair. A border of golden shrub daisy encloses a group of standard trees, a commemorative flagpole, and a rose arbor.

Rectangular beds give way as the garden moves north, and Florence Yoch's many revisions in both the planning and installation stages show how carefully she calibrated the eccentric forms in this part of the garden. The final, nameless shape of the meadow suggests several regular figures, but none is finished. Instead, one side is parallel to but does not match the edge of the rectangular bed on the south, another side bends to lead the east walk out of sight, a third creates a small piazza from which several different walks wend, and the fourth curves to frame a broad path going past the house. In the meadow she planted grass as a ground cover and joined to the existing old pepper tree a collection of fruit trees, which seem like the survivors of an antique orchard. She linked both ends of the garden with a robust hedge of roses ('Mermaid' and 'White Cherokee'), which parted for two radically different openings. Nearest the porch and the south end of the garden, she put in a broad bank of steps; on the north, she cut a narrow ramp to suggest a simple country footpath far removed from the actual urban site.

To these wide-ranging combinations of old and new forms, Yoch added a similar eclecticism in plants. All had in common ease of maintenance, whether they were imported or native. Besides many of her best-loved and longest-known friends (olive, white wisteria, Italian cypress, Rose 'Mermaid'), she included for the first time on any plan Catalina ironwood, Rose 'Golden Emblem', and the Blackberry Rose as well as peonies and apples she had been unable to specify in Southern California. Several grand old trees, including a band of windblown Monterey cypress and a venerable pepper tree growing through a fence, give character to the site.

Because this was a project involving a committee of seven women, rather than a single client, Yoch did not have total control. Yet in her eighty-first year, she participated in it with remarkable enthusiasm. She drew and lettered several versions of the plans, offered long lists of alternative plants drawn from her fifty-five years of experience, and even got out and raked the walks herself because she did not think they had been done properly.

Yoch's final landscapes celebrated the power of the imagination to create variety, order, and vistas in the most compact spaces. In Northern California she moved past the intellectual sportiveness that blended peasant utility with sophisticated taste in her earlier gardens, and she sought renewal in fresh sources. These included trips to study Australian plant habitats and native California meadows. A new version of the California

View along orchard, the Francis Doud House. Yoch changed the curve from concave to convex during installation. (Author's photograph)

style emerged from her expanding sensitivity to the nature of a site, an awareness that had begun with her love of California wildflowers and with her earliest projects for parks in wildernesses. Native ruggedness, frugality, and robustness came, at the end of her life, to seem kindred to her own taste for efficiency and independence.

An important expression of the development of Yoch's new style is contained in a letter she wrote a friend early in 1961. Harriet Doerr had asked for some advice about landscaping a house in Mexico. In her response, Florence Yoch revealed some of the attitudes and ideas that made her style "logical for use, becoming to the setting."

Dear Harriet:

I am assuming that the scale is 32, rather unusual, but perfectly usable, although not all the dimensions check out. This won't alter much if exact dimensions are off, as you are not paying a contractor by the square inch and a little inaccuracy or freedom may look authentically native.

Your descriptions in your letters are very explicit. As I see it you want to reduce in appearance the large area in front of the house—will need some shade—of course avoid any unnecessary or fussy upkeep.

By all means do not work against local conditions and spoil the genuine desert-country-ranch look, by bringing in too many suburban sophisticated plants that are unbecoming to the setting. Plant for genuine comfort and not for some effect. Would you accept a patch of Alfalfa for about two thirds of the lower part of this large front area? It is useful if you have animals, it gives the green and moisture of a lawn and looks a lot less pretentious. They often do this in the hot central valley. It is large enough to give spaciousness.

For a good big paved spot near the house I think about thirty feet out and clear across the entire width of the house looks well. Up here where paving is so expensive you'd reduce it all you could. Down there the bigger it is the more it will keep dust away from the house and make an excellent place for good bit plants in tubs, also furniture. They are certainly something your local people can take care of.

Without knowing which direction the house faces I cannot suggest any sensible planting—but the simple, wide rather crude design might be much the same and planting can be added to fit.

Water is always essential and is by far the most interesting feature in any garden. I suggest some kind of pool large enough to be obviously meant as part of the watering system, if only for dipping. What about a crude pool, stuccoed sides, rough stone coping, large enough to hold quite a lot of water so that you could put a faucet low on one side and use a hose gravity flow for things close to it. You probably would not need a heavy foundation.

You could fill it by the simplest intake in the bottom or even a hose as labor is not a consideration. If the inside of the bottom, or floor, were a few inches above the ground level it could be drained and scrubbed as needed, off to the side where the ground slopes away. I would not level up the ground any more than is necessary, as it looks more primitive and casual with some slope and is very practical if you have heavy rains.

Do you use the porch across the house front for living? Do you use the inner patio?

Keep as wide and spacious as possible in design.

Use local materials of course—you are lucky with tile & caliche.

Planting will depend on shadows, season of use, time of day.

As for plants be looking for things that are hardy there—logical for use—becoming to the setting.

Olives of course—Pomegranates mean it is not killingly cold—then also Roses—Tamarisk is a friend in that sort of setting. One of the most charming plant combinations I ever saw was Cactus (or Maguey) with Almonds in blossom. Peaches would do the same. I have always wanted to repeat that. Possibly a row down behind the Magueys, on one side or the other of the wall. The trees would not need to be nearer than 30 ft. apart because you are looking down a line. But if the Peppers would interfere with them, just a clump somewhere would be nice.

I noticed in Mex. D F they used Crape Myrtles for street trees. They slaughtered them horribly in pruning but they seemed to be hardy. I would like to see some very shiny dark green foliage somewhere as a touch of garden civilization, not too much, but to give contrast, near the house. It would be an interesting foil for the thinner desert type foliage. . . .

Best wishes,
Florence

Mexican sculpture embedded in the Ira Bryner/Albert Doerr Garden. (Photograph by Mr. George Waters)

VI

Public Gardens

The extraordinary range of her public commissions shows Florence Yoch's willingness to experiment with new plants and radically different climates and terrains. In many of these projects she used exciting new techniques and designs. Cranes lifted 40-foot trees several stories into the sky, boxcars carried hundreds of plants beyond their native habitats, and château geometries gave structure to a Mexican meadow.

Yoch often created public gardens for buildings that were Mediterranean in spirit. This important architectural style suited not only California's climate but also Yoch's conviction that classical forms were appropriate for celebrating American financial vigor. Landscape architect Beatrix Farrand rejected such classicism since it "stood for the burgeoning materialism of the Renaissance," preferring instead to use the Gothic in public institutions to express "timeless religious values." Farrand opposed classical buildings because they "were financed by merchant princes."[1] But it was precisely its base in commercial life that led Florence Yoch to realistically approve the Mediterranean style as suitable to an "era of machinery and commerce," for her clients were "too busy to give up the ideal amount of time in search of outdoor living."[2]

Court, The Athenaeum. Trees and pots relax the classical architecture. (Courtesy of Mr. Thomas C. Moore)

Many of Yoch's public gardens retain a soft-spoken, domestic quality. Vines loll along eaves and homey pots brighten corners and the edges of walks. There is little opportunity or even tolerance for the open spaces typical of the American northeastern landscaping style. Farrand's rule, "A campus is a place for trees and grass, nothing more,"[3] did not suit the California climate. Florence Yoch employed less maintenance-absorbing ground surfaces, including raked dirt, and she enclosed many areas with hedges. An overstory of trees usually gives shade from the oppressive sun.

The originality of Florence Yoch's public style distinguishes her landscapes from those of other noted practitioners. Farrand began her career as a private landscape gardener and became a landscape architect of public institutions, and she even adjusted the great private garden at Dumbarton Oaks to new requirements as a public showplace. Yoch, on the other hand, directed all of her efforts in an opposite direction: she made public places seem intimate, useful, and friendly. Thus the courtyards of the Athenaeum at the California Institute of Technology and the Women's Athletic Club in Los Angeles became elegant versions of the simple patios Yoch admired in Mediterranean countries; the avenue she planted at Cal Tech was of low-arching olives and gave the charming closeness of a Tuscan road to the space between the large dormitories. Even among the stately avenues of palms at the B.F. Johnston garden, there were benches, nooks, and smaller crosswalks to offer respites from the formal arrangements of the trees.

Florence Yoch designed parks from the earliest days of her career. Her projects included a proposal to develop a mountainous site near Shoshone Falls in Idaho; a park with picnic facilities and a bandstand among streamside groves of oaks in Orange County, south of Los Angeles; and a botanical garden for an irrigated plain in Los Mochis on the west coast of Mexico.

The B. F. Johnston Garden

Planting a botanical garden at Los Mochis, Sinaloa, Mexico, was part of the grand vision of B. F. Johnston, president and founder of the United Sugar Company. His nineteen-acre parcel was intended as the first stage of a plan that would eventually encompass an area more than three times that size. Johnston constructed irrigation canals from the Fuerte River and a pumping station second only in size to one owned by the city of Chicago. His domain was princely in scope: properties stretched over an area 100 miles wide. He built a new town and a railroad to serve it. The client's vision extended well beyond his own lifetime. He was building "for his son, his grandson, and for generations to come." Inspired by a visit to the Garden of Allah at Biskra and encouraged by Mrs. Johnston's garden experiments over a twenty-year period, the couple set a goal to exhibit plants from climates where sugar cane flourished—from southern

Front view, main house, the B. F. Johnston Garden. (Photograph by Florence Yoch, courtesy of Mr. Thomas C. Moore)

Garden façade, the B. F. Johnston Garden. Florence Yoch noted the "great palms" on the back of her photograph. (Courtesy of Mr. Thomas C. Moore)

"Looking down approach avenue from the Johnstons' home," the B. F. Johnston Garden. (Photograph and note by Florence Yoch, courtesy of Mr. Thomas C. Moore)

Entry gates, the B. F. Johnston Garden. An entrance in the grand Italian style. Drawing by Harrison Clarke. (Courtesy of Mr. Thomas C. Moore)

Circle of giant rubber trees at the principal intersection of the allées, the B. F. Johnston Garden. The plan calls for Indian laurel trees. Drawing by Harrison Clarke. (Courtesy of Mr. Thomas C. Moore)

Spain and the Hawaiian Islands, the Philippines, Cuba, California, Java, and Sumatra.[4]

Yoch's own informal snapshots of Johnston's house show the diversity of architectural styles that appealed to the owner. She tried to match this range in the garden. The front façade of the house is in the severe Tuscan style; the entrance hall is palatial.

Corresponding to Johnston's ambitious scheme, Yoch designed for the bare, sandy site a garden bigger and brasher in its imperial vistas and exotic plants than any of her other designs. After planning throughout 1929, Yoch and Council began work in May 1930 by laying out the principal walks and avenues on a heroic scale. The entrance gates are four huge white pillars, nearly 18 feet high, each crowned with a red terra cotta Italian ornament shaped like an oil jar. Modeled on a scene in the Botanical Garden in Algiers that Florence Yoch knew from her research trip for *The Garden of Allah*, a great plaza, 150 feet in diameter, forms the intersection of the principal avenues. Within a framing circle of Indian laurel trees, a large pool occupies a third of the space.

Beyond the formal entry court and parterre near the house, Yoch's plan divides the remaining space into four parts, as in a medieval monastery courtyard. The pairs of this huge parterre are largest near the house, and no single section exactly matches another. Two have straight and two have curved paths. As the plan recedes from the house, informal elements become more prominent. The farthest reaches of the garden combine a water labyrinth and a tropical grove on one side, a wild forest on the other. The strong axial lines of the canals and avenues of trees claim absolute authority over the large flat area in the manner of French gardens like Vaux-le-Vicomte and Versailles.

The abstract simplicity of the overall design resembles one of Florence Yoch's favorite seventeenth-century Italian gardens, the Villa Donà delle Rose at Valanzibio. There a canal crossed by a broad walk defines four areas: labyrinth, island, forest, and meadow. In her Italian guidebook she wrote: "I love this . . . get a taxi in Padua — ½ hour, worth it." In nearby Padua is one of the earliest botanical gardens (1545), which, like the Villa Donà delle Rose and the Johnston garden, is divided into four parts by axes connecting its main gates. On the Johnston plan, the princely cartouche proclaiming the owner's name connects his modern garden to antique Italian models.

Yoch also introduced her own interpretations of European garden conventions. Royal palms instead of beeches or plane trees line a canal, and scattered groups of Italian stone pines play against the regularity of the avenues. Even the more conservative renditions of traditional gardening practice, like the Italian cypress allée, the English groves and bogs, and the Persian swimming pool pavilion lead to unexpected conclusions. The stately cypresses end in an intimate pool court. Beyond its protective hedge, the plan calls for "ragged Monterey pines" to rustically conclude the formal vista.

Besides the mixture of garden styles, diverse plants vary the scene with horticultural splendors. The project allowed Yoch and Council to gratify their botanical zeal. From California they sent trainloads of plants to try in Mexico, and they kept records of successes and failures. Contrary to their usual practice of avoiding tropical plants, they specified many different palms; more than seventy-five kinds still survive in the garden, which has now become a public park. Florence Yoch rhapsodized about the research possibilities of planting in the future a section for

<blockquote>
succulents, cactus or desert natives. In later divisions there will be tropical shrubbery and a unit devoted to Mexico's native flora, many of which are very spectacular. In fact, the west coast of Mexico is a treasure house of strange and interesting plants upon which only the barest beginnings of collection have been attempted. Little is known about them, and Mr. Johnston's project offers a marvelous opportunity to grow, study and classify them.[5]
</blockquote>

A principal aim of the variety in design and in plants was to enliven the flat site, which had a fall of only 18 inches in a mile. Yoch's solution

View into the garden from the house, the B. F. Johnston Garden. Drawing by Harrison Clarke. (Courtesy of Mr. Thomas C. Moore)

Plan of the Botanical Garden at Padua. (Drawing by Mr. Timothy G. Scott)

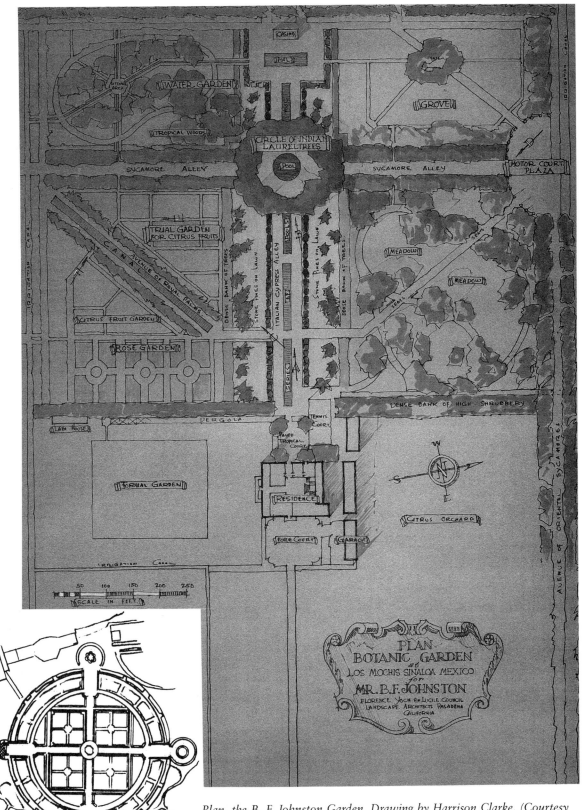

Inside the plan:

CASINO

POOL

WATER GARDEN

SITTING AREA

GROVE

TROPICAL WOODS

CIRCLE OF INDIAN LAUREL TREES

POOL

SYCAMORE ALLEY

SYCAMORE ALLEY

MOTOR COURT PLAZA

IRRIGATION CANAL

TRIAL GARDEN FOR CITRUS FRUITS

DENSE BANK OF TREES

STONE PINES ON LAWN

ITALIAN CYPRESS ALLEY

POOLS

STONE PINES ON LAWN

DENSE BANK OF TREES

MEADOW

MEADOW

C A N A L

AVENUE OF ROYAL PALMS

CITRUS FRUIT GARDEN

ROSE GARDEN

SERIES

STEPS

STEPS

DENSE BANK OF HIGH SHRUBBERY

LATH HOUSE

PERGOLA

TENNIS COURT

PAVED TROPICAL COURT

W

N

S

E

FORMAL GARDEN

RESIDENCE

CITRUS ORCHARD

FORE COURT

GARAGE

IRRIGATION CANAL

AVENUE OF ORIENTAL SYCAMORES

50   100   150   200   250

SCALE IN FEET

PLAN
BOTANIC GARDEN
at
LOS MOCHIS SINALOA MEXICO
for
MR. B.F. JOHNSTON
FLORENCE YOCH & LUCILE COUNCIL
LANDSCAPE ARCHITECTS PASADENA
CALIFORNIA

Plan, the B. F. Johnston Garden. Drawing by Harrison Clarke. (Courtesy of Mr. Thomas C. Moore)

was to "epitomize the productiveness and triumph over the challenge of flatness."[6] The problem called for considerable craft. Dramatic combinations were produced "to beguile the eye into the belief it is seeing a variegated cataract of vegetation on slopes and rolling ground."[7]

Florence Yoch commissioned Harrison Clarke to illustrate the plan and scenes from the garden. His sketches captured the clarity of her designs with a romantic dash she found appealing. Forty years after he did these drawings, she still preserved them in her collection. Three appeared in *Pencil Points,* August 1931, for an article commemorating Clarke's work.

In addition to the rich collection of designs, of periods, and of plants, the garden has a further set of tensions between the luxuriance of foliage and the orderly frames within which it is set. In a rare moment of exclamation about the refreshing, new aspects of this project, Florence Yoch proclaimed: "So everything is to be on a gigantic scale. We are not working with materials the size of garden flowers. Everything is defiant, barbaric, and wildly beautiful against the sky. No tree is too big, no plant too grim nor too insolently opulent to make jarring notes in this symphony of wild tropical strength and fecundity."[8] The vigor of this scene, too explosive for the courtyards and elegant grounds of her Pasadena practice, inspired her to designs like those of Henri Rousseau's jungle. The illusory changes of grade in the vast terrain, the scenic arrangement of the botanical exhibition, and the revolutionary transformation of historical garden formulas were a significant extension of her skills.

Vroman's Courtyard

In the 1920s and 1930s the rage for Mediterranean architecture produced many atriums, courtyards, and patios, particularly in public buildings. Yoch created designs for so many that she became a specialist in the form. One of her earliest courtyard commissions was for a "Seventeenth Century Spanish Garden" joined to Vroman's Bookstore in Pasadena. The colored plan, dated 1921, shows the subtle balance of this design.

The square courtyard with its bench and fountain alcoves establishes a firm architectural pattern that the plants obscure. The grace of the fountains and roses, the play of arcs and straight lines, the contrast of the balance and asymmetry make a geometrical puzzle that would suggest variety to the ordinary visitor and repay study for the frequent client of the shop. The original of Yoch's inspiration may have been in her admiration of peasant patios, which here take on a more complicated aesthetic pattern. Within the walled space, the fruit-bearing trees suggest the

Wall fountain and corner bench, Vroman's Courtyard. The mix of pebbles, tiles, and random-sized pots makes the garden seem old and personally tended. (Courtesy of Mr. Thomas C. Moore)

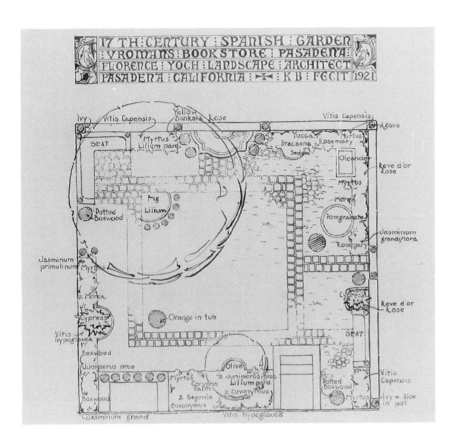

Courtyard plan, Vroman's Bookstore.
Drawing by Katherine Bashford.
(Courtesy of Mr. Thomas C. Moore)

agricultural roots of landscaping. But rather than the symmetrical planting of monastery courtyards, the arrangement of trees here is more subtly harmonious. An olive and pomegranate on one side of the garden balance a large fig tree on the other. Jasmine, roses, and grapes tumble over the walls in an unpredictable series. Within this grouping, different varieties introduce changes to entertain the discriminating eye. The richness and complexity of garden rhythms suggest why Yoch was called upon so often to work on courtyards.

The Serendipity Antique Shop Garden

One of Yoch's best-known projects is the sampler of courtyards and small terraces she created between the Pasadena home of the Bradford Perins and their Serendipity Antique Shop. The first published account of this garden, in the *Pasadena Star News*, 26 November 1927, described some of the features that Bradford Perin developed when he moved his antique shop from Los Robles to "a replica of a Spanish palace" set in a "notable grove of oak trees" on East Colorado Street.[9] In this former ranch setting, Florence Yoch and Lucile Council built up a collection of scenes in which the client could display his merchandise. The outdoor rooms include a principal patio, two paved terraces, a boxwood parterre, a formal rose garden, a shady lawn, and a cottage flower garden. Woods dominate the landscape, as the client wished; indeed, the trees were the inspiration for his move so far from the center of business in town.

The formal designs fit easily into the arboreal scene. Paths curve through the existing trees to link the garden rooms. The plan delicately suggests a controlling pattern in its symmetries of walls, gates, and ornaments; a generally Spanish tone prevails. Dramatic tension arises where the urban and the rustic elements meet. Cupids on pedestals suggest a formal gate, but the path branches informally from the road to wander through a field of iris.

The paved area nearest the shop also has statues gating the entrance to the main walk. Behind this elegant balance lean aged oak trees. The high wall screening the court from a side street descends and wraps around a tree outside the garden to join architectural and natural forms.

The relaxed way of treating the existing features of the site contrasts with the intense and learned eclecticism of its developed areas. The dazzled *Star News* reporter at one moment seemed to be in Granada, then in "old Virginia, or Maryland, or any back-home garden of our memories," then in California, and then in a nook that "Miss Yoch says . . . is exactly like a palace in Cordova."[10] This array of scenes, well suited to the genial entertaining Perin provided his customers, offered the pleasures of strolling through bits of Europe.

The spaces of these courtyards are open and the patterns loose to

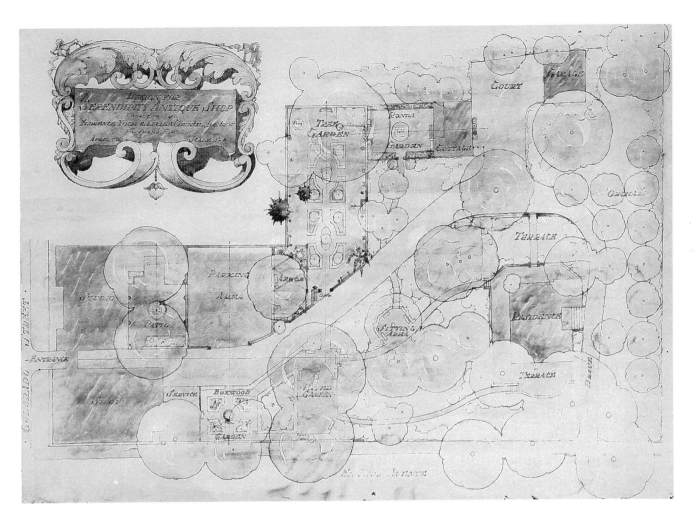

Plan, Serendipity Antique Shop.
(Courtesy of Mr. Thomas C. Moore)

Paved Garden, Serendipity Antique
Shop. The wall descending and
swirling around the distant oak was
an invention in the field. (Courtesy of
Mr. Thomas C. Moore)

allow flexibility in the display areas. The walks that lead from the shop to the owner's house ramble rather than proceed with axial directness. Even the broad service drive—the spine of the garden—bends to create glancing intersections with rooms and walks. The mix and excitement, even the mystery of the arrangement, represent in extreme form the creative confusion of unpredictable choices and routes that Florence Yoch's gardens have in their best moments.

The Women's Athletic Club

The commission for the Women's Athletic Club in 1925 required a solution to several new problems. Yoch and Council were asked to create a garden 40 feet in the air, on top of a building in downtown Los Angeles. Florence Yoch praised the architects, Allison and Allison, "for the grace and restraint of their interpretation of the best period of Italian architecture" as well as for their ingenuity in making the loggia, stairs, and terraces of the Italian *cortile* function as "a very adequate system of fire escapes." Yoch seems to have worked closely with the architects, who provided her, as she wrote in an article on this garden, with "a construction which would permit perfect drainage and proper depth of soil."[11]

Yoch's design kept the center open and simple, and restricted the planting to the wall spaces. Within these limitations, she said, "it was possible to arrange six or seven fairly secluded spots in loggias and terraces, where small parties might find semi-privacy."[12] The variety of planting contributed to the garden's interest and increased the individuality of the different areas. Seven olive trees, old and gnarled, give the feeling of age to so new a place. Contrasting elements from English practice—a broad lawn panel, colorful beds filled with hundreds of potted plants, and climbing roses on the wall—blend with the Italian scene.

In its small area, the garden ranges from urban to rustic moods. Alongside the elegant club façade, an inviting stair rises between an olive and a cypress. Farther into the garden, a crooked olive, leaning trees, loose vines, and varied shrubs suggest a wilder scene.

The pioneering technical achievement in creating this garden was getting five Italian cypress trees, weighing from three to ten tons each, over the wall. Yoch recorded this extraordinary tree-moving in a series of dramatic photographs. She was pleased with the solution to the hoisting problem: "the handling was very expeditious, once the proper equipment was obtained."[13] The cost of the crane for this task was slightly less than 10 percent of the job's total cost of $4,072. Modern methods made it possible to create on a rooftop the illusion of pastoral Italy.

Lawn, Women's Athletic Club. The varying rhythms and sizes of pots animate the scene. (Courtesy of Mr. Thomas C. Moore)

Rural nook, Women's Athletic Club. (Courtesy of Mr. Thomas C. Moore)

Hoisting an Italian cypress into the Women's Athletic Club. (Photograph by Florence Yoch, courtesy of Mr. Thomas C. Moore)

Garden and stair, Women's Athletic Club. (Courtesy of Mr. Thomas C. Moore)

The California Institute of Technology

Calling upon the partners' ability to handle both the constricted spaces of courtyards and long vistas down allées, the landscaping for the expansion of the California Institute of Technology in Pasadena occupied Yoch and Council from August 1930 to August 1931. Gordon Kaufmann designed the buildings in an Italianate style, and he presented to the Board of Trustees Yoch and Council's plans for the gardens, which drew on several related periods and styles.

The first phase of the expansion project was the Athenaeum, the faculty club, which Kaufmann designed as an Italian palazzo. For this urban building and site, the landscape plan drew on the softer aspects of a Florentine country house to create an inviting combination of well-defined avenues at the entrance, open spaces for games, and the suggestion of orchards and olive groves.

The first views of the club show traditional elements in unusual arrangements. Yoch designed the main drive to approach the entry court from the side, since the front was to be kept open for an additional building (not erected). A long row of olives lines the street façade to evoke an image of the Tuscan countryside. Yoch and Council carefully selected mature olives whose many twisted trunks give the illusion that the trees

Plan, The Athenaeum, the faculty club of the California Institute of Technology. (Redrawn by Mr. Timothy G. Scott)

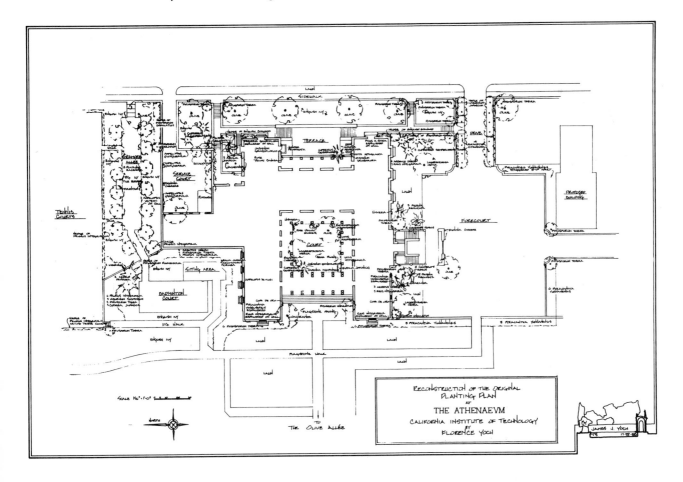

have always been there. In contrast to these softly rounded trees, tall, closely planted lemon gums edge the drive and announce the formal entrance to the club. Their gaunt, rose madder trunks achieve in a short run the effect of a villa avenue.

One of the surprises in this design is the planting at the high gate leading to the service court, which seems readier to receive Medici horsemen than garbage trucks. To support the Italian theme, Yoch massed a collection of Mediterranean plants, including palms, cypresses, and olives, in front of a vine-covered wall topped with large pots of bird of paradise. Her arrangement of these individual plants relieves the severity of the high walls and concludes the fluid line of olives running along the building with a solid block of greenery.

Along the porte-cochère and the south and west façades, she planted palms, pyracantha, crape myrtle, lemonade berry, and cup-of-gold vine to form an unpredictable sequence around the building. The pattern becomes more regular near the entrance, where India hawthorn backed by trumpet vine grows on the east side of the porte-cochère; on the west side grow hawthorn, an olive, and *Clematis montana*.

Yoch used plants here in unexpected ways. The lemon gums lining the drive are on very close centers (8 feet), creating a quick, staccato beat rather than the stately rhythms of cypress avenues customary at actual

Entry drive with lemon gum trees, The Athenaeum. (Photograph by Mr. George Waters)

Service gate, The Athenaeum. (Courtesy of Mr. Thomas C. Moore)

Italian villas. Where there was room for a long run beside the dormitories, she used olives instead of cypress and introduced a domestic scale rather than the monumentality preferred by princes. In her sycamore allée, however, trees usually found in boulevard plantings create a narrow pedestrian way.

Two major enclosed areas of the Athenaeum display landscaping elements in new arrangements. First, on the entrance porch, custom-made lead plant boxes formally edge the stairs. Playing rural diversity against the urban uniformity of these ivy-filled boxes, large round pots with seasonal flowers stand in a row on top of the side walls enclosing the stairs. The iron strapwork holding the pots in place sets a robust tone in contrast to the lighter flowers and vines.

The second enclosed area for planting is the central court which serves both as a light well and as an outdoor eating area. Its elegant columns frame the vista over the lawn to the informal allée of olives. A cypress and an olive tree set a dramatic diagonal across the square space. On a smaller scale, groups of pots, boxes, and tubs of flowers suggest amiable companionship in the foreground. Further relieving the restraint of the enclosing architecture, climbing roses, trumpet vine, grape ivy, and jasmine informally garland the arcades and walls.

In the design of this calm and eloquent courtyard, Yoch was more reserved than in her plan for the roof garden of the Women's Athletic Club. For the smaller space at Cal Tech, she used a simpler composition with considerably less ornament and only a suggestion of private areas in the nooks created by the two trees. The concentration of the Athenaeum *cortile* enhances the vistas into the extensive fields and avenues beyond the paved area.

The peaceful sycamore allée in the small space between the north façade and the tennis courts is among the most pleasing places on the campus. Yoch put the largest trees here in the project's smallest area, as she repeated the linear patterns of olives and lemon gums used in the more public avenues. Eccentric growth habits and spacing animate the rectangular form of the sycamore allée. On the south side is a single large panel; in contrast, on the north side, the area divides into three sections of similar but not exactly matched pieces. The parallel lines of trees begin with a pair placed exactly across the west end of the broad walk and then change to more casual correspondences. Yoch and Council placed and leaned each tree in this area to achieve exactly their ideal balance of continuity and interruption.

The conception and detailing of the Athenaeum landscape design were extraordinary even by Yoch and Council's exacting standards, and the cost per square foot was the highest of any job prior to World War II. Their time exceeded expectations, for the account book noted in parentheses, "loss on plan & supervision = $396.49." But Yoch and Council's thorough, perhaps extravagant, supervision accounts for why their work

Sycamore allée, The Athenaeum.
(Courtesy of Mr. Thomas C. Moore)

seems to have so many successes and so few errors. They caught and improvised solutions to design problems in the field. Plans were a minimum set of directions, only a sheet or two even for this most complex job. At the Athenaeum, the design of the angles and avenues established the basic patterns, which took on more particular, detailed forms during installation. The landscaping of the Athenaeum is one of Yoch's best achievements in adapting Renaissance ideas about proportion and arrangement into appropriate patterns for a modern mercantile republic.

VII

Gardens for the Homes of
Florence Yoch and
Lucile Council

In the gardens of her own homes Florence Yoch reveals her energetic pursuit of change. She admonished herself in a jotted note to make "frantic efforts to break shackles, however bejeweled," and she and Lucile moved and created for themselves new gardens about once a decade for fifty years. To avoid, as Yoch put it, "the palling of satiety and familiarity," she continually explored new directions and independently interpreted current fashions, whether for European gardens in the 1920s and 1930s, for the angularity inspired by Frank Lloyd Wright's architecture in the 1940s and 1950s, or for naturalistic groves and meadows in the 1960s. As her experience became broader and her humility before the site greater, Yoch was able to incorporate details, such as Italian motifs and Australian plants, within designs that made particular origins increasingly less important. Rather than the playful punning with European landscape vocabulary in her prewar work, in her own gardens in Pasadena and in Carmel she expressed her individuality with great reserve by reconciling the simplest ingredients of path, terrace, and tilled plot to the surrounding forests and hillsides.

Lucile Council pointing, Florence Yoch looking on, in the Mrs. C. Pardee Erdman Garden, about 1940. (Courtesy of Mr. Thomas C. Moore)

South Pasadena

In the early 1920s, Florence Yoch and Lucile Council laid out a garden for the house of Lucile's parents, Mr. and Mrs. W. H. Council. The new garden stretched in the long narrow space from the main house to the garage, which became the studio the two women used as an office until 1934.

The plan displays casual, country ease with formal features, a typical combination in Yoch's early work for clients in Pasadena. The small space contains a fountain, panel of lawn, terrace, rose garden, shrubbery, and shade walk. These elements of stately European gardens, so often imitated on great pre-Crash estates by the American plutocracy, here are tucked into an ordinary small-town lot. The *Pasadena Post* published a description of this garden in 1932:

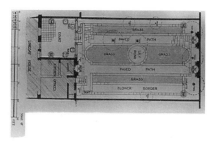

Plan, 100 Cheyne Walk, Chelsea. Designed by Edwin Lutyens. (Published in Gertrude Jekyll and Lawrence Weaver, Gardens for Small Country Houses *[London: Country Life, 1920], p. 64.)*

> The garden, approximately 60 × 200 feet, is a splendid example of one in which the luxuriant shrubbery has been kept in scale, partially by pruning, but more especially by careful selection of varieties. Planned to be viewed from the house, the little vista stretches out in lawn, bordered by two long paths and centered with a pool about which are set old copper watering pots from France and bits of Italian statuary. A tall yellow water iris emerges from one side. Terra cotta *amphorae* from the excavations at Naples are used effectively. . . . Once an orange orchard, the garden was planned to preserve seven of the trees, pruned high to reveal graceful branches and forming with two carefully placed "incense cedars" from the High Sierras, and other tall shrubs, an interesting skyline. . . . Having planned it primarily as a green garden, Miss Yoch and Miss Council use a conscious color scheme in spring. . . . The little garden is, in all its blooming season, a riot of color until September.[1]

Photographs taken during the decade spent developing this garden reveal Yoch's experiments in creating casual effects. Pictures show the off-center iris that recall Gertrude Jekyll's placement of wild marsh plants in architectural pools. Yoch assembled in one snapshot a pair of terriers and several loved objects to give a sentimental note to the scene. Informal groupings of furniture—a bench with several pots, a couple of chairs alongside an olive jar—beneath overhanging orange trees contrast with the elegant shape of the lawn, a *parterre à l'anglaise*.

The model for this garden was at 100 Cheyne Walk in Chelsea, where Edwin Lutyens wittily disrupted a formal scene of rectangular bands of grass by leaning a tree rakishly over the central pool. Lawrence Weaver published the plan of this garden in *Houses and Gardens by Sir Edwin*

Tree and pool, 100 Cheyne Walk, Chelsea. Designed by Edwin Lutyens. (Published in Jekyll and Weaver, Gardens for Small Country Houses, *p. 64.)*

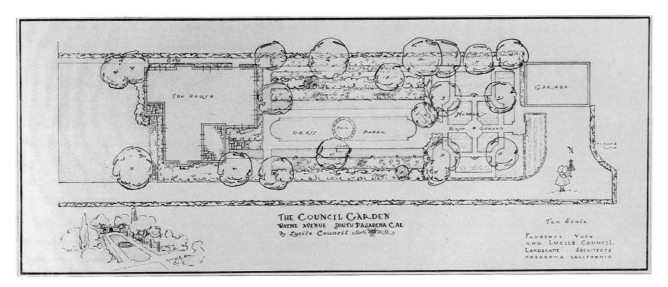

Plan, the W. H. Council Garden. Drawn by Lucile Council. (Courtesy of Mr. Thomas C. Moore)

Pool with entourage of pots and pets, the W. H. Council Garden. (Courtesy of Mr. Thomas C. Moore)

Undulating walk to the studio, the W. H. Council Garden. Yellow daylilies and Chinese bellflowers bloom with blue delphinium, iris and campanula. (Courtesy of Mr. Thomas C. Moore)

Chairs in the shade of an orange tree, the W. H. Council Garden. (Courtesy of Mr. Thomas C. Moore)

Lutyens, and he and Gertrude Jekyll also included it in their chapter, "The Treatment of Small Sites," in the popular *Gardens for Small Country Houses.* Yoch and Council expanded its suggestion of a country moment within a tight urban framework into a series of dramatic contrasts, bolder in sensual effects and more complex in geometry, throughout the Council garden. Their grass panel, in a shape echoing Lutyens's, has flower borders on both edges that obscure the periphery of the property. Moreover, the energetic and opulent planting increases the sense of rural wildness.

Choices abound. Rather than the parallel stone walks that proclaim symmetry in Lutyens's single scene, Yoch and Council created an interlocking pattern of useful and romantic decomposed granite paths that invite explorations into varied landscapes. Irregular and balanced, square and elongated, spaces of flowers and lawn and hedge form a series of views that make the garden seem much larger than it is. A broad path along the façade of the house gives access to the sun-lit, formal part of the garden as well as to the mysteries of the shade walk. At the end of the lawn, three walks offer different perspectives on the rose parterre, and one path turns to discover another surprise, the vine-garlanded studio, where the landscape architects had their first office together. Even the smallest details support the illusion of greater space to make the garden seem freer and more open. A postcard that Yoch and Council sent out in 1930 as

invitations for Sunday afternoon tea shows that the pots along a walk were graded from large to small to emphasize recession and distance.

Yoch greatly increased the role of casual elements not only from Lutyens's model but also from the English and Italian country houses that were the inspiration for her many garden rooms. Trees gate the walks by the house, close the vista on the lawn, and corner the rose garden yet seem to loosely drift across the landscape. The rendition of a traditional parterre has four sections, but none match. Other formal patterns pause for individual accents—an independent crape myrtle, an erect yew, a watering can, a statue, an olive jar, water reeds off-center in the pond, and a shaded bench. These endearing touches soften the classicism of the garden elements and make the place welcoming and affectionate.

San Marino

For their next house, begun in 1934, Yoch and Council decided to build on a sloping San Marino lot, outside of the most fashionable area of development. The second-floor loggia and the broad garden terrace give a surprising feeling of openness to the small site. Yoch might have expected visitors to recall Pliny's description of his Tuscan villa: "My house is on the lower slopes of a hill but commands as good a view as if it were higher up."[2]

Yoch and Council's postcard of a stair, the W. H. Council Garden. (Courtesy of Mr. John Peirce)

The W. H. Council Garden, 1933. (Courtesy of Mr. Thomas C. Moore)

The olive jar that formed the focal point of views from the lawn, the W. H. Council Garden. (Courtesy of Mr. Thomas C. Moore)

Yoch intended the house as a speculative investment and planned it to be attractive in several ways. She loosely adapted European architecture for its designs by borrowing freely from houses of the French countryside for the front façade and from Italian villas for the back. Although an abstract Mediterranean simplicity united both sides, the purchaser would get impressions of two worlds for the price of one.

To visually increase the feeling of space within the house, Yoch carefully calculated the detailing of the paneling, which combined elegant rounded and rectangular shapes resembling those she used in garden plans. On the fireplace wall, the wide central section seems to project into the room while the narrower panels on the sides appear to be set back. Although these are really in almost the same plane, her ingenuity with the proportions of the molding creates the impression of greater length to the room. This trick for getting space economically fulfills the axiom she gave Thomas Moore that designs should be "beautiful but not expensive."

Several perspective devices expand the sense of space on the site. A broad decomposed granite walk across the front of the house narrows as it turns the corner. The trees of the east garden draw in on the sides as do the edges of the central flower bed as it recedes from the viewer's sight. Broad-leaved camellias espaliered between the front windows set the foreground for views to the distant small-leaved rosemary.

Besides subtly creating illusions of space, Yoch also made the garden immediately appealing with colorful and informal plantings. She introduced a wide range of ornamentals, including an Arnold crabapple and camellias from Asia. However, the dominant plants are Mediterranean. The wide band of loosely growing rosemary along the street and the pair of large gnarled olives framing the house make the façade look mellowed by country custom and old time.

The arrangement of the garden behind the house reverses the open-centered plan of the Council garden by putting a mass of flowers in the middle and walks on the periphery. The changes in level, the walks angling out of sight, and the divided stair all give variety and a sense of freedom within a much smaller area than Yoch and Council had in their first home.

The increased efficiency of this plan shows in the remarkable concentration of garden features. To a composition that displays flowers in a thin band, in a meadow, and in pots along the terrace, Yoch added the major elements of an Italian villa. The east garden begins at the house in a sunny terrace exhibiting antique sculptures and ends in a classical fountain playing in a shady grove. The principal stair into the garden has landings set with pebbles like an ancient mosaic. Surveying the entire scene, the wisteria-covered loggia offers prospects beyond the garden borders.

Classical head and well, Florence Yoch and Lucile Council's San Marino home. Yoch loaned this figure to Dorothy Arzner a few years before using it in her own garden. (Author's photograph)

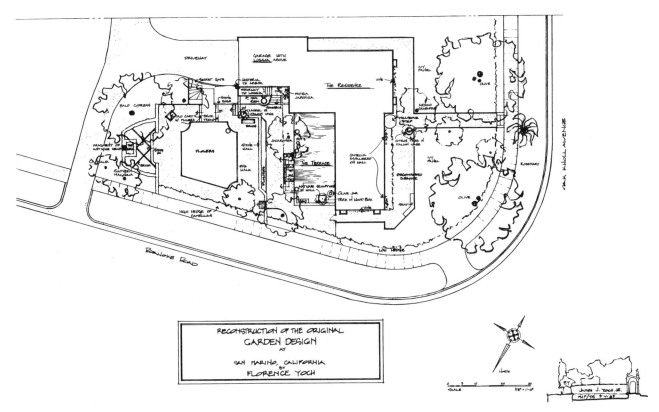

Reconstructed plan, Florence Yoch and Lucile Council's San Marino home. (Drafting by Ms. M. Jana Pereau and Mr. Timothy G. Scott)

Fireplace wall, Florence Yoch and Lucile Council's San Marino home. (Courtesy of Mr. Thomas C. Moore)

Left: View from terrace, Florence Yoch and Lucile Council's San Marino home. The sequence of eye-catchers concludes in a small classical head. (Courtesy of Mr. Thomas C. Moore)

Right: East Garden, Florence Yoch and Lucile Council's San Marino home. (Courtesy of Mr. Thomas C. Moore)

Lower right: Pebbled tread, divided stair, Florence Yoch and Lucile Council's San Marino home. (Courtesy of Mr. Thomas C. Moore)

Below: West façade, Florence Yoch and Lucile Council's San Marino home. (Courtesy of Mr. Thomas C. Moore)

In the Italian manner, a place for work fits comfortably into the garden. Yoch planned the tool room beneath the stair that rises to the loggia. Nearby, an Italian vase is the dipping basin for a fountain, in a composition perhaps inspired by Cecil Pinsent's charming stair at the Villa Le Balze, which she sketched on a visit in the 1920s. At her San Marino home, Yoch set scenes for her ideal leisure life in a suburban backyard.

Pasadena

In 1940, within six years of starting the San Marino house, Florence Yoch and Lucile Council were building again, this time on a hillside in north Pasadena. They laid out a garden that is assertively American to suit what their friend John Peirce remembers as the "barn red house trimmed in white" and the studio modeled on the Monterey Custom House. The massing and mix of roofs that so contribute to the unpretentious feeling of the architecture recall the happenstance arrangement at the Yoch family cottage at Laguna Beach, where Florence Yoch spent her childhood summers.

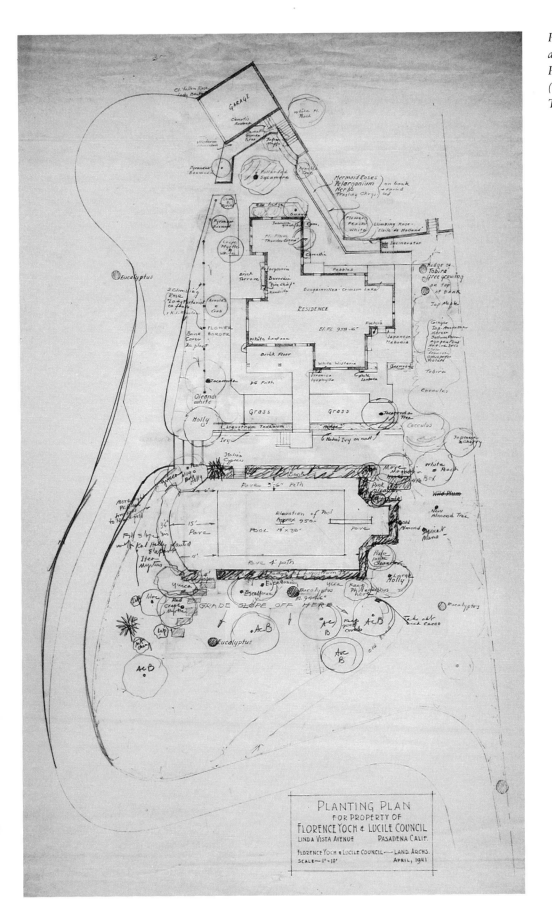

Plan, Florence Yoch and Lucile Council's Pasadena home. (Courtesy of Mr. Thomas C. Moore)

Pathways are the garden. On the upper level, flower-bordered walks surround the house and pause only briefly for a court between the main house and the studio and for a small area of lawn. The house itself is the central panel, and the routes around it offer views over colorful perennial beds to the distant mountains. In contrast to the outward-looking garden around the house, the lower garden turns in upon itself; at its center within a forest lies a pool, which Yoch surrounded with paths and hedges.

This lot was the first Yoch owned that had the advantage of character, and the development increases its drama. Beginning in simple wood rail gates, the long drive rises and curves to give the impression that the house sits within an immense estate. Pollarded plane trees and a hedge, screening off the nearby houses, suggest formal patterns that the seeming indirection of the road contradicts. The green enclosure of the drive breaks suddenly to reveal the bright red house, with its rich flower borders and spacious vistas.

Antique associations have a minor role in this garden. Yoch muted the individual power of loved mementos from the past by using them in witty combinations. A garlanded vase and a graceful column proclaim a civilized outpost on a barren mountain. A small classical statue leans rakishly against the large block of the chimney, and a fragment of a rustic stone column rises from a corner of the lawn.

The simple rail fence with plants poking through suggests a naïve

Front façade, Florence Yoch and Lucile Council's Pasadena home. The relics of the past have become incidental. (Courtesy of Mr. Thomas C. Moore)

Entry court and stair to the studio, Florence Yoch and Lucile Council's Pasadena home. (Author's photograph)

country style in the first view of the house, but exploration reveals many cunning devices. Contrary to custom, the entry court between the house and the studio is most irregular in shape and planting. A Japanese maple, an Arnold crabapple, a guava, and a large boxwood mark the four corners of this space. As though breaking through an ancient foundation, the maple grows out of the steps to the studio. Farthest away, the other enclosed garden, around the pool, is most formal. During installation Yoch reinforced its symmetry by making the ends of the evergreen hedges matching concave arcs. Plant combinations are unusual, for magnolias grow alongside Italian cypresses, and a cycad adds a strangely tropical note in an ivy bed.

Yoch treated the hillside site in a novel way, and her most original solutions are without European precedent. The formal entry door is far from the drive and not easily visible from it. Not foundation plants but borders set away from the house form foregrounds for the views. The pool lies so far downhill that it comes as a surprise. *Better Homes and Gardens* considered the design so successful they used it in color to illustrate their section on "limited planting space."[3]

The garden gives the freedom of many choices, beginning with selecting among the routes leading to the five doors of the house. The pathway that ambles around the perimeter of the house provides a variety of scenes as it narrows, jogs, swells, angles, changes surface from brick to decomposed granite to stone, and disappears out of sight. Yoch's many

Formal entry, Florence Yoch and Lucile Council's Pasadena home. A carefully worked out accompaniment of pots. (Courtesy of Mr. Thomas C. Moore)

Florence Yoch, 1964. (Courtesy of Mrs. Robert E. Ward)

photographs of this route suggest how she continually worked to improve the arrangement of pots, statues, and other ornaments that modulate the turns, give a restful focus, and then nudge and lure the visitor onward.

Refreshingly American in its bold effects, the garden is open and inviting. Flowers are up front, views are available everywhere, utility determines the walks, and a swimming pool is a major feature. Yoch and Council had found in themselves clients who took to heart Yoch's injunction to study "local demands and conditions" to produce "an inherently California type of house."

Carmel

Fluent in the language of European landscaping, Florence Yoch spent her life revitalizing traditional garden forms by adapting them to the new problems of American suburbia. She sought change, and she wrote in her notes, "Actually all thinking art lovers must welcome upheaval, change, revolution, however painful the process and regretful the apparent loss of loved patterns." Moving to a new climate and faced with a new vocabulary of plants in Carmel during her seventies, she developed some of her most original solutions to garden design, and her own home exemplified in a new way her ideal of "the supreme excellence of simplicity." The Carmel home is truly native American.

Hearing from the noted landscape architect John MacLaren of the do-nothing attitude ("a few geraniums in a pot and the garden's done") to

Lucile Council, 1964. (Courtesy of Mrs. Robert E. Ward)

landscaping in Northern California, she had chosen not to begin her practice there. Toward the end of her life, when a garden meant a place to entertain a few friends with a review of plants and have a meal, this presumed casual attitude in the north was an appealing invitation to purer forms after the intensity of her earlier work.

In 1960, Florence Yoch and Lucile Council remodeled "Lazycroft Cottage," their new house and its garden in Carmel. A client had sold them two lots with a view of the ocean, a great contrast to the enclosed site of their 1950s Pasadena home. In Carmel, they made their last home together until Lucile Council died in 1964; Yoch continued to live there and practice landscape architecture until her own death in 1972.

Lean and trim, the Carmel garden has few geometrical pranks or classical ornaments. Observing that "the greatest draftsmen express significance with a few strokes, whereas minor ones need to elaborate," Yoch used only elemental forms: a curve and a rectangle. With these, she established the basic facts of gardening life as moments of order within the splendid natural theater of an oak forest and a marine vista. From a gate at the road, a lazy path of ramps and steps winds up the hillside to the friendly terrace adjoining the house. Farther uphill is a working parterre, cornered with apple trees, displaying lilies eight feet tall and providing white asparagus for the table.

Like temporary encampments on an expedition into a wild territory, occasional spots in the garden offer repose and peace. Along the walk—and easing its purposeful climb—a bench invites momentary rest. At the oak-sheltered terrace, a classical bust mounted on a simple wooden

The walk, Florence Yoch and Lucile Council's Carmel home. (Photograph by Florence Yoch, courtesy of Mr. Thomas C. Moore)

The terrace overlooked by lilies, Florence Yoch and Lucile Council's Carmel home. In a patch of sun by the house, a grouping of olive jar and pots recalls the similar arrangement in the W. H. Council Garden. (Photograph by Florence Yoch, courtesy of Mr. Thomas C. Moore)

pedestal and plants in an informal mix of pots extend a comforting welcome. A similarly casual arrangement of logs, an old olive jar, and a chair and a bench furnish a place for the pleasures of outdoor conversations in a shaded nook. The wall angles slightly on its way to the corner to achieve a more relaxed effect, fitting the *Swiss Family Robinson* romance throughout the composition. This is indeed a place with "a cool side, a warm corner fit for all seasons," as Yoch once described the ideal garden.

In Carmel she was able to live at last among great trees, which she loved from her childhood. She preserved her own forest at great cost, and she paid a thousand dollars a year simply to keep the trees well trimmed. Venerating this native stand of trees, she felled only three to put in her garden, and almost a decade passed before she could decide to cut down a large oak that shaded the terrace and made growing flowers there impossible. Her notes reveal how she arrived at her radical plan for balancing her own needs and respecting the wilderness on the site: "This garden is proof of the limitation put upon design by the condition of the soil, climate, age, trees, roots, slopes. The answer is to have a naturalistic garden." She had come a long way from her first commissions, and wryly observed that "in the early days I thought I was creating," but now knew, adapting an aphorism of Francis Bacon, "you command Nature by obeying her."[4]

The winding path seems to trace a journey, a final pilgrimage, with a few treasured objects for company. Within the monumental natural landscape, the Mediterranean jars and a single English bench recall the principal inspirations of her early practice. New plants, most notably the gifts of her friend Thomas Moore, continually refreshed the scene.

The terrace, Florence Yoch and Lucile Council's Carmel home. A shaded corner. (Photograph by Florence Yoch, courtesy of Mr. Thomas C. Moore)

The design of the garden illustrated her continual search for renewal. She partially buried her great olive jars along the walk, as though they were in an abandoned villa garden, crumbling back into the earth as new forms rose up around them. She explained her enthusiasm for the freedom to choose and to change, the source of her artistic creed: "A vastly comforting thought sustains us while we wallow in the 'Silurian slime' of the period of change—where except in the ambivalence of design has mankind been so party to evolution, so privileged to see and to suffer as changes evolve."

In Carmel she abandoned all but a hint of her usual geometries. Forest and sea take on primary roles in the landscape drama, which goes well beyond her earlier focus on the more temperate pastoral entertainments of English country house weekends, of the Italian *villegiatura,* and of American picnics and games. Her last garden allowed grand natural features to stand free as models of her own robust independence. In the shade of her woods she wrote of "great trees, each symbolic of some flooding emotion." Reviewing the passionate contradictions within her precepts and practice during a life spent creating places for country freedom, she celebrated that "most legitimate and disconcerting complication, that essence of our democracy, individual taste."

Endnotes

NOTES TO PREFACE

1. Florence Yoch letter to Thomas C. Moore, 24 June 1971.

NOTES TO CHAPTER I

1. From Florence Yoch's notes for an uncompleted book, "Plants as Materials of Design in Planting." Unless a specific source is given, quotations attributed to Florence Yoch are all from her notes for this book that she began in 1958.
2. Mrs. J. E. Pleasants, *History of Orange County, California* (Los Angeles: J. R. Finnell, 1931), I, 449; Thomas B Talbert, *The Historical Volume and Reference Works Covering . . . Laguna Beach . . .* (Whittier, Calif.: Historical Publishers, 1963), III, 246.
3. Helena Modjeska, *Memories and Impressions* (1910. Reprint. New York: Benjamin Blom, 1969), p. 243.
4. Theodore Payne, *Life on the Modjeska Ranch in the Gay Nineties* (Los Angeles: Kruckeberg Press, 1962), pp. 40–41.
5. Axel Munthe, *The Story of San Michele* (1929. Reprint. New York: E.P. Dutton, 1937), pp. 336–37.
6. Charles Macomb Flandrau, *Viva Mexico!* (New York, 1908. Reprint. Appleton, 1928), p. 250.
7. Ruth Billheimer, "Women Achieve Fame as Landscape Artists," *Pasadena Post,* 29 May 1932, p. 5.
8. Florence Yoch letter to Thomas C. Moore, 12 May 1969.

NOTES TO CHAPTER II

1. After Florence Yoch's death, Miss Ruth Shellhorn carefully modified several areas of this garden in keeping with the spirit of the original design.

2. From the draft introductory chapter of Yoch's book "on the subject of 'Plants as Materials of Design in Planting.'" Ruth Billheimer ("Women Achieve Fame as Landscape Artists," *Pasadena Post* [29 May 1932], p. 5) admired the sense of permanence Yoch and Council achieved by planting venerable trees that made buildings seem "as though they had always been there." David Streatfield ("The Evolution of the California Landscape: Suburbia at the Zenith," *Landscape Architecture* 67 [September 1977], p. 418) observed the "effortless and unselfconscious quality" which induced a feeling of "inevitability" in Florence Yoch's work.

NOTES TO CHAPTER III

1. Margaret Olthof Goldsmith, *Designs for Outdoor Living* (New York: George W. Stewart, 1941), pp. 141–42.
2. Irene Mayer Selznick, *A Private View* (New York: Knopf, 1983), p. 198.

NOTES TO CHAPTER IV

1. Selznick Memorandum to Joseph J. Cohn: 11 March 1935. Quotations from David O. Selznick's papers used by kind permission of Selznick Properties, Ltd., and the Humanities Research Center, University of Texas, Austin.
2. Selznick Memorandum to Joseph J. Cohn: 5 March 1935.
3. Selznick letter to Florence Yoch, 22 March 1935.
4. *The New York Times,* 20 November 1936, p. 27, col. 2.
5. Bob Thomas, *Thalberg: Life and Legend* (Garden City, N.J.: Doubleday, 1969), pp. 299, 302.
6. Samuel Marx, *Mayer and Thalberg: The Make-Believe Saints* (New York: Random House, 1975), pp. 248–49.
7. Thomas, *Thalberg,* p. 301.

8. *The New York Times,* 21 August 1936, p. 12, col. 2.

9. *Memo from David O. Selznick,* ed. Rudy Behlmer (New York: Viking, 1972), p. 225 (20 October 1939); p. 145 (6 January 1937).

10. *Memo,* p. 212 (20 September 1939).

11. I am indebted to William J. Tomkin for this information from Art Director Lyle Wheeler's estimates.

12. Wilbur G. Kurtz, "Technical Adviser: The Making of *Gone With the Wind,*" ed. Richard Harwell, *Atlanta Historical Society Journal* 22, no. 2 (Summer 1978), p. 7.

13. "Technical Adviser," p. 124.

14. Susan Myrick, *White Columns in Hollywood* (Macon, Ga.: Mercer University Press, 1982), p. 34.

NOTES TO CHAPTER VI

1. Quoted in Diana Balmori, Diane Kostial McGuire, and Eleanor M. McPeck, *Beatrix Farrand's American Landscapes* (Sagaponack, N.Y.: Sagapress, 1985), p. 173.

2. Florence Yoch, "Fitting the Land for Human Use . . . ," *California Arts and Architecture* (July 1930), p. 72.

3. Quoted in Balmori et al., *Farrand,* p. 130.

4. Michael J. Phillips, "New Garden of Eden Laid Out in Great Mexican Estate," *Western Florist and Nurseryman,* 25 December 1930, pp. 4–5.

5. Quoted in "New Garden," p. 6.

6. Quoted in "New Garden," p. 6.

7. "New Garden," p. 6.

8. Quoted in "New Garden," p. 6.

9. "Dramatic Assemblage . . . ," *Pasadena Star-News,* 26 November 1927, sec. 4, pp. 31–32.

10. "Dramatic Assemblage . . . ," p. 32.

11. Florence Yoch, "The Court Garden of the Women's Athletic Club," *Landscape Architecture* 17 (1926), p. 37.

12. "Court Garden," p. 37.

13. "Court Garden," p. 39.

NOTES TO CHAPTER VII

1. Ruth Billheimer, "Women Achieve Fame as Landscape Artists," *Pasadena Post,* 29 May 1932, p. 5.

2. *Letters and Panegyricus,* trans. Betty Radice (Cambridge: Harvard University Press, 1922), I, 341.

3. *Better Homes and Gardens' Garden Book* (Des Moines: Meredith, 1951), pp. 26–27.

4. Francis Bacon, *Novum Organum,* Aphorism 1.129, in *Advancement of Learning and Novum Organum,* ed. James Edward Creighton. Rev. ed. (New York: Collier & Son, 1900), p. 366.

Florence Yoch's Commissions

A dagger (†) indicates that Florence Yoch only provided landscape ideas, or altered existing gardens.

1918

Mary Magdalen Church, Camarillo, California
Residence of Mrs. Howard Huntington (Mrs. James R. Brehm), Pasadena, California
Residence of Miss Eleanor Hague, Pasadena, California (1918–21)
Residence of Mr. W. K. Jewett, Pasadena, California (1918–28)

1919

†Shoshone Falls Park, Shoshone, Idaho

1920

The partnership of Florence Yoch and Lucia Fox began and ended this year.

Residence of C. B. Boothe, South Pasadena, California (1920–21)
Residence of Mrs. Dorothy Dobbins Freeman, Pasadena, California
Residence of Mr. and Mrs. Wellslake Morse, Pasadena, California
Residence of Mr. R. R. Goodell, Pasadena, California
Residence of Dr. A. A. Noyes, Pasadena, California
†Orange County Park, Santa Ana, California
Residence of Mr. Paul J. Pitner, Pasadena, California
†Residence of Miss Mattie Ritchey, Santa Ana, California
Residence of F. A. Weyerhauser, South Pasadena, California
Wilshire Country Club, Los Angeles, California

1921

Residence of Mr. and Mrs. Frank A. Bovey, Pasadena, California
Residence of Miss Sarah E. Carter, Los Angeles, California
Residence of Mr. Y. R. Del Valle, Piru, California
Residence of Mr. Joseph M. Hixon, Pasadena, California
Residence of Mrs. Hugh Lowther, San Gabriel, California
Pasadena Dispensary, Pasadena, California
Santa Ana Birch St. Park, Santa Ana, California
Santa Ana Schools, Santa Ana, California
Residence of H. W. Schultz, Pasadena, California
Residence of Mrs. A. M. Shields, Irvington, California
Residence of J. S. Thurston, Laguna Beach, California
Vroman's Bookstore, Pasadena, California

1922

†Rancho los Alamitos, Residence of Mr. and Mrs. Fred Bixby, Long Beach, California (1922–36)
Residence of Misses Elizabeth and Hallie Davenport, Pasadena, California (1922–23)
Residence of R. N. Frick, South Pasadena, California
Fair Oaks, Residence of Mr. and Mrs. C. W. Gates, Pasadena, California (1922–29)
†Mrs. Myron Hunt, Pasadena, California
Residence of Dr. W. H. Roberts, Pasadena, California
Residence of J. A. Smiley, Santa Ana, California
Residence of Capt. S. M. Spalding, Beverly Hills, California
Il Brolino, Residence of Mrs. Mary Stewart, Montecito, California (1922–23)
Residence of F. N. Warren, Pasadena, California

1923

Residence of Miss Emma Barnhisel, San Jose, California
Cumnock School of Expression, Los Angeles, California
Residence of Mr. and Mrs. Donald H. Fry, South Pasadena, California (1923, 1932)
Residence of Mrs. Max Hayward, South Pasadena, California
Residence of W. Lindley, Altadena, California
Polytechnic Elementary School, Pasadena, California
Residence of E. A. Titcomb, Los Angeles, California
Residence of Mr. William S. Waith, Beverly Hills, California
Residence of Mrs. Edwin Wilcox, San Jose, California
Residence of Mr. Alfred Wright, South Pasadena, California

1924

Residence of Mr. E. V. Armstrong, Pasadena, California
†Residence of Mrs. N. D. Carpenter, Los Angeles, California
Residence of Mr. and Mrs. W. H. Council, South Pasadena, California
Residence of Mrs. Jonathan S. Dodge, Altadena, California
Residence of Miss Laura J. Emery, Los Angeles, California
Residence of Mr. Frank S. Hodge, Los Angeles, California
Residence of J. W. Johnson, Glendale, California
Pasadena Preventorium, Altadena, California
Residence of Mrs. M. G. Ritchie, South Pasadena, California

1925

The partnership of Yoch and Council began in this year.

Residence of Mr. E. J. Bowen, Los Angeles, California
Residence of Mrs. Andrew Brown, Pasadena, California
Coast Royal Park, Laguna Beach, California .
El Mirador Subdivision developed by the Yoch Company, Laguna Beach, California (1925–27)
Residence of Mr. and Mrs. A. Parley Johnson, Downey, California (1925–27)
Residence of Mrs. J. H. Kelleher, South Pasadena, California
Residence of A. N. Kemp, Santa Monica, California
Residence of E. J. Miley, Los Angeles, California
Residence of Mrs. R. A. Puffer, Glendale, California
Residence of Mr. Joseph Skidmore, Laguna Beach, California
Residence of Dr. and Mrs. J. Morris Slemons, Los Angeles, California (1925–26)
Residence of Mr. Douglas Smith, Altadena, California
Women's Athletic Club, Los Angeles, California

1926

Residence of Mr. O. H. Barr, Santa Ana, California
Residence of Miss Elizabeth Berry, Pasadena, California
Residence of Mrs. George E. Coleman, Montecito, California
Residence of Dr. W. M. Dickie, Berkeley, California

Residence of Mr. C. W. Driver, Santa Monica, California
Residence of Mrs. J. A. Freeman, Pasadena, California
Residence of Mrs. Richard B. Fudger, Los Angeles, California (1926–27)
†W. K. Kellogg Ranch, Pomona, California (1926–27)
Residence of Miss Mary V. McCormick, Pasadena, California
†Residence of Mrs. Oswald Oliver, Los Angeles, California
Residence of Mr. A. B. Ruddock, San Marino, California
San Marcos Building, Santa Barbara, California
Residence of Mr. Robert H. Stephenson, Pasadena, California
Residence of Mrs. Irving J. Sturgis, Pasadena, California (1926–34)
Residence of Mr. E. S. Wade, Los Angeles, California

1927

Residence of Mrs. Francis Baer, South Pasadena, California
Residence of Mr. H. Stanley Bent, San Marino, California
Il Vescovo, Residence of Mr. and Mrs. W. T. Bishop, Bel Air, California
Residence of J. F. Burkhard, Pasadena, California (1927–30)
Residence of Mrs. Garrettson Dulin, Pasadena, California
The Ebell Club of Los Angeles, Los Angeles, California
Residence of Mrs. Frank W. Emery/Mrs. Ruth von Platen, Pasadena, California
Residence of Mrs. B. G. Hodges, Pasadena, California
The Jewish Alliance, Los Angeles, California
†Pasadena Public Library, Pasadena, California
Residence of Mrs. Robert Pitcairn, Jr., Pasadena, California
San Bernardino Schools, San Bernardino, California
Serendipity Antique Shop, Pasadena, California (1927–28)
Residence of Mrs. Reese Taylor, San Marino, California (1927–28)
The Town Club, Pasadena, California
Unitarian Church of Los Angeles, Los Angeles, California (1927–28)
Residence of Mrs. J. K. Urmston, Pebble Beach, California

1928

Boys' & Girls' Aid Society, Pasadena, California
†Casa Santa Cruz, Residence of Mr. and Mrs. Bernard Hoffman, Santa Barbara, California (1928, 1938)
Residence of Mr. Alfred Wright, South Pasadena, California

1929

Residence of Mr. Ira L. Bryner, Pasadena, California
Residence of Mr. Milton L. Davidson, Pasadena, California (1929–31)
Residence of Mrs. G. P. Griffith, Los Angeles, California (1929–30)
Residence of Mrs. Richard M. Griffith, San Marino, California (1929–30)

Residence of Mr. William B. Hart, Pasadena, California

Residence of Mr. and Mrs. Preston Hotchkis, San Marino, California

Residence and Botanical Garden of Mr. and Mrs. B. F. Johnston (Jardín Botánico Las Palmas), Los Mochis, Sinaloa, Mexico (1929–30)

Residence of Mr. Gordon B. Kaufmann, Bel Air, California

Residence of Mr. L. D. Kellogg, Pasadena, California (1929–31)

Residence of Mrs. James G. MacPherson, Pasadena, California (1929–30)

Residence of Mr. W. S. Mason, Pasadena, California

Residence of Mr. Daniel Murphy, Los Angeles, California (1929–30)

†Occidental College, Eagle Rock, California

Residence of Mr. and Mrs. Edwin M. Sherman, Pasadena, California

1930

Residence of Mr. and Mrs. Thomas Bell, Pasadena, California

†Residence of Miss Rose Bernard, Pasadena, California

California Institute of Technology: The Athenaeum (faculty club), and Undergraduate Housing, Pasadena, California (1930–31)

†Calvin House, Residence of Mrs. Cecil B. DeMille, Los Angeles, California

Residence of Mrs. G. Watson French, Montecito, California

Residence of R. N. Frick, South Pasadena, California

Good Hope Clinic, Los Angeles, California

Residence of Mr. Stuart O'Melveny, South Pasadena, California

Residence of Mrs. William A. Slater, Santa Barbara, California

1931

Bishop Johnson Memorial Chapel, Westwood, California (1931–32)

Residence of Mr. Cyril Chappellet, Bel Air, California

Residence of Mrs. W. S. Charnley, San Marino, California

Residence of Mrs. R. Y. Dakin, South Pasadena, California

Davidson Residence, location unknown

Residence of Mrs. Richard B. Fudger, Beverly Hills, California

Residence of Dr. L. G. Hunnicutt, Pasadena, California

Residence of Mr. James M. Irvine, Altadena, California (1931–32)

Rancho San Carlos, Residence of Mr. C. H. Jackson, Jr., Santa Barbara, California (1931–33)

Morgan Residence, location unknown

†Casa Alvarado, Residence of Miss Zelia Nuttall, Coyoacan, Mexico

Residence of Col. J. H. Poole, Pasadena, California

Residence of Mrs. L. D. Ricketts, Pasadena, California

Residence of Mr. John Newton Russell, Los Angeles, California (1931–32)

†Residence of C. O. Sparks, location unknown

Residence of Mr. and Mrs. Reese Taylor, Pasadena, California

Residence of Mrs. M. O. Terry, San Marino, California

†Williams Residence, location unknown

1932

Residence of Miss Dorothy Arzner, Los Angeles, California (1932--33)

Residence of Mrs. T. G. Franck, San Marino, California

Residence of Mr. and Mrs. F. D. Frost, Jr., San Marino, California

Residence of Mrs. H. H. Garstin, Redlands, California

†Mira Flores, Residence of Mrs. J. P. Jefferson, Montecito, California

Residence of Mrs. J. F. Sartori, Santa Monica, California

Residence of Mrs. W. L. Stewart, Jr., Pasadena, California

1933

Garfield School of South Pasadena, South Pasadena, California

Residence of Mr. Howard B. Hawks, Beverly Hills, California

†Holladay Residence, location unknown

Residence of Mr. R. B. Honeyman, San Marino, California

Residence of Mrs. Thomas P. Mathews, Monterey, California (1933–34)

Residence of Mr. H. W. O'Melveny, Bel Air, California

Residence of Mrs. Kenneth B. Wilson, San Marino, California

1934

Residence of Mr. and Mrs. G. Eshman, Bel Air, California (1934–36)

Residence of Mrs. R. S. Liebig, Bel Air, California (1934–35)

Residence of Mr. and Mrs. David O. Selznick, Beverly Hills, California (1934–35, 1939)

Residence of Miss Florence Yoch and Miss Lucile Council, San Marino, California

1935

Crocker Residence, location unknown

Residence of Mrs. J. G. MacPherson, Pasadena, California (1935–37)

Smiley Residence, Santa Ana, California

Residence of Mr. and Mrs. Jack Warner, Beverly Hills, California (1935–37)

1936

Residence of Mr. and Mrs. B. F. Bundy, Arcadia, California (1936–37)

Residence of Mr. and Mrs. Vernon S. Charnley, Pasadena, California

Residence of Mr. George Cukor, Los Angeles, California

The Garden of Allah (film), Selznick International

Romeo and Juliet (film), Metro Goldwyn Mayer

Residence of Mr. and Mrs. Homer Samuels (Amelita Galli-Curci), Los Angeles, California (1936–39)

1937

Residence of Mr. and Mrs. Sherman Asche, Pasadena, California

The Good Earth (film), Metro Goldwyn Mayer

Residence of Judge Ben B. Lindsey, Bel Air, California

Residence of Mrs. Daniel H. Martin, San Marino, California

Residence of Mr. and Mrs. Emerson Spear/Mrs. Georgie Van de Kamp, Pasadena, California (1937–38)

Residence of Mr. Leland K. Whittier, Holmby Hills, California (1937–38)

1938

Residence of Mr. Harry Borun, Beverly Hills, California (1938–39)

Residence of Mrs. C. Pardee Erdman, Pasadena, California (1938–41)

Residence of Mr. Harold S. Gladwyn, Montecito, California (1938–39)

†Scott Residence, Arcadia, California

Residence of Mr. and Mrs. Howard G. Smits, Pasadena, California

Residence of Mr. Charles Stanton, Pasadena, California

1939

Residence of Mr. and Mrs. Henry F. Haldeman, Los Angeles, California

Residence of Mr. and Mrs. Frank W. MacLennan, Los Angeles, California (1939–40)

†Residence of Mrs. Harry G. Steele, location unknown

Tara in *Gone With the Wind* (film), Selznick International

Residence of Mr. and Mrs. C. Van Niven, Beverly Hills, California (1939–40)

1940

†Residence of Miss Billie Burke, Brentwood, California

Residence of Mrs. E. W. Shirk, Redlands, California

Residence of Miss Florence Yoch and Miss Lucile Council, Pasadena, California (1940–41)

1941

Residence of Miss Ida M. Allerton, Pasadena, California

Residence of Mrs. Lawrence Barker, Santa Anita Rancho, California

Residence of Mr. and Mrs. Charles Edwin Davis, Pasadena, California

†Residence of Mr. and Mrs. Albert Doerr, Pasadena, California

How Green Was My Valley (film), Twentieth Century-Fox

Residence of Mr. Ben Smith, Santa Anita Rancho, California

1946

Rancho Los Cerritos, Residence of Mr. R. B. Honeyman, Jr., San Juan Capistrano, California (1946–47)

Residence of Mr. Edward R. Valentine, San Marino, California

1948

Residence of Mrs. Florence Banning, Pasadena, California

1952

Kendrick Residence, Pleasanton, California

Residence of Mrs. Richard W. Millar, San Marino, California (1952–54)

St. Edmund's Episcopal Church, San Marino, California

Residence of Mr. Frank Work, Monterey, California

Residence of Mrs. Reese Taylor, Pasadena, California

1955

Casa Alvarado, Residence of Dr. and Mrs. W. R. Heard, Monterey, California (1955–57)

Residence of Dr. and Mrs. Edmund von Hasseln, Monterey, California (1955–56)

Robinson's Department Store, Beverly Hills, California

1957

Casa Abrego Club, Monterey, California

Residence of Mr. Harrison Chandler, Pasadena, California

Residence of Mrs. David E. Park, Montecito, California (1957–61)

1958

Oakmead Farm, Residence of Mrs. Dorothy H. Cohn, Pleasanton, California

Residence of Mr. and Mrs. Charles Edwin Davis, San Marino, California

Garland Residence, location unknown

Residence of Mr. Reginald J. Johnson, Pasadena, California

1959

Residence of Mr. and Mrs. Sherman Asche, Montecito, California

1960

Residence of the Misses Erica and Kathy Ward, Ann Arbor, Michigan

Residence of Miss Florence Yoch and Miss Lucile Council, Carmel, California

1963

Residence of Dr. and Mrs. Donald Scanlon, Carmel, California

1964

Haines-Foster Studio, Hollywood, California

After Lucile Council's death in 1964, plans carry only Florence Yoch's name.

1965

Residence of Mr. and Mrs. Charles Edwin Davis, Pasadena, California (1965–69)
Residence of Mr. and Mrs. Hugo Oswald, Ukiah, California

1968

Residence of Mr. W. O. Minor, Merced, California

1969

Residence of Mrs. Reese Taylor, Pasadena, California

1970

Francis Doud House, Monterey, California (1970–71)

The following projects are documented without exact dates.
Residence of Mr. and Mrs. Harry J. Bauer, San Marino, California
Residence of Mr. Clark E. Bell, San Marino, California
Residence of Mr. and Mrs. Herbert Bell, San Marino, California
Residence of Mr. Kenniston Bell, San Marino, California
Residence of Mr. S. R. Burns, San Gabriel, California
Residence of Mr. H. C. Christians, Eagle Rock, California
Residence of Mr. Arthur W. Colby, Pasadena, California
Residence of Mr. Dardy Donnelly, Pasadena, California
Gila Pueblo, location unknown
Glendale Schools, Glendale, California
Residence of Mr. Walter A. Green, North Hollywood, California
†Residence of Mr. A. B. Hastings, Beverly Hills, California
Residence of Mr. George A. Hormel, Bel Air, California
Residence of Dr. Arthur Hurd, Pasadena, California
Residence of Mr. W. A. Johnson, Pasadena, California
Residence of Mrs. James T. Jordan, Los Angeles, California
Lobrero Theater, location unknown
Residence of Mr. James R. Mason, Pasadena, California
Orthopedic Hospital School, Los Angeles, California
†Sycamore Rosewood Apartments, location unknown
Mr. William Valentine, San Marino, California

Fitting the Land for Human Use

An Art That Is Closely Allied to Architecture

Florence Yoch

In progressive stages through the centuries since the atrophy and disintegration of the Renaissance, the architect has sloughed off many of his former attributes—such as, painter, sculptor, worker in fine marbles, and designer of great gardens.

The newer developments of science and modern living requirements have produced another category of applied arts—plumbing, various electrical arrangements, heating and ventilating, the handling of steel. All of these are expressions of the modern trend toward utilitarianism and increased physical comfort.

The older arts, however, were too highly developed to be discarded. Civilization has absorbed them and demands their continuance. In the readjustment they have fallen to the lot of specialists, or, if you prefer, lesser men. Each one of them has gone through the long period of decadence and the valley of shadow that is typified by the wooden glories of cookie-scalloped Gothic architecture. Now Bacon comforts the landscape gardener with his graceful but much quoted "You will ever find as the ages grow in ability and elegance, men come to build stately sooner than to garden finely, as though gardening were the higher art." A franker interpretation is probably that architecture is, and necessarily must be, the dominating and determinative art. All the others are fundamentally purely amenities. Architecture is equally as enduring and formative of men's minds as political institutions. Witness the living importance today of Grecian architecture with Roman laws.

Any article made by man, from the smallest and most useless bauble to the most complexly functioning building, is subject to rules of design and is conditioned by intentional use. I think all will agree that, in the applied arts, use is the prime factor influencing design. Materials can be beaten, bent, carved, and moulded to serve utility, but in the so-called "pure" arts, materials often dictate the expression.

Landscape gardening follows the parallel of architecture, and is only expressive and completely interesting when treated as an applied art with a definite and legitimate function. When a man-made landscape loses human relation and claims as its reason-for-being mere beauty, it rarely succeeds. Charles Eliot aptly described landscape architecture as "the art of fitting the land for human use and enjoyment."

Here, as elsewhere, all genuine design springs from absolute need. In landscape gardening the contributing and limiting elements are climate, water conditions, and materials available—whether plants or building. These are subjected to the influence of racial characteristics and demands, and the net result in every case is type or style.

Getting down to first principles in this manner is exactly comparable to studying primitives in the graphic arts. One is led to the realization that in the peasant gardens we find the essential qualities of each race or nation. The larger and most sophisticated run to a type. Just as there is a norm or glamorous ideal for other amenities in life, we find the more elaborate gardens trending toward a sameness, or universality, whichever you prefer to call the lack of distinctive national character. We have French cooking, German music, English servants, Italian gardens, advertised all over the earth's surface.

Very definite types of landscape art reflect the life of each people. The formal French city plan—the informal English village plan—is each perfect in its function and its expression of beauty. The austere settings for great public structures consummately handled by the French; the peaceful effect of the English park; the cozy charm of English domestic work; the regal splendor of the Italian pleasaunce, have never been successfully imitated by any other peoples.

Among the humbler folk we see outdoor living arrangements even more intriguing. No Italian peasant is too humble to have his scrap of paved terrace, where most of the domestic rites take place. They are frequently perched on steep hillsides, overlooking stupendous views, and always revealing the same unconscious, almost dramatic sense of the picturesque that is inherent in their race.

The Spanish peasant's patio provides indolent comfort in the most compact form. Interest and beauty are never lacking. The sharp contrast of white walls with interesting leaf texture and strong shadow, always some sort of fountain which is utilitarian as well as attractive, complete these beguiling little gardens.

The English cottage garden is famous the world over for its splashes of brilliant flower color. There is a poetic atmosphere of delicacy that we do not find in the more arid climates.

In France, the little potagers of the peasant indicate the Frenchman's thrift and his artisanry. Nowhere have economy of space, shipshape straight lines, and determination to wrest the last ounce of productivity from the soil; nowhere have these things produced such an effect of smartness and interest, as in France. The very name "potager"—place from which the potage comes—gives one a sense of its compactness. Peasant gardens owe a large part of their naive charm and interest to the materials of which they are ordinarily made. The poor man must construct walls, dipping wells, or other utilities, of the materials most near at hand and most practically adapted to general use.

One of the greatest points of interest in building gardens in California is the variety of materials available to harmonize with the many styles of architecture. It does not seem to me that our most interesting local gardens are necessarily those where alien and elaborate materials have been commandeered by the carload. Here, as elsewhere, an expressive and functioning use of logical materials tells the better story.

Landscape architecture properly approached is an art of design, and the adequately trained members of the profession nowadays receive an education in design as well as in horticulture and engineering, and should have a thorough appreciation of architectural types and requirements, so that each garden can be properly subordinated to the house and complement it. The old days of bushwhacking gardening are rapidly disappearing, and a genuine collaboration between the architect and landscape man results in many practical advantages to the home owner. A study of the site for contours, garden aspect, and location of outdoor utilities, should be thoroughly made even before the house is designed.

This is an era of machinery and commerce, compelling men to congregate in the cities, and we find with increasing wealth, following Lord Bacon's dictum, men are coming to desire to garden finely in their city homes. Most of the cities of Europe are relics of the past, and a thorough search for interesting garden settings, for finer homes, throughout the continent will result in disappointment, which is due to the fact that most of the really interesting old places were built when cities were very congested, had narrow streets, and no opportunity for gardens other than small interior courts. Since the days of modern building, most of the European countries have been absolutely inert in the matter of architecture. The great exception to this is, of course, Paris, where many fine and costly homes have some attempt at garden setting, but even here it is not the best period of French architecture or landscape work, but the more decadent recent types that we find. In a thorough canvassing of such widely separated cities as Madrid, Florence, Brussels, London, New York, the same general condition is found to prevail—work that is merely expensive, but not satisfying.

It is apparent from various indications that the coming era is typified by and probably belongs to America. It is natural enough that in the rapidly developing American cities we are finding the most logical and efficient, and therefore, pleasant expression of architecture and garden work. In America the general level of architecture is higher and the results are more interesting in California than in any other section of this broad land. This is due to the fact that while our southern architects have drawn freely upon the examples afforded by all of the climates of the world similar to ours, they have in the past few years come to a very definite study of our local demands and conditions, and are producing an inherently Californian type of house. It is interesting to analyze the reason for this. The majority of people are attracted here by the climate and the possibilities for outdoor living. On arrival, however, they find that here as in the rest of the world they are usually too busy to give up the ideal amount of time in search of outdoor living. Therefore, it becomes the function of the architect to provide for this contingency by designing a house which brings the outdoors in as close as possible relation to every day living. This results in the increasing use of patio, terrace, arbor, pergola, loggia, veranda, balcony and provides the principal link between the architect's work and that of the landscape man.

The Little Garden of Gaiety

With Alternate Planting Suggestions

Florence Yoch & Lucile Council, Landscape Architects

In the East even gaiety may slumber. California, however, has a twelve months' responsibility to keep the garden gay and charming. Decay has no charm. For the fundamental lines of our design we must employ only plants that remain thrifty and interesting throughout the year, avoiding the opposite pitfall of monotony which is never conducive to gaiety. Some of our most obligingly evergreen things become very monotonous and most of the easily attained and long enduring garden color becomes wearisome.

As elsewhere, design is our friend and comforter. It dictates feeling, guides choice of material and tides over the lean season. Given simple, satisfying lines worked out in substantial materials and interesting shapes and leaf texture, we have the framework on which to apply the everchanging element of color.

The first burst of spring is the one constantly recurring thrill that never palls and unless fully featured a garden fails of one of its foremost purposes. The colors expressing spring are crystal clear and gentle harmonies. In summer gaiety takes a higher pitch and the full gamut of effulgent brilliant discord is surprisingly satisfying. For autumn, rich minor notes, purple, mauve, smoky gold, and burnt rose embody the mood. In southern California there are quite a number of things that flower blithely on into winter and it is always surprising how a least flicker of color can light up an evergreen garden.

Some things that hold full beauty to the end—like Salvia leucantha and Lantanas—become important, but it is the few hardy souls like the earliest Acacias, Jasminum primulinum and Winter Peas and Bignonias which are cheerfully starting their new careers, bringing forth fresh color, while everything else is relinquishing the ghost. Though often obscured during the more colorful seasons, it is in winter that design comes into its own.

Of course, the voice of the garden is water and in the tiniest garden it is possible to get a maximum of effect by the simplest means—a central location, no coping, and an exaggeratedly high spray, can be almost dramatic.

Contrast is the foil for color, light, and music, so here we surround our gay little garden by rather a prim solid green hedge along the sides. At the rear we look into the shadowy depth of pleached trees. The borders are planted to things of woodsy character, few flowers, and delicate shades.

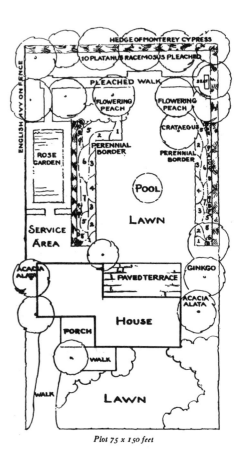

Plot 75 x 150 feet

PERENNIAL BORDER

Edgers

FOR THE EAST

1. Phlox-subulata
   Aubretia
   Iris Crimson King
2. Alyssum saxatile
   Viola, yellow
   Iris cristata
   Tulip Moonlight
3. Virginia Stock
   Pansy, mixed
   English Daisy
   Tulip Clara Butt
   Tulip Melicette
4. Blue Viola
   Verbena, purple and lavender
   Ageratum

FOR THE WEST

1. Statice perezi
   Convolvulus mauritanica
2. Alyssum saxatile
   Viola, yellow
   Iris stylosa
   Tulip Moonlight
   Lobelia
3. Virginia Stock
   Pansy, mixed
   English Daisy
   Tulip Clara Butt
   Tulip Melicette
   Dianthus
4. Blue Viola
   Verbena, purple and lavender
   Ageratum

Middle Ground

FOR THE EAST

5. Penstemon
   Iris pallida
   Single China Aster
6. Stock
   Perennial Aster
   Zinnia
   Iris in variety
7. Anemone coronaria
   Persian Ranunculus
   Perennial Blue Flax
   Peony

FOR THE WEST

5. Penstemon
   Iris pallida
   Single China Aster
6. Stock
   Perennial Aster
   Zinnia
   Iris in variety
7. Anemone coronaria
   Persian Ranunculus
   Perennial Blue Flax
   Agapanthus

For the Heights

FOR THE EAST

8. Chrysanthemum
   Purple Petunia
   Oriental Poppy
9. Delphinium
   Snapdragon

FOR THE WEST

8. Chrysanthemum
   Salvia leucantha
   Helianthemum angustifolius
   Canterbury-bell
9. Delphinium
   Salvia farinacea
   Salvia pitcheri
   Snapdragon

Shrubs

FOR THE EAST

A Spiraea thunbergi
B Weigela
C Bechtel's Crab
D Persian Lilac
E Flowering Almond
F Forsythia
H Hedge of Common Lilac

FOR THE WEST

Diosma
Quince
Bechtel's Crab
Persian Lilac
Flowering Almond
Jasminum primulinum
Hedge of Ceanothus cyaneus

Trees

FOR THE EAST

Flowering Peach
Tilia
Ulmus americana
Magnolia soulangeana
Crataegus oxyacantha
Crataegus lavallei
Ginkgo

FOR THE WEST

Cornus florida
Platanus racemosus
Acacia alata
Magnolia soulangeana
Crataegus oxyacantha
Crataegus lavallei
Ginkgo

Hedges

FOR THE EAST

Thuya occidentalis

FOR THE WEST

Monterey Cypress

Shady Border Along Pleached Walk

Same plant materials would be
   used for this border both in the
   East and the West.

Edgers
Nemophila
Nemesia
Brachycome Daisy
Myosotis
Primula in variety
Ajuga

Middle Ground
Funkia
Hemerocallis
Morea
Heuchera sanguinea
Ferns

Heights
Acanthus
Foxglove
Thalictrum dipterocarpum
Campanula grosseki
Anemone Japonica in variety
Columbine in variety

Selected Plant Lists

From reviewing the plans for representative gardens throughout Florence Yoch's career, I have prepared these lists of trees, shrubs, flowers, vines, and ground covers that she specified. The plans often went through several versions, and she frequently made major changes in the field. Moreover, her indications are sometimes as general as "tree" or "climbing rose" without naming the variety, and she often used a shortened form of the common or botanical name. From the available evidence, I have indicated the plants as specifically as possible and have roughly attempted to group them as she did, for such arrangements show her taste in horticultural and aesthetic harmonies. In addition to the green architecture of many gardens, and the now fashionable white and blue borders, these lists show that she often used patches of strong yellows, oranges, salmons, and reds.

Yoch's choices in plants went far beyond the usual nursery stock. For nomenclature, I have chosen as the standard, *Sunset's New Western Garden Book*. When, as frequently happened, I was unable to find in this text plants she used in her gardens, I consulted the botanical references that are listed in the Bibliography. I am indebted to John C. MacGregor IV for his specialized knowledge of plants and plant names of the period. To indicate changes in plant names since Florence Yoch's time, I give the name she used first, followed by the current name.

Vroman's 17th Century Spanish Garden

Pasadena, California

Plan, 1921

TREES AND SHRUBS

corypha palm (*Livistona australis*)
fig, edible (*Ficus carica*)
olive (*Olea europaea*)
cypress (*Cupressus*)
oleander (*Nerium oleander*)
pomegranate (*Punica granatum*)
Euonymus japonicus
juniper (*Juniperus squamata* 'Prostrata')
boxwood (*Buxus*)
myrtle (*Myrtus communis*)

VINES, FLOWERS, AND GROUND COVER

Spanish jasmine (*Jasminum grandiflorum*)
evergreen grape (*Vitis hypoglauca*, now *Cissus hypoglauca*)
ivy (*Hedera*)
yucca
Dracaena (probably *Dracaena draco*)
stonecrop (*Sedum*)
rosemary (*Rosmarinus officinalis*)
fortnight lily (*Moraea iridioides*, now *Dietes vegeta*)
leopard lily (*Lilium pardalinum*)
begonia
roses: 'Rêve d'Or', Lady Banks' (*Rosa banksiae* 'Alba plena')

IN POTS AND TUBS

ivy (*Hedera*)
aloe
boxwood (*Buxus*)
orange (*Citrus*)

The A. Parley Johnson Garden

Downey, California

Planting Plan, 27 May 1927

ALONG DRIVE

olive trees (*Olea europaea*) alternating with orange trees (*Citrus*)

cypress (*Cupressus*)
ivy (*Hedera*) ground cover
toyon (*Heteromeles arbutifolia*)
Italian buckthorn (*Rhamnus alaternus*),
    as hedge
oleander (*Nerium oleander*)
heliotrope (*Centranthus ruber*), as
    ground cover
lemon verbena (*Aloysia triphylla*)
roses:
    'Climbing Cécile Brunner', 'Climbing
    Mme. Caroline Testout', 'Rêve
    d'Or', 'Belle Portugaise'

FORECOURT AREA

California sycamores (*Platanus
    racemosa*)
Joshua tree (*Yucca brevifolia*)
manna gum (*Eucalyptus viminalis*)
camellia
passion vine (*Tacsonia mancata*, now
    Passiflora manicata)
blood-red trumpet vine (*Bignonia
    cherere*, now *Distictis
    buccinatoria*)
flame vine (*Bignonia venusta*, now
    Pyrostegia venusta)
anemone clematis (*Clematis
    montana*)
evergreen grape (*Vitis hypoglauca*,
    now *Cissus hypoglauca*)
hollyhocks (*Alcea rosea*)
Bougainvillea lateritia, now *B.
    spectabilis*
evergreen grape (*Vitis capensis*, now
    Rhoicissus capensis)

HOUSE WALL FACING FORECOURT

rose 'Climbing Cécile Brunner'
firethorn (*Pyracantha yunnanensis*, now
    P. fortuneana)
firethorn (*Pyracantha coccinea*
    'Lalandei')
Cotoneaster pannosus 'Nana', now *C.
    buxifolius*
dwarf myrtle (*Myrtus communis*
    'Compacta')

PATIO

hedge of tall English boxwood (*Buxus
    sempervirens*) along lawn side and
    the six perennial beds

1. statice (*Limonium*)
   heliotrope (*Centranthus ruber*)
   spuria iris 'Monspur'
2. Mexican bush sage (*Salvia
   leucantha*)
   beardtongue (*Penstemon*)
   chrysanthemum
   lavender (*Lavandula*)
3. German irises:
   'Leverrier', 'Lady Lou', 'Lady Foster',
   'Alcázar', 'Ballerina', 'Fontarabie', 'J.
   J. Dean', 'Claude Monet', 'Margery'
   lily-of-the-Nile (*Agapanthus
   orientalis*)
4. blue Spanish iris
   daylily (*Hemerocallis*)
   flame pea (*Chorizema*)
   geum, red, yellow
   African corn lily (*Ixia maculata*)
5. delphinium
   Canterbury bells (*Campanula
   medium*)
   Campanula grossekii
   Gladiolus primulinus
   African corn lily (*Ixia maculata*)
   anchusa
   snapdragon (*Antirrhinum majus*)
6. columbine (*Aquilegia*)
   Canterbury bells (*Campanula
   medium*)
   Campanula grossekii
   Gladiolus primulinus

ALONG LOGGIA

Spanish jasmine (*Jasminum
    grandiflorum*)
crape myrtle (*Lagerstroemia indica*)
rambler rose
anemone clematis (*Clematis montana*)
tobira (*Pittosporum tobira*)
flowering quince (*Chaenomeles*)
red yucca (*Hesperaloe parvifolia*)
red-hot poker (*Tritoma uvaria*, now
    Kniphofia uvaria)
rose 'Silver Moon'
wisteria
hibiscus
king palm (*Seaforthia elegans*, now
    Archontophoenix cunninghamiana)
oleander (*Nerium oleander*)

KITCHEN GARDEN

orange (*Citrus*)
peach 'George IV' (*Prunus persica*)

plum (*Prunus domestica*)
grapes (*Vitis*)
avocado (*Persea*)

KITCHEN GARDEN BORDER

mint (*Mentha*)
lavender (*Lavandula*)
rosemary (*Rosmarinus officinalis*)
pinks (*Dianthus*)
parsley (*Petroselinum crispum*)
thyme (*Thymus*)
taragon (*Artemisia dracunculus*)
sage (*Salvia*)
iris
violet (*Viola odorata*)
ranunculus
leeks (*Allium ampeloprasum*, Porrum
    group)
chives (*Allium schoenoprasum*)

TRIAL GARDEN FOR BULBS

chrysanthemum border
apricot (*Prunus armeniaca*)
nectarine 'Stanwick'
peach: 'George IV', weeping peach
persimmon (*Diospyrus*)
wild lilac (*Ceanothus cyaneus*)
rose 'White Cherokee' (*Rosa laevigata*)
trumpet vine (*Distictis buccinatoria*)
hollyhock (*Alcea rosea*)
grapes (*Vitis*)
Abutilon hybridum, yellow

ON WALL

roses:
    'Climbing Sunburst', 'Pink Cherokee'
    (*Rosa* × *anemonoides*
    'Anemone'), 'Climbing Mme.
    Caroline Testout', 'Climbing Los
    Angeles', 'Belle Portugaise'
violet trumpet vine (*Bignonia violacea*,
    now *Clytostoma callistegioides*)
blood-red trumpet vine (*Bignonia
    cherere*, now *Distictis buccinatoria*)

CUT FLOWER GARDEN

hedge of tall English boxwood (*Buxus
    sempervirens*)
beds hedged with true myrtle (*Myrtus
    communis*)

In parterre:
    scarlet gum (*Eucalyptus ficifolia*)
    saucer magnolia
        (*Magnolia × soulangiana*)
    dombeya
    incense cedar (*Libocedrus decurrens*,
        now *Calocedrus decurrens*)
    Senegal date palm (*Phoenix reclinata*)
    sweet olive (*Olea fragrans*, now
        Osmanthus fragrans)
    oleander (*Nerium oleander*)
    myrtle (*Myrtus communis*)

Outer wall:
    rose 'White Cherokee' (*Rosa
        laevigata*)
    poet's jasmine (*Jasminum officinale*)
    evergreen grape (*Vitis capensis*, now
        Rhoicissus capensis)
    evergreen grape (*Vitis sempervirens*)
    evergreen grape (*Vitis hypoglauca*,
        now *Cissus hypoglauca*)
    scarlet bougainvillea
    blood-red trumpet vine (*Bignonia
        cherere*, now *Distictis
        buccinatoria*)
    yellow trumpet vine (*Bignonia
        tweediana*, now *Macfadyena
        unguis-cati*)
    flame vine (*Bignonia venusta*, now
        Pyrostegia venusta)
    Spanish jasmine (*Jasminum
        grandiflorum*)
    Clematis 'Jackmanii'

TERRACE

pepper tree (*Schinus*)
violet trumpet vine (*Clytostoma
    callistegoides*)
evergreen grape (*Vitis capensis*, now
    Rhoicissus capensis)
English ivy (*Hedera helix*)
anemone clematis (*Clematis montana*)
evergreen grape (*Vitis hypoglauca*)
trumpet vine (Distictis buccinatoria)
Japanese aralia (*Aralia sieboldii*, now
    Fatsia japonica)
English boxwood (*Buxus sempervirens*),
    as standard

LEADING TO SHADY GARDEN

chain fern (*Woodwardia radicans*)
camellia
fuchsia

SHADY GARDEN

true myrtle (*Myrtus communis*), as
    hedge
holly fern (*Cyrtomium falcatum*)
saxifrage (*Megasea*, now *Bergenia
    crassifolia*)
Azara microphylla
lily-of-the-Nile (*Agapanthus orientalis*)
columbine (*Aquilegia*)
phlox
mist flower (*Eupatorium coelestinum*)
Japanese anemone (*Anemone japonica*,
    now *A. × hybrida*)
spuria iris 'Monspur'
spuria iris (*Iris ochrolenca*)
Kaffir lily (*Clivia miniata*)
fortnight lily (*Moraea iridioides*, now
    Dietes vegeta)

SECRET GARDEN

1. winter iris (*Iris stylosa*, now *I.
    unguicularis*)
   saxifrage (*Megasea*, now *Bergenia
    crassifolia*)
2. gladiolus 'The Bride'
   winter iris (*Iris stylosa*, now *I.
    unguicularis*)
   nepeta
   viola
   verbena, purple, lavender
   tulips: 'The Bishop', 'Melicette'
   narcissus 'Sea Gull'
3. dianthus
   English daisy (*Bellis perennis*)
   perennial blue flax (*Linum perenne*)
   hound's tongue (*Cynoglossum*)
   cockscomb (*Celosia*)
   tulips: 'Clara Butt', 'Rose Riante'
   narcissus 'Branston'
   evergreen candytuft (*Iberis
    sempervirens*)
   bluebell of Scotland (*Campanula
    rotundifolia*)
   Campanula ramosissima
4. basket of gold (*Alyssum saxatile*,
    now *Aurinia saxatilis*)
   dwarf lantana (*Lantana camara*),
    yellow, lemon
   daylily (*Hemerocallis*)
   narcissi: 'King Alfred', 'Vanilla'
   tulips: *Tulipa fulgens* 'Lutea Pallida',

Tulipa fulgens 'Lutea Maxima',
    'Moonlight'
5. watsonia 'Estrella'
   irises: 'Princess Beatrice', 'J. J.
    Dean'
6. Irises: 'San Gabriel', 'Fontarabie'
7. *Campanula grossekii*
   columbine (*Aquilegia*)
8. delphinium
   hollyhock (*Alcea rosea*)
Also included on plan:
    pomegranate (*Punica granatum*)
    hibiscus
    lilac (*Syringa*)
    marmalade bush (*Streptosolen
        jamesonii*)
    primrose jasmine (*Jasminum
        primulinum*, now *J. mesnyi*)
    yellow trumpet vine (*Bignonia
        tweediana*, now *Macfadyena
        unguis-cati*)
    wild lilac (*Ceanothus cyaneus*)
    Solanum rantonnetii
    boxleaf azara (*Azara microphylla*)
    grapes

The Ira Bryner Garden

Pasadena, California

Revised Planting Plans,

July 1929

ALONG FRONT DRIVE

India hawthorn (*Raphiolepis indica*)
arbutus
pepper trees (*Schinus molle*)
tobira (*Pittosporum tobira*)
Catalina cherry (*Prunus integrifolia*,
    now *P. lyonii*), as hedge
orange (*Citrus*)
rock cotoneaster (*Cotoneaster
    horizontalis*)
firethorn (*Pyracantha coccinea*
    'Lalandei')
Euonymus 'Reevsii'
Yucca pendula, now *Y. recurvifolia*
oleander (*Nerium oleander*)
strawberry tree (*Arbutus unedo*)
loquat (*Eriobotrya japonica*)
rose
wisteria
firethorn (*Pyracantha yunnanensis*, now
    P. fortuneana)

NORTHEAST OF HOUSE

tobira (*Pittosporum tobira*)
blueberry climber (*Ampelopsis brevipedunculata*)
loquat (*Eriobotrya japonica*)
Pfitzer juniper (*Juniperus chinensis* 'Pfitzeriana')
English laurel (*Prunus laurocerasus*)
fuchsia
eucalyptus
tecoma (*Tecomaria capensis*)
pepper tree (*Schinus molle*)
Spanish jasmine (*Jasminum grandiflorum*)
princess flower (*Tibouchina semidecandra*, now *T. urvilleana*)
Oregon grape (*Mahonia aquifolium*)
holly-leaf osmanthus (*Osmanthus aquifolium*, now *O. heterophyllus*)
aralia (*Fatsia japonicum*)
dracaena
violet trumpet vine (*Bignonia violacea*, now *Clytostoma callistegioides*)
flowering maple (*Abutilon*)
walnut (*Juglans regia*)
grapes (*Vitis*)

ROSE ARCH

'Climbing Cécile Brunner'

SOUTHEAST OF HOUSE

lemon verbena (*Lippia citriodora*, now *Aloysia triphylla*)
blue elderberry (*Sambucus glauca*, now *S. caerulea*)

ARBOR

boxwood (*Buxus*)
wisteria
flame vine (*Bignonia venusta*, now *Pyrostegia venusta*)
Cotoneaster pannosus, now *C. buxifolius*
vinca as ground cover
orange (*Citrus*)
evergreen grape (*Vitis hypoglauca*, now *Cissus hypoglauca*)
Spanish jasmine (*Jasminum grandiflorum*)
boxleaf azara (*Azara microphylla*)

AT STAIR FROM DRIVE TO TERRACE

rock cotoneaster (*Cotoneaster horizontalis*)
Italian cypress (*Cupressus sempervirens*)
Myrtus communis 'Tarentina'
rose 'Belle Portugaise'

ORCHARD

Oregon grape (*Mahonia aquifolium*)
plum 'Santa Rosa' (*Prunus salcina* 'Santa Rosa')
sweet olive (*Olea fragrans*, now *Osmanthus fragrans*)
boxwood (*Buxus*)
wisteria
flowering quince (*Chaenomeles*)
orange (*Citrus*)
Italian buckthorn (*Rhamnus alaternus*)
rosemary (*Rosmarinus officinalis*)
winter daphne (*Daphne odora*)
camellia
quince (*Cydonia oblonga*)
arborvitae (*Thuja occidentalis*)
roses
kumquat (*Fortunella margarita*)
oleander (*Nerium oleander*)
frosty wattle (*Acacia pruinosa*)
incense cedar (*Calocedrus decurrens*)
English boxwood (*Buxus sempervirens*)
Spanish jasmine (*Jasminum grandiflorum*)
evergreen grape (*Vitis hypoglauca*, now *Cissus hypoglauca*)
violet trumpet vine (*Bignonia violacea*, now *Clytostoma callistegioides*)

SOUTH END OF ORCHARD

Sydney golden wattle (*Acacia latifolia*, now *Acacia longifolia*)
flowering plum (*Prunus*)
Jasminum and *Gelsemium sempervirens* on south and east fences
eucalyptus
rose 'Climbing Cécile Brunner'
heliotrope (*Centranthus ruber*)
English ivy (*Hedera helix*)
plum 'Santa Rosa'

lemon verbena (*Lippia citriodora*, now *Aloysia triphylla*)

AREA BETWEEN HOUSE AND GARAGE

cup-of-gold vine (*Solandra maxima*)
flowering plum
English laurel (*Prunus laurocerasus*)
Catalina cherry (*Prunus integrifolia*, now *P. lyonii*)
eucalyptus
acacia
holly-leaf osmanthus (*Osmanthus aquifolium*, now *O. heterophyllus*)
abutilon
heavenly bamboo (*Nandina domestica*)
lilac (*Syringa*)
arborvitae (*Thuja*)

MOTOR COURT

California sycamore (*Platanus racemosa*)
holly-leaf cherry (*Prunus ilicifolia*)
blackwood acacia (*Acacia melanoxylon*)
firethorn (*Pyracantha yunnanensis*, now *P. fortuneana*)
myrtle (*Myrtus*)
eucalyptus
India hawthorn (*Raphiolepis indica*)
tobira (*Pittosporum tobira*)
Catalina cherry (*Prunus lyonii*) as hedge
Myrtus communis 'Tarentina'

MOCK WOODS AROUND SUMMERHOUSE

Monterey cypress (*Cupressus macrocarpa*)
holly flame pea (*Chorizema ilicifolium*)
California laurel (*Umbelularia californica*)
coast live oak (*Quercus agrifolia*)
Cotoneaster buxifolius
strawberry tree (*Arbutus unedo*)
avocado (*Persea*)
incense cedar (*Calocedrus decurrens*)
Victorian box (*Pittosporum undulatum*)

firethorn (*Pyracantha fortuneana*)
peach tree (*Prunus persica*)
carob tree (*Ceratonia siliqua*)

ON CURVED WALK TO SUMMERHOUSE

toyon (*Heteromeles arbutifolia*)
peach tree (*Prunus persica*)
lemonade berry (*Rhus integrifolia*)
firethorn (*Pyracantha fortuneana*)

ON WALK LEADING FROM SUMMERHOUSE TO LAWN

Oregon grape (*Mahonia aquifolium*)
true myrtle (*Myrtus communis*)
blackwood acacia (*Acacia melanoxylon*)
Natal plum (*Carissa grandiflora*)
holly flame pea (*Chorizema ilicifolium*)
English boxwood (*Buxus sempervirens*)

BETWEEN SUMMERHOUSE AND WESTERN EDGE OF GARDEN

matilija poppy (*Romneya coulteri*)
California laurel (*Umbelularia californica*)
Catalina cherry (*Prunus lyonii*)
carob tree (*Ceratonia siliqua*)
Monterey pine (*Pinus radiata*)

ON WESTERN BOUNDARY

common butterfly bush (*Buddleia davidii*)
Catalina cherry (*Prunus lyonii*)
coast live oak (*Quercus agrifolia*)
Monterey cypress (*Cupressus macrocarpa*)
pearl acacia (*Acacia podalyriifolia*)
Monterey pines (*Pinus radiata*)
toyon (*Heteromeles arbutifolia*)
peach tree (*Prunus persica*)
Catalina cherry (*Prunus lyonii*)
Sandankwa viburnum (*Viburnum suspensum*)

Pool Garden
9 February 1929

BORDERS OF LAWN AREA

verbena
violets (*Violas*) as edging
irises: 'Alcazar', 'J. J. Dean',
    'Fontarabie', 'Mesopotamica',
    'Lady Foster', 'Caterina', 'Lady
    Lou', 'San Gabriel', 'Crimson
    King', 'Monsignor', 'Corrida',
    'Princess Beatrice', 'Archevêque'
Phlox 'Chamois Rose'
floss (*Ageratum*)
stock (*Matthiola*)
statice (*Limonium latifolium* and *L. perezii*)
snowball (*Viburnum*)
giant tritoma (*Kniphofia uvaria*)
crabapple (*Malus*)
zinnias
annual aster (*Callistephus chinensis*)
perennial aster (*Aster* sp.)
Pimelea prostrata
Canterbury bells (*Campanula medium*)
delphinium
holly (*Ilex*)
watsonia
tulips: 'Clara Butt', 'Melicette',
    'Merreille', 'Gesneriana' (yellow),
    'Ariadne', 'Duchess of Hohenberg',
    'Prince of Orange', 'fulgens Lutea
    Pallida', 'Sabrina', 'Marconi',
    'Groote Samson', 'Blue Amiable'
Petunia hybrida
Swan River daisy (*Brachycome iberidifolia*)
basket-of-gold (*Alyssum saxatile*, now *Aurinia saxatilis*)
pansy (*Viola* × *wittrockiana*)
Transvaal daisy (*Gerbera jamesonii*)
primrose (*Primula*)
fortnight lily (*Moraea iridioides*, now *Dietes vegeta*)
foxglove (*Digitalis purpurea*)
Hydrangea macrophylla
daylily (*Hemerocallis*)
windflower (*Anemone*)
African daisy (*Dimorphotheca*)
Kaffir lily (*Clivia miniata*)
lily-of-the-Nile (*Agapanthus orientolis*)
lavender (*Lavandula angustifolia* 'Munstead')
anchusa

SEASONAL PLAN

Winter	*substitute*	*Summer*
pot marigold (*Calendula officinalis*) stock (*Matthiola incana*)	for	zinnias
snapdragon (*Antirrhinum majus*) African daisy (*Dimorphotheca*) annual phlox (*Phlox drummondii*)	for	asters (*Callistephus chinensis*)
Virginian stock (*Malcolmia maritima*)	for	petunias
violets and pansies (*Violas*)	for	floss (*Ageratum*)
nemophila Swan River daisy (*Brachycome iberidifolia*) English daisy (*Bellis perennis*)	for	floss (*Ageratum*)

Pitcher's salvia (*Salvia pitcheri*, now
 Salvia azurea var. *grandiflora*)
Mexican bush sage (*Salvia leucantha*)
hollyhock (*Alcea rosea*), lemon, yellow,
 and apricot
belladonna lily (*Amaryllis belladonna*)
snapdragon (*Antirrhinum majus*)
chrysanthemum
morning glory (*Convolvulus*)
heath (*Erica*)

TREES IN BORDERS

dwarf pomegranate (*Punica granatum*
 'Nana')
coast live oak (*Quercus agrifolia*)
flowering peach (*Prunus persica*)
pine (*Pinus*)
arborvitae (*Thuja occidentalis*)

SHRUBS IN BORDERS

English boxwood (*Buxus sempervirens*)
lilac (*Syringa*)
quince (*Chaenomeles*)
breath of heaven (*Diosma* or
 Coleonema)

BED BY THE POOL

irises: *Iris stylosa* (now *I. unguicularis*),
 'J. J. Dean', 'Alcazar',
 'Mesopotamica'
hollyhock (*Alcea rosea*)
watsonia, pink
wild lilac (*Ceanothus*)
ranunculus
giant poker plant (*Tritoma uvaria*, now
 Kniphofia uvaria)
sunflower (*Helianthus*)
tulips: 'Valentine', 'Prince Albert'
nemophila
Virginian stock (*Malcolmia maritima*)
petunia 'Silver Blue'

California Institute
of Technology
The Athenaeum

Pasadena, California

Plan, 1931

ENTRY DRIVE

lemon-scented gum (*Eucalyptus
 citriodora*)
tobira (*Pittosporum tobira*)
olive (*Olea europaea*)

PORTE-COCHERE AREA

India hawthorn (*Raphiolepis ovata*)
anemone clematis (*Clematis montana*)
blood-red trumpet vine (*Bignonia
 cherere*, now *Distictis buccinatoria*)
Mediterranean fan palm (*Chamaerops
 humilis*)
Senegal date palm (*Phoenix reclinata*)
jacaranda (*Jacaranda mimosifolia*)
Arbutus unedo
lemonade berry (*Rhus integrifolia*)
crape myrtle (*Lagerstroemia indica*)
Victorian box (*Pittosporum undulatum*)
tobira (*Pittosporum tobira*)
firethorn (*Pyracantha yunnanensis*, now
 P. fortuneana)

WEST FACADE

jacaranda (*Jacaranda mimosifolia*)
tobira (*Pittosporum tobira*), as hedge
Victorian box (*Pittosporum undulatum*)
firethorn (*Pyracantha yunnanensis*, now
 P. fortuneana)
lemonade berry (*Rhus integrifolia*)
rose
cup-of-gold vine (*Solandra maxima*)

COURT

star jasmine (*Rhynchospermum
 jasminoides*, now
 Trachelospermum jasminoides)
grape ivy (*Vitis rhombifolia*, now
 Cissus rhombifolia)
Italian cypress (*Cupressus sempervirens*)
Lady Banks' rose (*Rosa banksiae*
 'Lutea')

wisteria
blood-red trumpet vine (*Bignonia
 cherere*, now *Distictis buccinatoria*)

AROUND TERRACE

fig (*Ficus microcarpa* var. *nitida*),
 espaliered on wall
southern magnolia (*Magnolia
 grandiflora*), espaliered on wall
English boxwood (*Buxus sempervirens*)
 as hedge
juniper (*Juniperus prostrata*, now *J.
 chinensis* 'Parsonii')
Spanish jasmine (*Jasminum
 grandiflorum*)

SYCAMORE ALLEE

California sycamore (*Platanus
 racemosa*)
English ivy (*Hedera helix*), as ground
 cover
Boston ivy (*Ampelopsis veitchii*, now
 Parthenocissus tricuspidata
 'Veitchii')
Victorian box (*Pittosporum
 undulatum*), as hedge

**BADMINTON COURT AND AREA
TO THE WEST**

English ivy (*Hedera helix*), as ground
 cover
Victorian box (*Pittosporum undulatum*)
tobira (*Pittosporum tobira*)
Boston ivy (*Parthenocissus tricuspidata*
 'Veitchii')
Catalina cherry (*Prunus integrifolia*,
 now *P. lyonii*)
Sandankwa viburnum (*Viburnum
 suspensum*)
flowering quince (*Cydonia japonica*,
 now *Chaenomeles lagenaria*)

SERVICE COURT

gum (*Eucalyptus*)
olive (*Olea europaea*)
English ivy (*Hedera helix*), as ground
 cover
blood-red trumpet vine (*Bignonia
 cherere*, now *Distictis buccinatoria*)
Virginia creeper (*Ampelopsis
 quinquefolia*, now *Parthenocissus
 quinquefolia*)

The George Cukor Garden

Los Angeles, California

Plan, October 1936

Upper Garden

BEDS OUTSIDE DINING ROOM WINDOW

Spring:
cineraria, intermediate
    (*Senecio × hybridus*)
bleeding heart (*Dicentra*)
lilies (*Lilium*)
ferns
Summer:
mist flower (*Eupatorium coelestinum*)
Japanese anemone (*Anemone
    japonica*, now *A. × hybrida*)
phlox (*perennial*). 'Elizabeth
    Campbell', 'Miss Lingard'

FLOWER BEDS ON NORTH SIDE OF POOL DECK

delphinium
beardtongue (*Penstemon*)
watsonias
Spanish iris
Dutch iris
pansies (*Viola × wittrockiana*)

BED ON SOUTH SIDE OF POOL

hollyhock, white (*Alcea rosea*)
Parney cotoneaster (*Cotoneaster
    lacteus*)
cut-leaf Japanese maple, now laceleaf
    maple (*Acer palmatum
    'Dissectum'*)
coast live oak (*Quercus agrifolia*)
oleander (*Nerium oleander*)

FLOWER BEDS ALONG RAMP UP HILL TO CUT FLOWER TERRACES

hibiscus
sweet olive (*Olea fragrans*, now
    Osmanthus fragrans)
saucer magnolia
    (*Magnolia × soulangiana*)
coast live oak (*Quercus agrifolia*)
oleander (*Nerium oleander*)
euonymus

Parney cotoneaster (*Cotoneaster
    parneyi*, now *C. lacteus*)
cut leaf Japanese maple, now laceleaf
    maple (*Acer palmatum
    'Dissectum'*)
jacaranda (*Jacaranda mimosifolia*)
loquat (*Eriobotrya japonica*)

CUT FLOWER TERRACES

giant Burmese honeysuckle (*Lonicera
    hildebrandiana*)
blood-red trumpet vine (*Bignonia
    cherere*, now *Distictis buccinatoria*)
copa de leche (*Solandra longiflora*)
rubber tree (*Ficus elastica*)
cup-of-gold vine (*Solandra guttata*, now
    S. maxima)
Viburnum tinus 'Robustum'
irises: 'Margery', 'San Gabriel'
common aubrieta (*Aubrieta deltoidea*)
beardtongue (*Penstemon*)
rosemary (*Rosmarinus officinalis*)
lavender (*Lavandula*)
snapdragon (*Antirrhinum majus*), pink
delphinium
columbine (*Aquilegia*), pink, blue
stock (*Matthiola*), lavender
pincushion flower (*Scabiosa*)
blue marguerite (*Agathaea coelestis*,
    now *Felicia amelloides*)
pink (*Dianthus*)
Virginian stock (*Malcolmia maritima*)
nemophila
tulips: 'Clara Butt', 'Altesa'
narcissi: 'Diane Kasner', 'Hera'

HILLSIDE EAST OF CUT FLOWER TERRACES

Sydney golden wattle (*Acacia latifolia*,
    now *A. longifolia*)
lemonade berry (*Rhus integrifolia*)
California holly (*Heteromeles
    arbutifolia*)
Canary Island pine (*Pinus canariensis*)
Victorian box (*Pittosporum undulatum*)

HILLSIDE BETWEEN CUT FLOWER TERRACES AND SPRING FLOWER BORDER

Upper walk edged with tidytips (*Layia
    platyglossa*) and Cape marigold
    hybrids (*Dimorphotheca*)
coast live oak (*Quercus agrifolia*)

trumpet vine (possibly *Distictis*, or
    Clytostoma)
Natal plum (*Carissa*)
California holly (*Heteromeles
    arbutifolia*)
Sydney golden wattle (*Acacia latifolia*,
    now *A. longifolia*)
Canary Island pine (*Pinus canariensis*)

EDGING WALK ALONG SPRING FLOWER BORDER

St. Thomas tree (*Bauhinia tomentosa*)
Solanum
lemon (*Citrus limon*)
loquat (*Eriobotrya japonica*)
rose
wisteria

SPRING FLOWER BORDER

hibiscus, yellow
ranunculus, white
Cape marigold (*Dimorphotheca*), white
nemophila
dianthus, white
Virginian stock (*Malcolmia maritima*)
pincushion flower (*Scabiosa*)
bellflower (*Campanula*)
Iceland poppy (*Papaver nudicaule*)
ranunculus, yellow
Cape marigold (*Dimorphotheca*)
pansy (*Viola*), yellow
snapdragon (*Antirrhinum majus*),
    yellow
beardtongue (*Penstemon*), lavender
aubrieta, lavender
Swan River daisy (*Brachycome
    iberidifolia*)

ARBOR

purple glory plant (*Sutera grandiflora*)
heliotrope (*Centranthus ruber*)
cranesbill (*Geranium*)
California bay (*Umbellularia
    californica*)
hawthorn (*Raphiolepis*)
Ternstroemia gymnanthera
golden wonder senna (*Cassia splendida*)

SCREENING ARBOR

coast live oak (*Quercus agrifolia*)
Canary Island pine (*Pinus canariensis*)
rose apple (*Syzygium jambos*)
Sydney golden wattle (*Acacia longifolia*)

LAWN WEST OF SPRING FLOWER BORDER

flowering peach (*Prunus persica*)
coral tree (*Erythrina*)
star jasmine (*Trachelospermum jasminoides*)

WEST EDGE OF SPRING FLOWER BORDER

shrub aster (*Aster fruticosus*, now *Felicia fruticosa*)
lupine (*Lupinus*), as ground cover under coral tree (*Erythrina*)
flowering peach (*Prunus persica*)

FLAGSTONE TERRACE

coast live oak (*Quercus agrifolia*)
camellia
osmanthus
hollyleaf sweetspire (*Itea ilicifolia*)
oleander (*Nerium oleander*)
crimson-spot rockrose (*Cistus ladanifer*)
clematis
violet trumpet vine (*Bignonia violacea*, now *Clytostoma callistegioides*)
red bauhinia (*Bauhinia galpinii*, now *B. punctata*)
Japanese honeysuckle (*Lonicera japonica* 'Halliana')
coralpea (*Kennedya rubicunda*)
flowering peach (*Prunus persica*)

BANK BETWEEN SPRING FLOWER BORDER AND LOWER GARDEN

trailing rosemary (*Rosmarinus officinalis* 'Prostratus')
flowering peach (*Prunus persica*)
coast live oak (*Quercus agrifolia*)
Parney cotoneaster (*Cotoneaster parneyi*, now *C. lacteus*)
Cotoneaster procumbens
California holly (*Heteromeles arbutifolia*)
lemonade berry (*Rhus integrifolia*)
sugar gum (*Eucalyptus cladocalyx*)
Pfitzer juniper (*Juniperus chinensis* 'Pfitzeriana')
rock cotoneaster (*Cotoneaster horizontalis*)
white bauhinia (*Bauhinia variegata* 'Candida')

hollyleaf cherry (*Prunus ilicifolia*)
herbs
laurel sumac (*Rhus laurina*)
waxleaf privet (probably *Ligustrum japonicum* 'Texanum')
flowering almond (*Prunus triloba*)
Cactus (*Opuntia*)
jacaranda (*Jacaranda mimosifolia*)
flowering peach (*Prunus persica*)
Myoporum laetum
Cape chestnut (*Calodendrum capense*)
common buckthorn (*Rhamnus cathartica*)
golden wonder senna (*Cassia splendida*)
Natal plum (*Carissa grandiflora*)
crimson spot rockrose (*Cistus ladanifer*)

BORDERS ON WALK FROM STAIR TO ROSE PARTERRE (FALL)

edgers:
petunias, purple, lavender, white
floss flower (*Ageratum houstonianum*)
French marigold (*Tagetes patula*)
Zinnia haageana
chrysanthemums

backed by:
perennial aster, purple, blue
African marigold (*Tagetes erecta*), lemon, orange
chrysanthemum, yellow, bronze, red
Mexican sunflower (*Tithonia rotundifolia*)
cannas
Helianthus angustifolia
common sneezeweed (*Helenium autumnale*)
sage (*Salvia*)
marguerites, Paris daisy (*Chrysanthemum frutescens*)

BORDERS ON WALK FROM STAIR TO ROSE PARTERRE (SPRING)

border of violets backed by delphinium
flowering peach (*Prunus*)

Lower Garden

THE ORCHARD

border of trees and shrubs:
coast live oak (*Quercus agrifolia*)
flowering fruit trees

sycamore (*Platanus racemosa*)
California bay (*Umbellularia californica*)
avocado (*Persea*)
sugar gum (*Eucalyptus cladocalyx*)
crape myrtle (*Lagerstoemia indica*)
maidenhair tree (*Ginkgo biloba*)
Canary Island pine (*Pinus canariensis*)
blackwood acacia (*Acacia melanoxylon*)

underplanted with:
wild lilac (*Ceanothus*)
toyon (*Heteromeles arbutifolia*)
Catalina cherry (*Prunus lyonii*)
strawberry tree (*Arbutus unedo*)
rock cotoneaster (*Cotoneaster horizontalis*)
border of flowering almond (*Prunus triloba*) and Persian lilacs on west side
rose 'Frau Karl Druschki' added to border shrubbery on south side

orchard planting:
Valencia oranges (*citrus*)
deciduous fruit trees
figs (*Ficus*)
Cupaniopsis anacardiodes

ALONG WALK NORTH OF ROSE PARTERRE

Washington navel oranges underplanted with pansies (spring), chrysanthemums (fall)

GROUPING OF PLANTS NORTH OF ROSE PARTERRE

coast live oak (*Quercus agrifolia*)
hollyleaf cherry (*Prunus ilicifolia*)
white orchid tree (*Bauhinia variegata* 'Candida')
lily-of-the-valley tree (*Tricuspidaria dependens*, now *Crinodendron patagua*)
bridal-wreath spiraea (*Spiraea prunifolia*)

ROSE PARTERRE

European boxwood (*Buxus sempervirens*)
pomegranate (*Punica granatum*)
Roses (Bed #1), white:
'Caledonia'

'Madame Jules Bouché'
'Kaisin Auguste Viktoria'
'Innocence'
Roses (Bed #2), yellow and yellow
    blends:
    'Mrs. E. P. Thom'
    'Ville de Paris'
    'William F. Dreer'
    'Feu Joseph Looymans'
Roses (Bed #3), pink blends:
    'Los Angeles'
    'Hinrich Gaede'
    'President Herbert Hoover'
    'Talisman'
    'Condesa de Sástago'
Roses (Bed #4), red:
    'Etoile de Holland'
    'Victoria Harrington'
    'Black Knight'

Plant List for Spring Border, September 1936

BED #1

FOREGROUND OF BORDER

tulips:
    'Lemon Queen', 'Madame Buyssems',
        'Arethusa', 'Praestans'
narcissi:
    'Hera', 'Diana Kasner'
irises:
    'Corrida', 'Lady Paramount'
ranunculus, white
Iceland poppy, white (*Papaver
    nudicaule*)
nemophila
dimorphotheca, white

BACKGROUND

penstemon
Canterbury bells
delphinium
lupine

BED #2

FOREGROUND

tulips:
    'C. J. Hunt', 'Zwanenburg',
        'Carrara', 'White Duchess',
        'Regulus', 'Snowdrift'
narcissus 'Mrs. O'Melveny'
ranunculus, white
dimorphotheca, white
nemophila
dianthus, white

BACKGROUND

stock, white
penstemon
snapdragon, lemon
iris 'Shining Waters'
delphinium
iris 'Margery'
Osteospermum ecklonis

BED #3

FOREGROUND

rosemary
lavender
tulips:
    'Clara Butt', 'Altesa'
narcissi:
    'Diana Kasner', 'Hera'
dianthus
Virginian stock (*Malcolmia maritima*)
nemophila

BACKGROUND

aubrieta
penstemon, lavender
rosemary
lavender
columbines, pink, blue
agathaea (*Agathaea coelistis,* now
    Felicia amelloides)
scabiosa
stock, lavender
snapdragons, pink
delphinium
iris 'Margery'

BED #4

FOREGROUND

Alyssum saxatile (now *Aurinia
    saxatilis*)

tulips:
    'Mrs. Moon', *fulgens* 'Lutea Pallida'
Iceland poppy (*Papaver nudicaule*)
narcissus 'Conspicuous'
ranunculus, yellow
Dutch iris 'Wedgewood'
scabiosa
Campanula grossekeii
iris 'Rose Ash'

BACKGROUND

dianthus
Virginian stock (*Malcolmia maritima*)
nemophila
tulips:
    'Clara Butt', 'Cardinal Manning'
verbena, blue and pink
narcissus 'Mrs. O'Melveny'
lavender
flax (*Linum perenne*)
iris
stock, pink
penstemon, pink
Osteospermum ecklonis
iris 'Aurelle', lavender
columbine, pink
snapdragons, pink
irises:
    'Gargantua', 'San Gabriel',
        'Pale Moonlight'

BED #5

FOREGROUND

dimorphotheca hybrids
pansy 'Roggli Rheingold', yellow
tulips:
    'Perseus', 'Avis Kennicott'

BACKGROUND

irises: 'J. J. Dean', 'Portola'
gaillardia
primrose
calendula 'Nankeen'
daylily
watsonia 'Sturdevant'
delphinium
lupine
snapdragon 'Buff Beauty'
irises: 'Red Flare', 'Mauna Loa',
    snapdragon 'Flame'
watsonia 'Flame'
iris 'San Gabriel'

heuchera
ranunculus 'Cherry Red'
tulip 'Prince of Wales'
narcissus 'Glory of Isse'
iris 'Ambassadeur'
lavender
columbine, yellow
narcissus 'Croesus'
stock, yellow
watsonia, coral
delphinium
iris 'Sienna Blue'

BED #6
FOREGROUND

rosemary
viola, blue
tulip 'Arethusa'
narcissus 'Conspicuous'
aubrieta, lavender
Swan River daisy
tulips: 'Bishop', 'C. J. Hunt'

BACKGROUND

iris 'J. J. Dean'
agathaea
Dutch iris 'Wedgewood'
scabiosa, blue
flax (*Linum perenne*)
Campanula grossekii
iris 'Royal Salute'
columbine, blue
stock, purple
Osteospermum ecklonis
lavender
eryngium
iris 'San Diego'
snapdragon, lemon
delphinium
iris 'Gargantua'
penstemon, lavender
aubrieta, lavender
lupine
snapdragon, yellow
watsonia 'Estrella'
hollyhock, white

Florence Yoch and Lucile Council Garden
Pasadena, California
Planting Plans, April 1941

GARDEN BORDER ON SOUTH FRONT OF HOUSE

trees and shrubs:
  Bechtel crabapple (*Malus ionensis* 'Plena')
  Arnold crabapple (*Malus* × *arnoldiana*)
  oleander (*Nerium oleander*)
  jacaranda (*Jacaranda mimosifolia*)
  myrtle (*Myrtus communis*)
  boxwood (*Buxus*)
  camellia 'Purity'
  olive (*Olea europaea*)
  crape myrtle (*Lagerstroemia indica*)
  boxleaf myrtle (*Myrtus communis* 'Buxifolia')
flowers and bulbs:
  irises:
    'Cacique', *Iris savannarum*, 'Welcome', 'Westlander', 'Crimson King', 'Sun Gold', 'Fair Enough', 'San Diego', 'Blue River', 'Paramount', 'Fort Knox', 'Sierra Blue'
  Pacific Coast iris (*Veronica lyophylla*, now *Hebe leiophylla*)
  columbine (*Aquilegia*)
  dianthus, pink with deep pink center, pink with dark red eye, pink striped
  dianthus: 'Ruth Elaine', 'Best Salmon Fringe'
  daylily (*Hemerocallis*): 'Flame'
  lily-of-the-Nile (*Agapanthus orientalis*)
  sage (*Salvia pitcheri*, now *Salvia azurea* var. *grandiflora*)
  poet's narcissus (*Narcissus poeticus*)
  narcissi: 'John Evelyn', 'Diana Kasner'
  beardtongue (*Penstemon*)
  roses: 'Louise Catherine Breslau', 'Lady Forteviot'

POOL AREA

acacia
flowering apricot (*Prunus mume*)
almond (*Prunus amygdalis*)

escallonia
peach (*Prunus persica*), white
Japanese cherry (*Prunus serrulata*)
gum (*Eucalyptus*)
lilac (*Syringa*)
magnolia

ON NORTH SIDE OF PROPERTY

tobira (*Pittosporum tobira*), as free-growing hedge
ginger (*Hedychium gardnerianum*)
peach (*Prunus persica*), white
sweet olive (*Osmanthus fragrans*)
Japanese cherry (*Prunus serrulata*)
wild plum
windflower (*Anemone*)
fortnight lily (*Moraea iridioides*, now *Dietes vegeta*)
lily-of-the-Nile (*Agapanthus orientalis*)
native iris
Mexican orange (*Choisya ternata*)
freesia
violas
Cocculus laurifolius

ENTRY COURTYARD BY STUDIO

Arnold crabapple (*Malus* × *arnoldiana*)
Japanese maple (*Acer palmatum*)
anemone clematis (*Clematis montana*)
royal fern (*Osmunda regalis*)
lavender (*Lavandula*)
wisteria
boxwood (*Buxus sempervirens* 'Pyramidata')
crape myrtle (*Lagerstroemia indica*), white
guava

Mrs. Florence Banning Garden
Plans, January and February 1948

TREES

arbutus with *Cocculus laurifolius*
camphor tree (*Cinnamomum camphora*)
cork oak (*Quercus suber*)

deodar cedar (*Cedrus deodara*)

dogwood (*Cornus*)

Japanese maple (*Acer palmatum*) with white azaleas

lady palm (*Rhapis excelsa*) with cast-iron plant (*Aspidistra elatior*)

olive (*Olea europaea*)

saucer magnolia (*Magnolia × soulangiana*)

star magnolia (*Magnolia stellata*)

sycamore (*Platanus*)

flowering almond (*Prunus triloba*)

Japanese flowering apricot (*Prunus mume*)

evergreen pear (*Pyrus kawakamii*)

lime (*Citrus*)

orange (*Citrus*)

peach (*Prunus persica*)

PARTERRE

azaleas: 'Alta', 'Torch'

Kaffir lily (*Clivia miniata*)

golden flax (*Linum flavum*)

Azalea mollis, now *Rhododendron molle*

Azalea altaclarense (*Rhododendron rustica* var. *altaclarense*)

canna, flame-colored

monkshood (*Aconitum*)

bridal wreath spiraea (*Spiraea prunifolia*)

rice paper plant (*Tetrapanax papyriferus*)

boxwood (*Buxus*) as hedge

Sandankwa viburnum (*Viburnum suspensum*), or Portugal laurel (*Prunus lusitanica*), as hedge

Hahn's ivy (*Hedera helix* 'Hahn's Self-Branching), as ground cover

AT BOTTOM OF LAWN

Camellia japonica 'Debutante' with 3 widely spaced white camellias, then 3 closely spaced camellias, white, pink, and 'Silver Moon'

Cape pittosporum (*Pittosporum viridiflorum*)

Chinese holly (*Ilex cornuta*), as hedge

cocculus (*Cocculus laurifolius*)

SHRUBS

Victorian box (*Pittosporum undulatum*)

Delavay osmanthus (*Osmanthus delavayi*)

oleander (*Nerium oleander*)

Mexican orange (*Choisya ternata*)

navel orange, dwarf bush, as hedge

waxleaf privet (*Ligustrum japonicum* 'Texanum'), as hedge

PERENNIALS, INCLUDING FERNS

fortnight lily (*Moraea iridioides*, now *Dietes vegeta*)

bird of paradise (*Strelitzia reginae*)

calla (*Zantedeschia*)

canna, lemon, ivory, and flame

monkshood (*Aconitum*)

cast-iron plant (*Aspidistra elatior*)

chain fern (*Woodwardia*)

coast sword fern (*Polystichum dudleyi*)

Kaffir lily (*Clivia miniata*)

azaleas, including 'Torch', as border

daylily (*Hemerocallis*)

ginger (probably *Hedychium gardnerianum*)

sandwort (*Arenaria*)

howea palms in band behind rustic seat

Pacific Coast iris

Lady Banks' rose (*Rosa banksiae* 'Alba Plena')

Casa Alvarado Garden

Plan, February 1957

FRONT GARDEN

boxwood (*Buxus*)

Monterey cypress (*Cupressus macrocarpa*)

fuchsia

GARDEN NORTH OF HOUSE

bed along façade:

camellia

parrot-beak (*Clianthus puniceus*)

boxwood (*Buxus*), as hedge

perennials

Yulan magnolia (*Magnolia denudata*)

lily magnolia (*Magnolia liliiflora*)

saucer magnolia (*Magnolia × soulangiana*)

peonies (*Paeonia*)

hellebore (*Helleborus*)

in square planters set in open terrace:

apple (*Malus*), pyramidal

California buckeye (*Aesculus californica*)

tree wisteria, white

beds on west side of terrace:

rose 'Climbing Golden Emblem'

wisteria

Abutilon megapotamicum

boxwood (*Buxus*), as hedge

apricot (*Prunus armeniacum*), espaliered

loquats (*Eriobotrya japonica*), pollarded

roses

bulbs

beds around arbor:

boxwood (*Buxus*), as hedge

clematis

tree wisteria

climbing rose 'Sombreuil'

white Lady Banks' rose (*Rosa banksiae* 'Alba Plena')

Monterey cypress (*Cupressus macrocarpa*)

climbing rose 'Violetta'

climbing rose 'Madame Alfred Carrière'

cherry (*Prunus*)

rose 'Irish Fireflame'

Chinese wisteria (*Wisteria sinensis* 'Alba')

WEST GARDEN

along façade:

climbing rose 'Silver Moon'

Chinese wisteria (*Wisteria sinensis*)

fragrant azalea

fortnight lily (*Moraea iridioides*, now *Dietes vegeta*)

watsonia

valentine plum (*Prunus*)

rose

flowering maple (*Abutilon vitifolium*)

laurustinus (*Viburnum tinus*)

bed dividing house from children's play yard:

ivy (*Hedera*), as border

fortnight lily (*Dietes vegeta*)

flowering quince (*Chaenomeles*)

spring bulbs, blue

incense cedar (*Libocedrus decurrens*, now *Calocedrus decurrens*)

apple (*Malus*)

parterre:

trailing rosemary (*Rosmarinus officinalis* 'Prostratus'), as borders

Veitch magnolia (*Magnolia veitchii*)

roses

irises

daylilies (*Hemerocallis*)

boxwood (*Buxus*), as hedge

blueberries (*Vaccinium ovatum*), as hedge

doublefile viburnum (*Viburnum plicatum* var. *tomentosum*)

hydrangea

escallonia

dogwood (*Cornus*)

curved beds edging children's play yard:
boxwood (*Buxus*), as hedge
rosemary (*Rosmarinus officinalis*), as border along walk
apricot (*Prunus*)
trailing manzanita (*Arctostaphylos*), as ground cover
olives (*Olea europaea*)
bamboo
doublefile viburnum (*Viburnum plicatum* var. *tomentosum*)
fortnight lily (*Dietes vegeta*)
Escallonia rubra, as clipped hedge
pink escallonia (*Escallonia organensis*, now *E. laevis*)
strawberry tree (*Arbutus unedo*)
camellia
lilac (*Syringa*)
"old blue rose of Monterey"

Mrs. David E. Park Garden

Montecito, California

Plan, 1959–1960

CRABAPPLE WALK

Arnold crabapple (*Malus × arnoldiana*) on both sides of walk
irises on both sides of walk in groups of 3:
'Painted Desert', 'Snow Flurry', 'Lady Mohr', 'Ormohr', 'Blue Ribbon', 'Little Darling', 'Blue Shimmer'
tulips on both sides of walk in groups of 25:
'Geo. Dick', 'Chinese Ivory', 'Cherry', 'White Wings', 'Mariette', 'Testout', 'China Pink', 'Renown', 'Picotee', 'Bonnie Lass', 'O. Oswald', 'Bullock'

lemon trees in bed with ground cover of winter annuals

African daisy (*Dimorphotheca*)

Nemophila

Phacelia

At ends of crabapple walk:
espaliered apple trees
trellis covered with ivy (*Hedera helix*)
avocado trees
holly hedges (*Ilex cornuta* and *Ilex × altaclarensis* 'Wilsonii')

JACARANDA WALK

summer bloom and permanent perennials:
yarrow (*Achillea taygetea*)
lily-of-the-Nile (*Agapanthus orientalis*)
Japanese anemone (*Anemone japonica*, now *Anemone × hybrida*)
columbine (*Aquilegia*)
Campanula in variety
maiden's wreath (*Francoa ramosa*)
hellebore (*Helleborus*) in variety
daylily (*Hemerocallis*) in variety
Iris in variety
polyanthus primroses (*Primula × polyantha*)
fairy or baby primroses (*Primula malacoides*)
pansy or violet (*Viola*) edgings
delphinium
meadow rue (*Thalictrum*)
Salvia pitcheri, now *Salvia azurea* var. *grandiflora*
speedwell (*Veronica*)
beardtongue (*Penstemon*)
dwarf plumbago (*Plumbago larpentae*, now *Ceratostigma plumbaginoides*)
Rauwolfia samarana
oleander (*Nerium oleander*)
Irish yew (*Taxus baccata* 'Stricta')
Victorian box (*Pittosporum undulatum*)
flowering apricot (*Prunus mume*)
Ilex latifolia

by fountain area:
Edging of *Carissa grandiflora*
Yulan magnolia (*Magnolia denudata*)
heliotrope (probably *Centranthus ruber*)
winter daphne (*Daphne odora*)
oleander (*Nerium oleander*)
midget crabapple (*Malus kaido*, now *Malus micromalus*)

edging of breath of heaven (*Diosma ericoides*)

JACARANDA WALK

spring bloom (1961 plan)

tulips:
'The Bishop', 'Harvest Moon', 'Cum Laude', 'Fascinating', 'Wall Street', 'Geo. Grappe', 'New Hope', 'Lemon Ice', 'The Clown', 'Niphetos', 'Olsen's Favorite', 'Ming', 'Virdiflora praecox'
narcissi:
'Fortune', 'Thalia', 'Golden Harvest', 'Spring Glory', 'Geranium', 'Silver Star', 'Beersheba', 'Sunshine', 'Actaea', 'Scarlet Elegance', 'Mount Hood', 'Pink Glory'
Neapolitan cyclamen (*Cyclamen hederifolium*)
feathered or plume hyacinth (*Muscari comosum* 'Plumosum', now *M. comosum* 'Monstrosum')
lilies:
'Citronella', 'Lemon Cup', 'Pumila', 'P. Golden Gleam'
dutch irises:
'Yellow Queen', 'Moonlight'
delphiniums:
'Blue Ribbon', 'Royal Blue'
fritillary crown imperial (*Fritillaria imperialis*)

slope by fountain:
gardenias
Carissa grandiflora 'Tuttle' as edging
cranesbill (*Geranium*) with Scilla
rhododendron
Japanese maple (*Acer palmatum*)
Azalea mollis, now *Rhododendron molle*
Kaffir lily (*Clivia miniata*)
oleander (*Nerium oleander*)
lily 'Citronella'
lavender (*Lavandula*)
wisteria

around wall:
hibiscus 'White Wings'
Jasminum azoricum
polyanthus primroses (*Primula × polyantha*)
olive (*Olea europaea*)
valentine plum

purple-leaf plum (*Prunus pissardii*,
   now *Prunus cerasifera*
   'Atropurpurea')
Japanese flowering crabapple (*Malus
   floribunda*)
narcissus
geranium with scilla

EXEDRA

Tulips on both sides of walk:
   'Olsen's Favorite', 'C. W. Leak',
   'Mrs. Scheepers'
Louisiana iris (*Iris fulva, I.
   giganticaerulea, I. brevicaulus
   hybrids*)
Pacific Coast iris
snowflake (*Leucojum aestivum*)
scillas
Muscari 'Heavenly Blue' as border
Monbretia, now *Tritonia*, among shrubs
narcissi:
   'Actaea', 'Thalia', 'Silver Star',
      'Trevithian', 'February Gold'
rose trees

The Charles Edwin Davis Garden

Pasadena, California

Plans 1965–1969

ROSE GARDEN

border of carnations (*Dianthus
   caryophyllus*)
roses:
   'Golden Showers', 'Dainty Bess',
   'Sarabande', 'White Bouquet' or
   'Ivory Fashion', 'Green Fire',
   'Little Darling', 'Climbing
   Peace', 'Mister Lincoln',
   'Oklahoma', 'Olé', 'Christian
   Dior', 'Grand Slam',
   'Matterhorn', 'Jack Frost', 'Helen
   Traubel', 'Picture' or 'First
   Love', 'Margo Koster', 'Climbing
   Golden Emblem', 'Climbing
   Etoile de Hollande'

In corners of Rose Garden:
   bougainvillea 'San Diego'
   Meyer lemon (*Citrus limon* 'Meyer')

MAGNOLIA WALK

border of walk: large California violets
   (*Viola*)
by seat at top of walk:
   rose 'Climbing Lady Forteviot'
   wisteria
   lavender (*Lavandula*)
trees and shrubs:
Arnold crabapple
   (*Malus × arnoldiana*)
Akebono cherry (*Prunus yedoensis*
   'Akebono')
Catalina cherry (*Prunus lyonii*)
Catalina ironwood (*Lyonothamnus
   floribundus*)
dogwood (*Cornus*)
lemon-scented gum (*Eucalyptus
   citriodora*)
Yulan magnolia (*Magnolia denudata*)
myrtle (*Myrtus*)
coast live oak (*Quercus agrifolia*)
pepper tree (*Schinus molle*)
Wilson holly (*Ilex × altaclarensis*
   'Wilsonii')
Camellia sasanqua
ferns and flowers:
anemones, blue, red
epimedium
foxglove (*Digitalis*)
hellebores (*Helleborus*)
iris 'New Zealand'
orchid 'Sprite'
ranunculus, yellow, white, and mixed
Rhododendron fragrantissima
tulips:
   'Mrs. Scheepers', 'Dillenburg',
   'Matador', 'Niphetos', 'Clara
   Butt', 'Scotch Lassie'
tree fern (*Dicksonia antarctica* or
   Sphaeropteris cooperi)
fairy primrose (*Primula malacoides*)
maiden's wreath (*Francoa ramosa*)
Ternstroemia gymnanthera

IRIS WALK

trees and shrubs:
   Azalea 'White April'
   Japanese black pine (*Pinus
      thunbergiana*)

Catalina cherry (*Prunus lyonii*)
English holly (*Ilex aquifolium*)
gum (*Eucalyptus*)
Italian cypress (*Cupressus
   sempervirens*)
flowering nectarine (*Prunus persica
   'Alma Stultz'*)
coast live oak (*Quercus agrifolia*)
oleander (*Nerium oleander*)
Japanese maple (*Acer palmatum*)
flowering peach (*Prunus persica
   'Peppermint'*)
snowball (*Viburnum opulus
   'Roseum'*)
southern magnolia (*Magnolia
   grandiflora*)
flowers:
daylilies
irises:
'Queen Quest', 'Cloud Dancer',
   'Harbinger', 'Black Taffeta',
   'Lovely Diana', 'Glittering Gold',
   'Fleet Admiral', 'One Desire', 'Pink
   'n' Pretty', 'Ribbon Round',
   'Millionaire', 'Jet Black', 'Bronze
   Belle', 'Allegiance', 'Demetria',
   'Swan Ballet', 'Adorn', 'Pacific
   Panorama', 'Edith Edmon',
   'Burney', 'Ruth's Love', native
   irises (Pacific Coast hybrids)

CUT FLOWER GARDEN

African daisy (*Arctotis* hybrids), red
border of white freesias
blue marguerite (*Agathaea coelestis*,
   now *Felicia amelloides*)
Aster × frikartii
columbine (*Aquilegia*)
coral bells (*Heuchera sanguinea*)
dahlias, red and purple
dianthus
fleabane (*Erigeron*)
gaillardia
Gladiolus tristis
harlequin flower (*Sparaxis tricolor*)
kalanchoe
marguerite (*Chrysanthemum
   frutescens*)
meadow rue (*Thalictrum*)
Lobelia vedraiensis
Ornithogalum
pincushion flower (*Scabiosa*), in blue,
   red, and black
ranunculus

Shasta daisy (*Chrysanthemum maximum*)
tritonia (*Montbretia*)
tulip

CRAPE MYRTLE WALK

trees and shrubs:
Catalina cherry (*Prunus lyonii*)
Camellia sasanqua
carrotwood (*Cupaniopsis anacardioides*)
crape myrtle (*Lagerstroemia indica*), white
fringe tree (*Chionanthus*)
hibiscus, yellow
incense cedar (*Libocedrus decurrens*, now *Calocedrus decurrens*)
Jacaranda mimosifolia
maidenhair tree (*Ginkgo biloba*)
Victorian box (*Pittosporum undulatum*)
Wilson holly (*Ilex × altaclarensis* 'Wilsonii'), as hedge
tulip tree (*Liriodendron tulipifera*)
yew (*Taxus*)
viburnum

flowers:
baboon flower (*Babiana*)
bear's breech (*Acanthus mollis*)
camellia
grape hyacinth (*Muscari*)
hyacinth (*Hyacinthus orientalis* 'Albulus'), blue
iris 'Blue Tileston'
lily-of-the-Nile (*Agapanthus orientalis*), as border
narcissi:
    'Beersheba', 'Carleton', 'Deanna Durbin', 'February Gold', 'Fortune', 'Irish Lucky', 'Limone', 'Mount Hood', *N. jonquilla*, 'Pink Trumpet', 'Red Marley', 'Thalia', 'Zircon'
squill (*Scilla*)
violet trumpet vine (*Bignonia violacea*, now *Clytostoma callistegioides*)

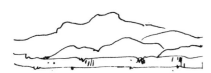

The W. O. Minor Garden
Merced, California

Plan, June 1968

DRIVE

native black oaks (*Quercus kelloggii*)
Raphiolepis ovata, now *R. umbellata*, as hedge
Catalina cherry (*Prunus lyonii*)

SOUTH OF HOUSE AND SWIMMING POOL

southern magnolia (*Magnolia grandiflora*)
locust (*Robinia*), underplanted with rosemary (*Rosmarinus officinalis*)
flowering quince (*Chaenomeles*)
pomegranate 'Wonderful' (*Punica granatum* 'Wonderful')
English ivy (*Hedera helix*), on fence
pistache (*Pistacia*)
yellow Lady Banks' rose (*Rosa banksiae* 'Lutea'), on arbor
lavender (*Lavandula*)
Chinese wisteria (*Wisteria sinensis*)
orange trees

SOUTH END OF PORCH

Italian cypress (*Cupressus sempervirens*)
rosemary (*Rosmarinus officinalis*)
scarlet tecoma, now Cape honeysuckle (*Tecomaria capensis*)
giant honeysuckle (*Lonicera hildebrandiana*), on loggia

NORTH END OF PORCH

tobira (*Pittosporum tobira*)
India hawthorn (*Raphiolepis indica* 'Springtime')
crape myrtle (*Lagerstroemia indica*), white
irises and annuals
boxleaf myrtle (*Myrtus communis* 'Buxifolia'), as hedge
star jasmine (*Trachelospermum jasminoides*), on slope

MEADOW AREA, NORTHWEST OF HOUSE

African grass (African bermuda, *Cynodon transvaalensis*)
Monterey cypress (*Cupressus macrocarpa*), as a windbreak
Italian stone pines (*Pinus pinea*)

NORTHEAST EDGE OF BARLEY FIELD

Italian stone pines (*Pinus pinea*)
Italian cypress (*Cupressus sempervirens*)

ON SLOPE BY GARAGE SIDE OF HOUSE

area for birds and chickens
haystack
cut flowers and vegetables
fruits and grapes

BY GARAGE

loquat (*Eriobotrya japonica*)
weeping willow (*Salix babylonica*)

PARKING COURT

olives (*Olea europaea*)
California black oaks (*Quercus kelloggii*)
Canary Island pine (*Pinus canariensis*)

The Francis Doud House
Monterey, California

Suggested Plant List, August 1970

TREES

Monterey pine (*Pinus radiata*)
Monterey cypress (*Cupressus macrocarpa*)
Italian cypress (*Cupressus sempervirens*)
olive (*Olea europaea*)

California bay (*Umbellularia californica*)
apple (*Malus*)
apricot (*Prunus armeniaca*)
plum (*Prunus domestica*)
pear (*Pyrus*)
orange (*Citrus*)
fig (*Ficus carica*)
crabapple (*Malus*)

SHRUBS

English boxwood (*Buxus sempervirens*)
flowering quince (*Chaenomeles*)
lemon verbena (*Aloysia triphylla*)
toyon (*Heteromeles arbutifolia*)
Spanish broom (*Spartium junceum*)
golden chain tree (*Laburnum watereri* 'Vossii')
pomegranate (*Punica granatum*)
Chilean guava (*Psidium*)
India hawthorn (*Rhaphiolepis indica*)
Azara microphylla
Escallonia

VINES

scarlet bougainvillea
moon-flower (*Ipomoea alba*)

honeysuckle (*Lonicera*)
jasmine (*Jasminum*)
wisteria

BULBS

gladiolus
baboon flower (*Babiana*)
harlequin flower (*Sparaxis tricolor*)
tiger lily (*Lilium tigrinum*, now *L. lancifolium*)
freesia
tritonia (*Montbretia*)
Dianella tasmanica

ROSES

'Mermaid'
'White Cherokee' (*Rosa laevigata*)
'Yellow Lady Banks' (*Rosa banksiae* 'Lutea')
'Duchesse de Brabant'
'Mme. Alfred Carrière'
'Belle Portugaise'
'Cécile Brunner'
'Persian Yellow' (*Rosa foetida* 'Persiana')
'Austrian Copper' (*Rosa foetida* 'Bicolor')

'Reine des Violettes'
Rose of Castile (*Rosa* × *damascena* 'Bifera')
chestnut rose (*Rosa* × *roxburghii*)
blackberry rose (*Rosa rubus*)
'Golden Emblem'
'Kathleen'

HERBACEOUS PLANTS

Agathaea coelestis, now *Felicia amelloides*
yarrow (*Achillea*)
fuchsia
heliotrope (probably *Centranthus ruber*)
geranium (*Pelargonium*)
sea lavender (*Statice*, now *Limonium*)
beardtongue (*Penstemon*)
marguerite (*Chrysanthemum frutescens*)
violets (*Viola*)
daylily (*Hemerocallis*)
lily-of-the-Nile (*Agapanthus orientalis*)
dwarf iris
gazania
poppy (*Papaver*)
pinks (*Dianthus*)
perennial aster
delphinium
hollyhocks (*Alcea rosea*)
mallow (*Malva*)

Garden Maintenance Directions for Mrs. Preston Hotchkis

Florence Yoch—Lucile Council, Landscape Architects

I. GENERAL GARDEN INFORMATION

A. Climate

Garden practice in California differs from that of the East in exactly the same way as does the climate, and for the same reasons.

We have NO RAINS during the growing season which is a condition totally unlike that in any other temperate climate. This means that we depend upon irrigation and other artificial means for growth and propagation, thus throwing the normal seasonal practices of other climates completely off schedule here.

We consider that we have two Springtimes in California. The first commences with the Fall rains, usually in October. This is the natural Spring when California native grasses and annual flowers start their growth. It is the most important gardening season in southern California and this is when we plant bulbs and annuals which would bloom in the regular calendar Spring and early summer in other climates, but, many of which start to bloom here in December and continue until May. We also put in seeds and plants of perennials that continue to flower from May until December.

Ours is so arid as to be actually a desert climate, which fact is responsible for the difference in soils and treatment of plants. In cold climates the term "hardy plant" is taken to mean one that is resistant to low temperatures. With us, it is more frequently used to mean a plant capable of a certain amount of resistance to drought.

B. Soils

Due to the effects of the climate, practically none of the soils in southern California are ideal for garden use; some, in fact, are very poor, but all are quite easily corrected with ordinary preparation and care.

ALL plants must both breathe and feed through their roots. This necessitates an open, porous type of soil through which air can pass readily. Modern tests and experience find that air is much more important to plant growth than was realized some years ago. The outstanding accomplishment in our section of the country has been the recent success with Azaleas and Camellias which were formerly considered difficult to grow here.

The prime essential for all plant growth is sufficient moisture. It has been proved that loose, fibrous soil distributes underground water more readily and evenly, because of its structure.

The two types of soil most commonly met with in this region are:

(a) the thin sandy soil where drainage is too sharp;
(b) heavy dark clays, known locally as Adobe, which are so fine-grained as to be too compact and which do not drain well enough.

Of the two, the Adobe is much more fertile than sand but both are seriously deficient in humus. For both of these extreme types of soil the same treatment produces optimum results, and that is the addition of humus.

C. Humus

All living organisms are supported by material that has previously been living matter, that is of plant or animal origin. Humus is obtained as the result of the breaking down and decomposition of organic material. No plant lives in the ground on materials of mineral origin only and all are more thrifty when there is sufficient humus to build a proper soil texture. The underground airways not only permit the transfer of water and therefore food which must be in solution, but also correct the physical structure of the soil increasing its ability to absorb and hold moisture and to distribute the chemical content.

The principal organic materials used for adding humus to the soil are:

(a) barnyard or dairy manure. It is not particularly high in fertilizing content, but has that even more valuable characteristic of supplying humus;

(b) other animal manures, if old enough and added to de-composed plant material;

(c) plant materials like bean straw, alfalfa and leaf mold.

A compost of plant materials made with a proper amount of manure, topsoil and certain chemicals makes the most efficient, and scientific form of humus for soil improvement. As our soils need constant and consistent maintaining it is the worst possible mistake to destroy or carry off the very materials plants need most.

The ideal garden soil is that most nearly like the soil in a mountain meadow, dark in color, soft to touch, moist but not soggy wet, light in weight, fibrous and fragrant.

For instructions for making compost see our diagram and sheet following.

II. MAINTENANCE

A. Watering:

As we have practically no rainfall during the prolonged growing season in this climate it is necessary to get in mind the few principal facts concerning irrigation.

Frequency and depth of watering depend upon:

1. the depth and character of the root growth. Surface roots, like grass, require shallow and therefore frequent watering. As plants increase in size they will require deeper and less frequent waterings. Trees and shrubs must be watered deeply enough to ensure that their deep feeding roots receive sufficient moisture. This is PARTICULARLY important to those that have been moved in large boxes. They do not want to be overwatered, as no plant likes to stand in continuous moisture, and roots require air. But remember that all plant food has to be in solution in order for the plant to assimilate it.

2. the character of the soil. Heavy soils do not dry out as rapidly as thin, sandy soil, or light peaty mixtures.

3. weather, of course, and seasons.

Cultivation:

After each thorough irrigation, the open topsoil should be lightly cultivated to form a dirt mulch and allow air to penetrate. Be careful around shallow rooted subjects, particularly Roses, Camellias, and annual flowers, not to go deep enough to injure surface roots.

Caution about the Use of Peat:

Peat has a strange quality known as hygroscopic action not shared by ordinary soil. It has the ability to attract water away from surrounding areas if it, itself, is not thoroughly saturated. A great deal of harm is done by the use of dry peat put on the top of moist soil in the mistaken idea of mulching. ALWAYS BE SURE peat is in a state of thorough saturation before mixing it into the soil. This requires about SIX HOURS. Don't think it can be done in less. NEVER use a surface mulch of peat. It dries out and robs adjacent areas. Even when used properly in an underground mixture, peat disintegrates rapidly and, in the case of certain plants that are definitely peat-lovers, it is necessary to replace it once a year.

Important:

The best way to determine whether the ground needs watering is to pick up a handful of soil and squeeze it. If there is sufficient moisture in the soil to retain the mold of the hand on opening it, the soil is wet enough as the water surrounding the soil particles is capable of cohesion. If the handful of soil breaks and falls apart, it needs water. This is worth doing, as mere dark color does not always mean the proper amount of moisture.

General Observation:

Green leaved plants show distress by the foliage turning yellowish. This may be due to too much water, or too little water, or wrong chemical content, usually an improper pH factor. The pH factor is the measure of acidity and alkalinity in the soil. In our arid climate all water and most soils are somewhat alkaline. The tolerance of the majority of plants is amazing in this respect, but for some, a correction must be made.

B. Fertilizing:

"Never feed a sleeping baby." That is, plants can only take in food during their growing season.

General Rules:

All plant food has to be in liquid form to be assimilable by the minute root hairs at the tips of the roots.

There are three essential chemicals in plant feeding which must be supplied in ordinary soils:

1. Nitrogen expressed as (N). This is always of organic origin. It supplies the protein content of food, and, in plants, builds the green coloring matter—chlorophyll—an overabundance of which may cause too lush foliage growth and spoil flowering plants.

2. and 3. *Phosphate* (P) and *Potassium* (K) are always considered together. They are of mineral origin and contribute to the formation of flowers and seeds. This will guide you in feeding.

Most California natives are tolerant of alkali in varying degrees, as are many desert and sun loving plants. Indeed a good many of these do not tolerate animal manure. Most shade loving, and most very shiny green leaved plants, are acid lovers. See directions for feeding Camellias, etc.

A good many so-called fertilizers are actually not plant foods but are used for the purpose of modifying the pH of the soil or to stimulate growth.

Humus material as explained above is the best soil conditioner and best carrier for food elements in the ground. If you do not allow the humus content to become exhausted, relatively little actual plant food will be required.

Plants in sun require more food than in the shade, because they require more water.

TYPES OF PLANTS

For garden purposes we classify plants in several ways:

1. *Evergreen and Deciduous:*
   In California we designate all plants that keep their leaves throughout the year as Evergreens. You will see that this includes not only the needle-leafed (Conifers) as is usual in Eastern gardens, but most of the handsome broadleafed trees and shrubs. Deciduous plants lose their leaves in Fall, even here.
2. *Sun-lovers and Shade-lovers:*
   These categories are so distinct as to make great differences in our gardening.
3. *Drought resistant and Moisture loving:*
   Most California natives are more or less drought resistant, some even of desert origin.
4. *Season of bloom:*
   Winter, Spring, Summer, Fall—depending upon what part of the globe they come from.
   In general, we plant flowering things at the opposite time of the year than we expect them to bloom.
5. *Habit of growth:*
   Trees
   Shrubs—woody plants
   Vines (Scandent Shrubs)
   Herbaceous perennials—non-woody plants that live on for an indefinite number of years.
   Annuals—plants that complete their life in one year.
   Bulbs
   Grasses

MAINTAINING THE HEALTH OF THE GARDEN

Lack of thrift in the garden may be due to any or all of the following reasons:
A. *Physical Conditions of Soil* (not necessarily disease)
   1. Too much or too little water—can be rectified by proper irrigation, proper drainage.
   2. Improper soil structure—to correct this apply additional humus-bearing material.
   3. Too Alkaline soil or water—can be rectified by commercial product known as "Acidate" (see label for directions) or Agricultural Sulphur.
   4. Too Acid—this is rare in California—found on old places with poor drainage—remedy is application of gypsum (get special advice).
B. *Actual Diseases of plants* are rare in California. The few prevalent are usually of virus types and need special advice in each case.
C. *Pests or Plant Enemies* constitute the greatest menace to garden thrift. They are living organisms and can be classified under the two main headings of:
   1. *Animal pests* such as snails, caterpillars, aphis, thrips, etc., are divided into two classes:
      a. *Chewers: Those large enough to see* and handle conveniently—like snails, slugs, sow bugs, wire worms, caterpillars, cutworms, etc. These are best picked off and killed—follow by using generous amounts of some commercial bug bait. *Those that chew holes* in foliage—these have mouth parts and stomachs and are controlled by stomach poison. To date the best of those contain some form of arsenic.* The trouble is immediately discernible by holes chewed in foliage.
      b. *Smaller creatures*—sometimes microscopic, that *do not chew but suck* the juices and life out of plants, usually on tender, new growth—these are many in kind but are all controlled by some form of smothering contact poison. The old-fashioned tobacco derivations or plant powders which act as repellants or contact poisons are used.
      These minute pests are often classed as Red Spider which is simply one of them, but typical of most.
      The trouble shows as wilted yellow, and sometimes spotted looking growth. *Remedies:*
      Pyrethreum products
      Tobacco products

*This method is now unacceptable. Safer remedies are available and should be used. J.Y.

2. *Microscopic Plant Organisms* which show as mildew, rusts, and other fungus growth, are controlled by dusting sulphur for the most easily killed, like mildew on roses. But for more tenacious growth, special sprays and follow-up are necessary—ask dealers.

Two generalizations are true to date:

1. Keeping planting well fed and watered, growing rapidly, and keeping up humus content of soil, has proved the most effective way of resisting damage by pests and enemies. *This is true.*

2. The new products of war science seem in many cases to do a great deal of avoidable harm, in that they are very effective—too effective—in killing fairly mild pests they also sterilize soil and kill out the essential beneficial bacteria and small soil life.

There are a few friends to gardening in Nature—first, the earthworm—which should not be confused with injurious worms like cutworm and wireworms; then soil bacteria which you will not see, but whose effects are evident. Certain birds are also helpful.

COMPOST

This Compost takes fifteen weeks to make instead of two years as the old method took, is much more mellow and does NOT SMELL in the making.

DO NOT use a pit or box. Make it directly on the top of the ground, as air is essential to the process. DO NOT neglect soaking the pile as directed, as moisture is one of the essentials.

1. Make a layer of green materials, leaves, grass, garden and kitchen refuse	6 inches deep
2. Spread 2 inches of FRESH (not rotted) cow manure	2 "
3. Spread $1/2$ inch Gypsum (NOT LIME) Spread $1/8$ inch Potassium sulphate Spread $1/8$ inch Superphosphate	$3/4$ "
4. Spread 2 inches of Good live topsoil	2 "
Total approximately	10 inches deep

Repeat these three layers until you have a flat topped heap about 30 inches high. Make a ridge around the outer edge so as to hold water on top. Put a set spray on and soak until thoroughly saturated.

In one week turn over the entire pile. Do this again as follows:

Once a week for three weeks 3	weeks
Once in two weeks for two weeks 4	weeks
Once in a month for 2 months 8	weeks
	15 weeks

Then it is ready for use. Remember, this is a process of growth, NOT DECAY, and air, moisture and warmth are necessary. Ordinary California temperatures at all times of the year are sufficient. The chemicals aid in a rapid breakdown of the organic materials and give a slight fertilizing effect. BUT YOU ARE MAKING HUMUS AND NOT a rich fertilizer here. This makes a clean compost, the best form of HUMUS.

GARDEN CALENDAR

Month to Plant		To Bloom In
February	*Divisions of*	
	Japanese Anemone	Fall
	Achillea in variety	Spring & Summer
	Gerbera	Fall & Winter
	Hemerocallis	Sprg. & Summer
	Native Iris	April
	Shasta Daisies	July
	Veronica (perennial)	Summer
	Bulbs of Gladiolus	Fall
	Plants of Cinerarias	May
March and April	*Seeds of*	
	Ageratum	Summer
	Annual Phlox	Summer

March and April cont.

Seeds of

Asters	Summer
Cosmos and other summer annuals	Summer
Dimorphotheca perennial (Ecklonis)	Following winter
Lobelia	Summer
Petunias	Summer
Zinnias	Summer

Divisions of

Chrysanthemum	Fall
Dahlia	Fall
Perennial Asters	Fall
Perennial Campanulas	Summer
Rudbeckia	Summer
Salvia	Summer

May

Calliopsis	Summer
French and African Marigolds	Summer
Portulaca	Summer
Primula malacoides	Following winter
Tithonia	Following winter

Seeds of Perennials & Biennials

Agathea	Gaillardia
Aquilegia	Hollyhocks
Canterbury Bells	Myosotis
Campanula in variety	Penstemon
Delphinium	Scabiosa in variety
Digitalis	

June

Seeds of   Winter
Primulas in variety
Violas
Cineraria

July

Seeds of

English Daisy	Winter
Stocks for early bloom	Winter
French & African Marigold	Fall
Calliopsis	Fall
Ranunculus & Anemone	Fall
Violas	Fall

August	*Seeds of*	Winter
	Dimorphotheca	
	Stocks	
	Calendula	
	Sweet Pea—August 15	
	Annual Phlox—tall type	
	Viscaria	
	Brachycome Daisy	
	Virginian Stock	
	Cineraria	
	Iceland Poppy	
	Johnny Jump Up	
	Pansy	
	Snapdragon	
	Bulbs of (Impatient types)	
	Madonna Lily	Spring
	Freesia	Spring
	Amaryllis in var.	Spring
	Iris—Bearded	Following Sprg.
	Muscari	Following Sprg.
	Nerine (Lycoris)	Following Summer
September	*Seeds of*	Spring
	Nemophila	
	Clarkia and other native Calif. annuals	
	Agathea	
	Virginian Stock	
	Arctotis—annual	
	Brachycome Daisy	
	Bulbs of	Spring
	Muscari	
	Spanish Iris	
	Watsonia	
	Freesias	
	Plants of	Summer
	Penstemon	
	Columbine	
	Campanula grossekii	
	Agathea	
	Delphinium	
	Statice	
	Foxglove	
	Dianthus	
	Heuchera	
	Scabiosa	

September (cont'd)
Salvia farinacea
Canterbury bells
Primula in variety:
    P. Malacoides
    P. Obconica
    P. Chinensis
    P. Polyanthus

October
In general, *same as for September* in planting seeds and plants.

With the first
rains put in:

Seeds of:
Cornflower
Shirley Poppy
Salpiglosis
Larkspur
Native Annuals

Divisions of:
Hemerocallis
Myosotis
Francoa

Bulbs of: ALL DUTCH & OTHER LATER BULBS—
Narcissus
Hyacinths
Regal and other Lilies
Scillas in variety
Tulips
Anemone

ALTERNATIONS AND SUCCESSIONS

Sweet Peas
Annual Dianthus

To Bloom In:
Winter and Spring

Sun or Semi-Shade
Viola

Full Sun
Calendula
English Daisy
Dimorphotheca
Pansy
Stocks
Snapdragon
California Poppy
Columbine
Annual Larkspur
Canterbury Bells
Virginian Stock
Nemophila
Iceland Poppy

Semi-shade or Full shade
Cineraria
Primula malacoides
Myosotis
Foxglove
Perennial types of Primulas

Summer and Fall

Full Sun
African and French Marigold
Petunia
Zinnia
Calliopsis
Helianthus angustifolia
Portulaca
Annual Phlox

Sun or Semi-Shade
Ageratum
Annual Phlox
Annual Aster
Perennial Aster
Salvia Pitcheri
Lobelia
Viscari

Semi-shade or Full shade
Tuberous Begonia
Eupatorium coelestinum
Hydrangea
Japanese Anemone

N.B. Plants which need to stay in place all year are not included in this list.

The choices given here are open to much variation and juggling to suit color, height or other requirements.

Reliable Garden Flowers That Bloom Practically All Year Round In California

Agathea
Arctotis
Campanula grossekii
Erigeron
Scabiosa
Gaillardia
Hemerocallis
Iris Crimson King
Morea iridioides
Petunia (unless frost)
Statice perezi

Valerian
Verbena
Geranium

Note: These are perennials useful for cutting.

CUTTING GARDENS

All Year Perennials

Agathea
Dianthus Allwoodi
Ecklonis
Gaillardia
Yellow Marguerite

Spring Perennials

Violets
Primula polyantha
Heuchera
Geum
Carnation
Columbine
Cynoglossum
Lupine
Delphinium
Campanula in variety

Summer and Fall Perennials

Delphinium
Campanula in var.
Perennial Aster
Salvia in var.
Rudbeckia in var.
Helianthus in var.
Goldenrod
Chrysanthemum
Gerberas—Carry over

Midwinter Annuals

Sweet Peas
Calendula
Dimorphotheca
Annual Phlox
Stock
Snapdragon
Annual Dianthus

Late Spring Annuals

Larkspur
Lupine
Shirley Poppy
Salpiglossis
Godetia

Summer and Fall Annuals

Salpiglossis
Zinnia
Aster
Lupine

Marigold
Calliopsis   Carry over into
An. Phlox   Mid-Winter

Bulbs

Anemone
Ranunculus
Scilla
Roman Hyacinths
Spanish Iris
Narcissus
Leucocoryne
Ixia
Gladiolus in var.
Tritoma
Watsonia

NOTE: This list purposely omits flowers which are chiefly valuable for garden decoration such as:
Pansy
Petunia
Ageratum
Canterbury bells
Anemone japonica
Perennial phlox

OR Seaside things such as:
Cornflower
Dahlia
Annual Chrysanthemum
Statice

POTTED PLANTS

For Large Pots:

Flower Color

Spring
Azaleas
Agaves
Geranium

Summer
Bougainvillea
Oleander
Dahlia

Fuchsia
Plumbago
Agapanthus

Fall
Chrysanthemum

Winter
Clivia
Saxafrage cordata

Evergreen Foliage

Sun
Climbing Aloe
Boxwood
Citrus in variety
Palms
Sedum

Shade
Aralia sieboldi
Asparagus acutifolius
Ivy
Palms
Holly Fern
Tree Fern
Ruscus
Begonia—tall

For Small Pots:

Spring
Narcissus
Tulips
Dudley
Mesembryanthemum—orange

Summer
Geranium
Petunia

Fall
Chrysanthemum

Winter

Shade
Primula
Cineraria
Cyclamen

Sun
Chorizema
Jerusalem Cherry

INSTRUCTIONS FOR PANSIES

Soil preparation

4″ manure
4″ leaf mold
Prepare 6 to 8 weeks in advance. Fork over lightly.
NEVER CULTIVATE PANSIES—They have surface feeder roots.
Sow seed in July if you want flowers for Thanksgiving and Christmas.

Fertilizer

Feed "4-10-5" or "4-10-4" or "5-10-5" or "4-12-4" every two weeks—a small sprinkling around each plant.

Pansies for Pots

Start feeding two months after planting in pots. Use "4-10-4", one teaspoon to a gallon of water once a week.

FERTILIZING THE ROSE BED

Give the rose bed a good inch of cow manure and bean straw or manure alone some time in February when the main rainfall has passed by. Follow this up throughout the year, about six weeks apart, with ¼ cup of Vigoro or blood and bone. Carry on this treatment until September and then wait until Spring again to put some more manure on.

(Sent by John van Barneveld)

VIOLETS

Outdoor culture should be almost identical to that of Strawberry.

Best Situation—Under a high shade of deciduous trees where there is little direct sun but plenty of light. They do not flower freely in dense shade.
Soil—Slightly acid workable soil which does not dry out rapidly at the surface. Use plenty of manure. (Carl Purdy says he made a Violet bed using 10″ of manure.)
DO NOT CULTIVATE—Violets have surface feeder roots which should not dry out or be disturbed. Remake Violet beds every two years.

CAMELLIAS

Feeding Instructions:

For a plant in an 18″ pot, feed a mixture of ½ Cup Cottonseed Meal to 1 teaspoon of blood meal. Scratch into the soil and water in immediately. Use two to three times during the Spring (six weeks apart) and early summer. Start using as soon as the plant stops blooming and new growth starts. Never use after the hot summer weather starts or during the fall and winter. If the plants are in a shady location where soil is inclined to get sour, a working-in of charcoal into the soil once or twice a year will be very beneficial.

Camellias are shallow rooting. They resent disturbance of their roots by deep cultivation. They cannot survive if planted too deeply. *Take care to plant exactly at original ground line and maintain this level always.*

FERTILIZER FOR CHRYSANTHEMUMS

Use *Liquid Manure* or *Vigoro*.
Have solution very weak—just slightly colored. Fertilize every three weeks after plant is put in, watching that leaf stays dark green and velvety.
Don't fertilize if leaf snaps when bent. Pinch back to 3 or 4 buds two or three times—that is, until July 1. Keep feeding during the growing season until flower buds start to form. Then stop for season.
Sulphate of Ammonia can be used: 1 teasp. to 1 gallon water. Sprinkle this solution around plants then wash with water, once ev. 2 wks.

TRAINING CASCADE CHRYSANTHEMUMS

1. Use any scandant type. Start cuttings March 1st.
2. Use light soil mix.
3. When plant is well started, about 6″ high, pinch back top. From new growth select main leader and do not pinch it back.
4. Pinch back lateral growth until August 15.
5. When leader is 12″ high put heavy wire (3′ to 4′ long) in pot. Bend to 45 degree angle and tie leader to wire with raffia.
6. Tie leader to wire every week as growth increases.
7. Point wire toward north.
8. September 1–15th (when flower buds are forming) bend support to horizontal position. Turn plant to face south—finally bend down to vertical position.
9. If pots can be plunged in propagating bed it is much easier to keep constant moisture.

AZALEAS

These directions apply to Kurume Azaleas—*AS GROWN IN POTS.*

Some varieties are evergreen and foliage stays good throughout the year. Others are deciduous or semi-deciduous so that one must learn to judge whether plants are merely obeying seasonal habits or are in bad condition.

In fall, the leaves of a healthy deciduous plant (of any kind) turn yellow or brown and drop off *freely*, leaving a fresh smooth bark that will show a bright green underlayer if a tiny cut is made with the thumbnail. An unhealthy plant droops, retains wilted looking leaves of poor color, and the bark looks shriveled. If underlayer (cambium) is examined it shows a yellowish color or is completely dry.

1. Azaleas should never be allowed to go without water for a long enough period so that their potting soil (or mixture) can become completely dry. Neither can they stand continuous soppy, wet mixture, which prevents proper aeration.
2. They are shallow rooting plants and are better in pots wider than they are deep.
3. The best potting medium seems to be a mixture of:
   $^1/_3$ each of sand
   leafmold
   peat (See special discussion of peat)

Repotting should be done *immediately after flowering* is finished (about May 1st here)—just before new growth on twigs starts. If plant is being transferred from pure peat to the mixture above, *BE SURE TO* wash all peat out from underneath the central crown of roots. If not, it will decay further and cause incurable toxic condition. *DO NOT OVERPOT*—any potted plant is healthier in a pot just large enough to contain its roots comfortably. Slow growing plants particularly do not thrive in too large a pot.

Do not confuse actual fertilizing (feeding) of Azaleas, Camellias, Fuchsias and other ACID LOVING plants with acidifying.

We use acid fertilizer to feed the plant. For Azaleas, COTTONSEED MEAL has been found very satisfactory in our conditions. Fertilize only during the growing season. For small potted plants, feed once a month from June 1st to September 1st. Large pots should be fed two or three times during the same period and in a corresponding amount.

Sprinkle fertilizer and work in lightly to prevent a crust of mold growing on surface of the peaty mixture.

To counteract the alkalinity of local water and soil, apply the commercial product called "ACIDATE" as per directions on the bottle. It is wise also to give one application of garden sulphur once during the growing season.

If a bad case of Chlorosis develops (sickly yellow foliage—no growth) *REPOT PLANT* AT ANY TIME—wash decayed material out of root mass, change to fresh soil mix, and keep in a cool place.

Do not fail to keep plant pruned to develop flowering wood. Long, straggling twigs spoil the shape of a plant and reduce flowering wood. Nip the terminal buds when growth is three or four inches long.

All small flowered Azaleas can be nipped until the first of July; large flowered types only until June 1st.

Flower buds will set better if plants are carried over the summer in *HALF DAY SUN*, or under partial shade of tall deciduous trees.

When in Full bloom the flowers last better if they can be placed in full shade to prevent sun scalding in early spring.

Wash foliage frequently in dry periods as the plant breathes through its leaves. *BUT NEVER* water foliage in the sunshine.

CAUTION: Make sure to provide adequate drainage in each pot. Use two or three pieces of broken pot.

BULBS

	Bulb	Plant	to	Bloom
M	CLIVIA	July to August		November–March
M	GRAPE HYACINTH	do.		December–March
P	IRIS STYLOSA	Aug. to September		November–February
P	SNOWFLAKE			January–February
R	CALLAS	All year		February on
R	CROCUS	September–October		January–February
M	HYACINTH—ROMAN	August–October		do.
M	NARCISSUS in variety (Daffodils & Jonquils included here)	September–October		March 1–May 1

	Bulb	Plant	to	Bloom
R	RANUNCULUS & ANEMONES*	do.		do.
M	FREESIAS	August–September		March–April
M	HYACINTHS—DUTCH	September–October		February–March
P	MOREA	All year		All year
P	NATIVE IRIS (perennial) (Divide clumps during rain)			
M	SCILLA in variety	August to September		April
M	SPANISH IRIS	September–October		March–April
P	IRIS—Garden Var. (Perennial—a few repeat flowering in summer and fall)	July–September		February–May
R	TULIP	October		March–April
M	AMARYLLIS in variety	August		April–August
M	LILIES in variety	August–December		do.
M	WATSONIAS	August–October		May to June
M	GLADIOLUS	January–July		May–October (with repeated plantings)
P	AGAPANTHUS	January–March		June–July
P	CANNAS	January–March		May–December
M	DAHLIAS	April thru June		June–November
P	DAY LILIES	All year		June thru Summer
M	NERINE OR LYCORIS (Spider Lily)	November–January		September
P	TRITOMA	All year		Summer
M	STERNBERGIA (Amusing fall Crocus; flowers within a month of planting)	August		September

KEY: P—Perennial
M—Multiplies
R—Replace

FOOTNOTES:

#1- P- Perennial, of which foliage remains good throughout the year and can stay in the ground for indefinite number of years.

M- Foliage dies down, but bulbs multiply and can be counted upon for repeated flowering. Most of these should be dug up and separated alternate years.

R- Some, as Tulips, Anemones and Ranunculus have to be replaced with new bulbs every season.

#2- See Catalog for Color

#3- Note: A good many things on this list are used as common herbaceous perennials in southern California. (See Footnote #1)

#4- Spring flowering bulbs usually referred to as "Dutch Bulbs" include Narcissus, Hyacinths, and Tulips.

#5- A few types of bulbs—staples in southern California—are known as "Impatient"—meaning that they resent being out of the ground long after flowering and ripening of bulbs. Most popular among these are: Grape Hyacinths, Freesias, Madonna Lily, Amaryllis in variety.

If kept out of the ground for a period of several weeks, these bulbs deteriorate.

Bibliography

GENERAL BACKGROUND

American Academy. *A Guide to Villas and Gardens in Italy.* Florence: Parenti, 1938.

Armor, Samuel B. *History of Orange County, California, with Biographical Sketches.* Los Angeles: Historic Record Company, 1921.

Balmori, Diana, Diane Kostial McGuire, and Eleanor M. McPeck. *Beatrix Farrand's American Landscapes.* Sagaponack, N.Y.: Sagapress, 1985.

Behlmer, Rudy, ed. *Memo from D. O. Selznick.* New York: Viking Press, 1972.

Blomfield, Sir Reginald. *The Formal Garden in England.* London: Macmillan, 1892.

Bridges, Herb. *The Filming of Gone With the Wind.* Macon, Ga.: Mercer University Press, 1984.

Buck, Pearl S. *The Good Earth.* New York: Grosset and Dunlap, 1931.

Burk's Southern California Business Directory. Los Angeles: Los Angeles Directory Company, 1898.

Carr, Jay. "Director Arzner: A Mind of Her Own." *Boston Globe,* 23 April 1984, pp. B1, B8.

City Directory: Santa Ana, Tustin, Garden Grove, Orange, Olive, El Molino, Villa Park. Long Beach: Western Directory Company, 1923.

Cran, Marion. *Gardens in America.* New York: Macmillan, 1932.

Dent, Alan. *Vivien Leigh: A Bouquet.* London: Hamish Hamilton, 1969.

Dézallier d'Argenville, Antoine-Joseph. *La Théorie et la Pratique du Jardinage.* Paris, 1709.

Downing, Andrew Jackson. *A Treatise on the Theory and Practice of Landscape Gardening, Adapted to North America; with a View to the Improvement of Country Residences.* New York: Wiley and Putnam, 1841.

———. *The Architecture of Country Houses.* New York: D. Appleton, 1850. Reprint. New York: Dover, 1969.

Earle, Alice Morse. *Old-Time Gardens ... A Book of the Sweet O' the Year.* New York: Macmillan, 1901.

Eliot, Charles W. *Charles Eliot, Landscape Architect.* Boston: Houghton Mifflin, 1902.

Flandrau, Charles Macomb. *Viva Mexico!* 1908. Reprint. New York: D. Appleton, 1928.

Garnett, Porter. *Stately Homes of California.* Introduction by Bruce Porter. Boston: Little, Brown, 1915.

Gebhard, David, ed. *Myron Hunt, 1868–1952: The Search for a Regional Architecture.* California Architecture and Architects series, no. 4. Los Angeles: Hennessey and Ingalls, 1984.

Girouard, Mark. *Sweetness and Light.* London: Oxford University Press, 1977.

Gowan, Alan. *The Comfortable House: North American Suburban Architecture 1890–1930.* Cambridge: MIT Press, 1986.

Hall, Moraunt. "A Delight to the Eye: Rich in Beauty but Poor in Drama." *The New York Times,* 11 September 1927, p. 8. Review of 1927 *Garden of Allah.*

Hanson, A. E. *An Arcadian Landscape: The California Gardens of A. E. Hanson, 1920–1932.* Edited by David Gebhard and Sheila Lynds. California Architecture and Architects series, no. 5. Los Angeles: Hennessey and Ingalls, 1985.

Hawthorne, Hildegarde. *The Lure of the Garden.* New York: The Century Company, 1911.

Hichens, Robert. *The Garden of Allah.* New York: Frederick A. Stokes, 1904.

Hills, Patricia. *John Singer Sargent.* New York: Abrams, 1986.

Jekyll, Gertrude. *Home and Garden.* London: Longmans, Green, 1900.

———. *Wall and Water Gardens.* London: Longmans, Green, 1901.

———. *Some English Gardens*. London: Longmans, Green, 1904.

———. *Colour in the Flower Garden*. London: Country Life, 1908.

Jekyll, Gertrude, and Lawrence Weaver. *Gardens for Small Country Houses*. London: Country Life, 1920.

———. *Garden Ornament*. New York: Dodd, 1926.

Lambert, Gavin. *GWTW: The Making of Gone With the Wind*. Boston: Little, Brown, 1973.

Langer, Suzanne. *Feeling and Form*. London: Routledge & Kegan Paul, 1953.

Le Blond, Mrs. Aubrey. *The Old Gardens of Italy: How to Visit Them*. London: B. T. Batsford, 1912.

Llewellyn, Richard. *How Green Was My Valley*. New York: Macmillan, 1941.

Loudon, Mrs. John Wiley (Jane Webb). *Gardening for Ladies; and, Companion to the Flower Garden*. Edited by A. J. Downing. New York: John Wiley, 1851.

Lowell, Guy. *American Gardens*. Boston: Bates and Guild, 1901.

———. *Smaller Italian Villas and Farmhouses*. New York: P. Wenzel and M. Krakow, 1916.

McGuire, D. K., and L. Fern. *Beatrix Jones Farrand: Fifty Years of American Landscape Architecture*. Washington, D.C.: Dumbarton Oaks, 1985.

McLaren, John. *Gardening in California: Landscape and Flower*. San Francisco: A. M. Robertson, 1909.

Marx, Samuel. *Mayer and Thalberg: The Make-Believe Saints*. New York: Random House, 1975.

Maynard, Samuel T. *Landscape Gardening as Applied to Home Decoration*. New York: Basil Wiley, 1895.

Meadows, Don. *Historic Place Names in Orange County*. Balboa Island, Calif.: Paisano, 1966.

Mitchell, Margaret. *Gone With the Wind*. New York: Macmillan, 1936.

———. *The "Gone With the Wind" Letters, 1936–1949*. New York: Macmillan, 1976.

Modjeska, Helena. *Memories and Impressions*. 1910. Reprint. New York: Benjamin Blom, 1969.

Moore, Charles W., and Wayne Attoe. "Ah Mediterranean! Twentieth-Century Classicism in America." *Center: A Journal for Architecture in America*, 2 (1986).

Mullgardt, Louis Christian. *The Architecture and Landscape Gardening of the Exposition*. San Francisco: Paul Elder, 1915.

Munthe, Axel. *The Story of San Michele*. 1929. Reprint. New York: E. P. Dutton, 1937.

Neubauer, Erika. "The Garden Architecture of Cecil Pinsent, 1884–1964." *Journal of Garden History*, 3 (1983), pp. 35–48.

Palmer, Olive (Mrs. Silas). *Vignettes of Early San Francisco Homes and Gardens*. December 1935 program of the San Francisco Garden Club.

Payne, Theodore. *Life on the Modjeska Ranch in the Gay Nineties*. Los Angeles: Kruckeberg Press, 1962.

Platt, Charles Adams. *Italian Gardens*. New York: Harper and Brothers, 1894.

Pleasants, Mrs. J. E. *History of Orange County, California*. 3 vols. Los Angeles: J. R. Finnell and Sons, 1931.

Pliny. *Letters and Panygericus*. Translated by Betty Radice. Cambridge: Harvard University Press, 1969.

Praz, Mario. *An Illustrated History of Interior Decoration: From Pompeii to Art Nouveau*. Translated by William Weaver. New York: Thames and Hudson, 1982.

Ramsey, Merle, and Mabel Ramsey. *The First Hundred Years in Laguna Beach: 1876–1976*. Edited by Ramsey Lee Riddell. 1976.

Ruskin, John. *The Stones of Venice*. 3 volumes. London: Smith, Elder, 1851–53. Abridged and edited by J. G. Links. Reprint. New York: Da Capo, 1985.

Rybczynski, Witold. *Home: A Short History of an Idea*. New York: Viking, 1986.

San Michele Foundation. *Axel Munthe's San Michele*. Stockholm: San Michele Foundation, 1980.

Sedding, John D. *Garden-Craft Old and New*. London: John Lane, 1903.

Shepherd, John Chiene, and Geoffrey Alan Jellicoe. *Italian Gardens of the Renaissance*. New York: Scribner's, 1925. Reprint. London: Tiranti, 1966.

Starr, Kevin. *Americans and the California Dream, 1850–1915*. New York: Oxford University Press, 1973.

———. *Inventing the Dream: California Through the Progressive Era*. New York: Oxford University Press, 1973.

Streatfield, David C. "The Evolution of the California Landscape: Settling into Arcadia." *Landscape Architecture* 66 (January 1976), pp. 39–46, 78.

———. "The Evolution of the California Landscape: Arcadia Compromised." *Landscape Architecture* 66 (March 1976), pp. 117–26, 170.

———. "The Evolution of the California Landscape: The Great Promotions." *Landscape Architecture* 67 (May 1977) pp. 229–39, 272.

Tabor, Grace. *The Landscape Gardening Book*. New York: McBride, Winston, 1911.

Talbert, Thomas B., ed. *The Historical Volume and Reference Works Covering Garden Grove, Tustin, Santa Ana . . . Laguna Beach. . . .* 3 vols. Whittier, Calif.: Historical Publishers, 1963.

Thomas, Bob. *Thalberg: Life and Legend*. Garden City, N.J.: Doubleday, 1969.

Tompson, Tommy. "Some Gardens in the Pacific Coast Region." *Landscape Architecture* 29 (January 1939), pp. 53–71.

Van Rensselaer, Mrs. Schuyler. *Art Out-of-Doors: Hints on*

Good Taste in Gardening. New York: Charles Scribner's Sons, 1903.

Wharton, Edith. *Italian Villas and Their Gardens*. New York: Century, 1905.

Wyatt, David. *Fall into Eden: Landscape and Imagination in California*. Cambridge: Cambridge University Press, 1986.

Calif.: Windsor, 1986. Description and picture of Mr. Douglas Smith Garden; picture of California Institute of Technology.

Selznick, Irene Mayer. *A Private View*. New York: Knopf, 1983. Pictures and description of Mr. and Mrs. David O. Selznick Garden.

BOOKS CONTAINING INFORMATION ABOUT FLORENCE YOCH'S DESIGNS OR YOCH AND COUNCIL WORK

Andree, Herb, and Noel Young. *Santa Barbara Architecture*. Santa Barbara: Capra Press, 1980. Picture of Il Brolino.

Better Homes and Gardens. *Better Homes and Gardens' Garden Book*. Des Moines: Meredith, 1951. Yoch and Council's own Pasadena Garden as an uncredited example of treating "limited planting space."

Bissell, Ervana Bowen. *Glimpses of Santa Barbara Gardens and Montecito Gardens*. Santa Barbara: Schaver Printing Studio, 1926. Picture of Il Brolino.

Cran, Marion. *Gardens in America*. New York: Macmillan, 1932. Description of Mrs. Fred Bixby's 'Friendship' garden.

Dobyns, Winifred Starr. *California Gardens*. New York: Macmillan, 1931. Thirty-six of 207 plates devoted to Yoch and Council gardens.

Gebhard, David, and Robert Winter. *A Guide to Architecture in Los Angeles and Southern California*. Santa Barbara: Peregrine Smith, 1977. Locates Mr. Gordon B. Kaufmann Residence and Il Brolino.

Goldsmith, Margaret Olthof. *Designs for Outdoor Living*. New York: George W. Stewart, 1941. Pictures and description of Mr. George Cukor Garden.

Haver, Ronald. *David O. Selznick's Hollywood*. New York: Knopf, 1980. Pictures and description of Tara.

———. *David O. Selznick's Gone With the Wind*. New York: Crown 1986. Pictures and description of Tara.

Myrick, Susan. *White Columns in Hollywood: Reports from the GWTW Sets*. Edited by Richard B. Harwell. Macon, Ga.: Mercer University Press, 1982. Description of preparations for landscaping Tara.

Newcomb, Rexford. *The Spanish House for America: Its Design, Furnishing and Garden*. Philadelphia: Lippincott, 1927. Pictures of the Misses Davenport Garden.

———. *Mediterranean Domestic Architecture in the United States*. Cleveland, 1928. Picture of Il Brolino.

Padilla, Victoria. *Southern California Gardens, An Illustrated History*. Berkeley: University of California Press, 1961. Includes Yoch and Council in list of landscape architects of unrivaled excellence.

Scheid, Ann. *Pasadena: Crown of the Valley*. Northridge,

ARTICLES CONTAINING INFORMATION ABOUT FLORENCE YOCH'S DESIGNS OR YOCH AND COUNCIL WORK

Adams, Charles Gibbs. "If I Were to Build a Little Country Place." *California Arts and Architecture* 51 (April 1937), pp. 16–25. Mrs. G. P. Griffith and Mr. and Mrs. Homer Samuels gardens.

Adams, Tony. "Patios Are Their Pleasure." *Los Angeles Times*, 26 February 1950, Magazine section, p. 17. Picture of Rancho Los Cerritos patio.

"Architectural Digest Visits George Cukor." *Architectural Digest* 35 (January–February 1978), pp. 92–99.

Billheimer, Ruth. "Women Achieve Fame as Landscape Artists." *Pasadena Post*, 29 May 1932, p. 5. Athenaeum at California Institute of Technology; Mr. and Mrs. W. H. Council Garden.

Blackiston, Pamela. "California in Bloom: Georgie Van de Kamp." *W*, 13–20 July 1987, p. 38. A noted modern gardener's use of Florence Yoch's principles.

Bottomley, William Lawrence. "Small Italian and Spanish Houses as a Basis of Design." *Architectural Forum* 44 (1926), pp. 185–200. Picture of the Misses Davenport Garden.

"Brick Is Fitting for California-Colonial." *California Arts and Architecture* 40 (December 1931), pp. 29–31. Mr. William B. Hart Residence.

"California Gardens." *House Beautiful* 62 (October 1927), pp. 377–79. Mr. Douglas Smith, Mr. and Mrs. Frank A. Bovey, Misses Davenport gardens.

Crowther, Bosley. "A Beautiful and Affecting Film Achievement Is 'How Green Was My Valley' at the Rivoli." *The New York Times*, 29 October 1941, p. 27, col. 2.

"Dramatic Assemblage of Old World Structures Makes Picturesque Business Home for Antique Shop." *Pasadena Star-News*, n.s. vol. 12, 26 November 1927, sec. 4, pp. 31–32. Pictures and description of Serendipity Antique Shop.

"Five-Room Colonial Achieves Spaciousness—Residence of Mr. and Mrs. Vernon S. Charnley." *American Home* 18 (September 1937) pp. 26, 138–39.

"Four Stucco Houses in Pasadena, California." *House Beautiful* 67 (April 1930), p. 443. Picture of Mrs. Irving J. Sturgis Residence.

Frank, Mrs. Dudley. "New Ebell Clubhouse Will Be Opened

Formally." *Los Angeles Times*, 2 October 1927, Home section, pp. 33–34.

"A Hanging Garden at Bel-Air." *California Arts and Architecture* 39 (April 1931), p. 45. Pictures of Il Vescovo.

"A Hillside Villa of Italian Inspiration." *California Arts and Architecture* 39 (April 1931), pp. 26–27. Pictures of Il Vescovo.

"The House in Good Taste." *House Beautiful* 62 (September 1927), pp. 249–52. Mrs. Richard Fudger Residence in Los Angeles.

"The House in Good Taste." *House Beautiful* 67 (April 1930), pp. 453–56. Mr. Gordon B. Kaufmann Residence.

"House of Mrs. Richard B. Fudger in Beverly Hills, California." *Architecture*, 69 (April 1934), pp. 207–10.

"Keeping Bachelor's Hall." *Country Life* 72 (June 1937), pp. 52–56. Mr. George Cukor Residence.

Kurtz, Wilbur G. "Technical Adviser: The Making of Gone With the Wind: The Hollywood Journals of Wilbur G. Kurtz." Edited by Richard B. Harwell. *Atlanta Historical Society Journal* 22 (Summer 1978), pp. 7–131. Tara.

Leech, Ellen. "Landscaping a Country Club's Grounds." *California Southland* 17 (March–April 1921), pp. 15–16. Includes Florence Yoch's sketch for the patio of the Wilshire Country Club.

McCall, Gabrielle Drake. "Fifty Iris—and a Few More." *Garden and Home Builder* 47 (May 1928), pp. 560–561. Picture of Miss Eleanor Hague Garden.

McCay, William. "A Garden House." *California Arts and Architecture* 38 (July 1930), pp. 30–31. Serendipity Antique Shop Garden.

McManus, John T. "The Music Hall's 'Garden of Allah' Is Technicolor Triumphant." *The New York Times*, 20 November 1936, p. 27, col. 2.

Murray, Robert Dennis. "Harrison Clarke, Artist and Architect." *Pencil Points* 12 (August 1931), pp. 563–581. Discussion of Florence Yoch's standards; pictures of Mr. B. F. Johnston and Mr. W. K. Kellogg gardens.

Nevins, Deborah. "The Triumph of Flora: Women and the American Landscape, 1890–1935." *Antiques* 123 (April 1985), pp. 904–22. Lists Florence Yoch.

"Novel Designs for Women's Athletic Club." Unknown newspaper, early April 1925. Includes picture of Florence Yoch, misidentified as Frances Yoch.

Nugent, Frank S. "Metro's Film of 'Romeo and Juliet' Opens at the Astor." *The New York Times*, 21 August 1936, p. 12, col. 2.

———. "The Screen in Review." *The New York Times*, 20 December 1939, p. 31, col. 2. Review of *Gone With the Wind*.

"Old England Comes to California." *California Arts and Architecture* 37 (January 1930), pp. 32–37. Mrs. Frank W. Emery Residence.

"One of Pasadena's Famous Studio Gardens." *California Arts and Architecture* 38 (July 1930), frontispiece, pp. 28–29. Pictures of Serendipity Antique Shop Garden.

"Pebble Mosaics." *Sunset* 107 (August 1951), p. 44. Picture of mosaic at Mr. Harold S. Gladwyn Residence.

Phillips, Michael J. "New Garden of Eden Laid Out in Great Mexican Estate." *Western Florist and Nurseryman*, 25 December 1930, pp. 4–6, 17. Description of Mr. B. F. Johnston Garden.

"Plates and Illustrations." *Western Architect* 34 (May 1925), frontispiece, plates 1–8. Mrs. Howard Huntingon, Mr. Douglas Smith, Mr. and Mrs. Frank A. Bovey, Mrs. C. W. Gates, Misses Davenport gardens.

"Portfolio of Current Architecture." *Architectural Record* 53 (April 1923), pp. 367–368. Picture of Mr. W. K. Jewett Garden.

"The Proper Use of Gardens." *California Southland* 13 (November 1920), p. 10. Praise of Florence Yoch's imagination and pioneer efforts in landscape architecture; picture of Mrs. Dorothy Freeman Dobbins Garden.

"The Residence of Mr. and Mrs. Homer Samuels." *California Arts and Architecture* 51 (April 1937), pp. 18–19.

"The Residence of Mr. and Mrs. Reese Taylor at San Marino, California." *California Arts and Architecture* 38 (July 1930), p. 26.

"The Residence of Mr. and Mrs. Sherman Asche in Pasadena, California—Florence Yoch and Lucile Council, Collaborators." *California Arts and Architecture* 55 (April 1939), pp. 18–19.

"The Residence of Mr. Leroy D. Kellogg in Pasadena." *California Arts and Architecture* 36 (December 1929), pp. 24–27.

Sadler, Hammond. "The Decorative Use of Tile Outdoors." *Garden and Home Builder* 47 (July 1928), p. 473. Serendipity Antique Shop Garden.

Sajbel, Maureen O., and Glynnis G. Costin. "The Lush Life of Santa Barbara." *W*, 12–19 July 1985, pp. 38–39, 42–43. Color illustration of the topiary garden at Il Brolino.

"Scarlett O'Hara's Family Home." *House and Garden* 76 (November 1939), pp. 28–40. Pictures and description of Tara.

Schnabel, Robert O. "Palms Along Mexico's West Coast Highway." *Principes* 8 (January 1964) pp. 4–13. Lists surviving palms in Mr. B. F. Johnston's Garden.

Seares, Millamy. "California Institute of Technology." *California Arts and Architecture* 39 (May 1931), pp. 34–36. The Athenaeum.

"Second Prize in the 8 to 12 Room Group." *House Beautiful* 69 (May 1931), pp. 489–91. Mr. William B. Hart Residence.

Smaus, Robert. "The Big Bed." *Los Angeles Times*, 27 May 1984, Home section, cover and pp. 4–7. Useful discussion, with color photos, of a skilled gardener's restoration of the Mr. and Mrs. Sherman Asche Garden.

"Some Pleasant Pictures from the Pasadena Garden of Mrs. Irving J. Sturgis." *California Arts and Architecture* 39 (March 1931), cover and pp. 25–27.

Streatfield, David C. "The Evolution of the California Landscape: 4. Suburbia at the Zenith." *Landscape Architecture* 67 (September 1977), pp. 417–24. Includes insightful review of Yoch and Council work prior to 1940.

"Typical Home Life of California." *California Arts and Architecture* 40 (October 1931), pp. 17–25. Mr. Douglas Smith, Mr. and Mrs. Edwin Sherman gardens.

"When an Architect Realizes a Dream." *California Arts and Architecture* 37 (June 1930), pp. 28–30. Mr. Gordon B. Kaufmann Residence.

" 'Where Art Thou Romeo?' " *California Arts and Architecture* 39 (June 1931), p. 25. Pictures of Women's Athletic Club.

"With Santa Barbara's Hills for Background." *House and Garden* 53 (May 1928), pp. 119–21. Mr. and Mrs. Bernard Hoffman Garden.

Wren, Helen. "Informal Charm of Old Spain in a City Home." *Arts and Decoration* 29 (October 1928), pp. 45–47, 88. Description and photographs of the Mrs. Richard Fudger Garden in Los Angeles.

Yoch, James J., Jr. "Gardens for a Director: Florence Yoch's Italian Renaissance Landscapes for *Romeo and Juliet* and for George Cukor's Home." *Center: A Journal for Architecture in America* 2 (1986), pp. 58–62.

ARTICLES BY FLORENCE YOCH

Yoch, Florence. "Planting of a Hacienda." *California Southland* 19 (June 1921), p. 20.

———. "The Court Garden of the Women's Athletic Club." *Landscape Architecture* 17 (1926), pp. 37–39.

———. "Sympathetic Attitude of Architect Is Aid to Art of Landscaping." *Southwest Builder and Contractor* 75 (11 April 1930), pp. 29–30. This is the original article, later reprinted with illustrations from the Mrs. Richard Fudger Garden in *California Arts and Architecture* 38 (July 1930).

———. "Fitting the Land for Human Use, An Art Closely Allied to Architecture." *California Arts and Architecture* 38 (July 1930), pp. 19, 20, 72. Yoch's landscaping philosophy illustrated with sketches and pictures of Mrs. Richard Fudger Garden. Reprinted in this volume, p. 186–87.

Yoch, Florence, and Lucile Council. "The Little Garden of Gaiety." *Garden and Home Builder* 47 (May 1928), p. 205. Reprinted in this volume, p. 188–89.

UNPUBLISHED WORK BY FLORENCE YOCH

Yoch, Florence. Introductory chapter of a book "on the subject of 'Plants as Materials of Design in Planting.' " Courtesy of Mr. Thomas C. Moore.

———. Notes Toward a Book on Landscaping. Courtesy of Mr. Thomas C. Moore.

———. Four Notebooks of Sketches and Observations on Travel in Europe and in the Eastern United States, principally during the 1920s. Courtesy of Mr. Thomas C. Moore.

Yoch, Florence, and Lucile Council. Garden Directions for Mrs. Doerr. 16 October 1941. Courtesy of Mrs. Harriet Doerr.

———. Garden Maintenance Directions for Mrs. Preston Hotchkiss. Courtesy of Mr. Thomas C. Moore.

———. [Horticultural Instructions]. General Garden Information and Maintenance. Courtesy of Mr. Thomas C. Moore.

Yoch and Council Office Account and Record Book, 1922–40. Courtesy of Mr. Thomas C. Moore.

PHOTOGRAPHIC RECORDS

Yoch and Council Collection of Photographs (including Florence Yoch's Album of Gardens). Courtesy of Mr. Thomas C. Moore and Mrs. Robert E. Ward.

Florence Yoch's Photograph Album of European and Mexican Landscapes. Courtesy of Mr. Thomas C. Moore.

Lucile Council's Photograph Album of European and Mexican Landscapes. Courtesy of Mr. Thomas C. Moore.

Florence Yoch's Glass Slides (1920s & 1930s) of her and of Yoch and Council Work. Courtesy of Special Collections, University Research Library, the University of California at Los Angeles.

William M. Clarke Collection of Architectural Negatives. Courtesy of the Henry E. Huntington Library, San Marino, California.

CORRESPONDENCE

Mr. Herb Bridges: 31 March 1988.

Correspondence regarding *The Garden of Allah,* courtesy of Selznick Properties, Ltd., and the Harry Ransom Humanities Research Center, the University of Texas at Austin.

David O. Selznick to Florence Yoch: 22 March 1935.

Florence Yoch (signing for Yoch and Council) to David O. Selznick: 22 March 1935.

David O. Selznick to George Cukor: 22 March 1935.

David O. Selznick's secretary to Florence Yoch: 22 March 1935.

Florence Yoch to George Cukor: 3 May 1935.

Florence Yoch to David O. Selznick: 10 May 1935.

Ms. Elizabeth Lewton: 6 December 1982.

Mr. Thomas C. Moore: 17 September 1982; 7 June 1983.

Mr. John Peirce: 1 July 1982; 26 May 1983; 21 August 1983; 30 November 1983; 23 January 1984; 5 February 1984; 24 February 1984; 3 March 1987; 26 March 1988; 24 March 1988.

Daniel Selznick: 29 April 1988.

Irene Mayer Selznick: 15 March 1988.

L. Jeffrey Selznick: 9 May 1988.

Ms. Ruth Shellhorn: 20 April 1981.

Mr. William J. Tomkin: 2 February 1988.

Mrs. Robert E. Ward: 3 November 1982; 14 November 1982; 27 November 1982; 5 October 1985.

Florence Yoch to Mrs. Lockwood de Forest: 29 November 1940.

Florence Yoch to Harriet Doerr: 21 January 1961.

Florence Yoch to Thomas C. Moore: 12 May 1969; 9 November 1969; 12 June 1970; 7 February 1971; 26 March 1971; 29 June 1971.

MEMORANDA REGARDING THE GARDEN OF ALLAH

Courtesy of Selznick Properties, Ltd., and the Harry Ransom Humanities Research Center, University of Texas at Austin

David O. Selznick to Joseph J. Cohn, 5 March 1935.

David O. Selznick to Joseph J. Cohn, 7 March 1935.

David O. Selznick to Joseph J. Cohn, 11 March 1935.

David O. Selznick to J. Robert Rubin, 20 March 1935.

Marcella Bennett to F. L. Hendrickson, 21 March 1935.

David O. Selznick to Louis B. Mayer, 22 March 1935.

David O. Selznick to William Wright, 29 March 1935.

F. L. Hendrickson to David O. Selznick, 7 August 1935.

David O. Selznick to F. L. Hendrickson, 8 August 1935.

INTERVIEWS

Mr. William Aplin: 21 October 1982.

Mrs. Florence Banning: 9 August 1983.

Lady Ruth Crocker: 20 July 1981.

Mr. George Cukor: 14 July 1981.

Mrs. Adelaide Davis: 28 July 1982.

Mrs. Harriet Doerr: 19 July 1981.

Mrs. Lockwood de Forest: 21 June 1981.

Mrs. Carolyn Hotchkis: 16 July 1981.

Mrs. A. Parley Johnson: 5 August 1983.

Ms. Elizabeth Lewton: 10 December 1982.

Mr. Thomas C. Moore: 29 March 1982, 31 December 1982, 15 April 1985, 1 June 1985, 20 March 1986, 22 April 1988.

Mrs. Margaret Pashgian: 12 July 1980.

Mr. John Peirce: 10 July 1980, 8 February 1982, 16 April 1988.

Mr. James Ross: 9 July 1981.

Mr. Alex Salcido: 5 June 1985.

Mrs. Ann Warner: 1 September 1981.

BOTANICAL REFERENCES

Bailey, L. H. *Manual of Cultivated Plants.* New York: Macmillan, 1949.

Beales, Peter. *Classic Roses.* New York: Holt, Rinehart and Winston, 1985.

Dobson, Beverly R., ed. *Combined Rose List.* N.P., 1988.

Hillier's Manual of Trees and Shrubs. 1971. Reprint. Newport, Isle of Wight: Yelf Brothers, 1974.

Hortus. Compiled by L. H. Bailey and Ethel Zoe Bailey. 1930. Revised edition. New York: Macmillan, 1935.

Hortus Second. Compiled by L. H. Bailey and Ethel Zoe Bailey. New York: Macmillan, 1947.

Hortus Third. Compiled by Liberty Hyde Bailey and Ethel Zoe Bailey and the Staff of the Liberty Hyde Bailey Hortorium. New York: Macmillan, 1976.

Hoyt, Roland Stewart. *Check Lists for Ornamental Plants of Subtropical Regions.* N.P., n.d.

Index Kewensis Plantarum Phanerogamarum. 16 vols. Compiled by Joseph Hooker, B. Daydon Jackson et al. Oxford: Oxford University Press, 1893–1981.

Index Nominum Genericorum (Plantorum). 3 vols. Utrecht: Bohn, Scheltema and Holkema, 1979.

Mathias, Mildred E. *Flowering Plants in the Landscape.* Los Angeles: University of California Press, 1982.

McFarland, J. Horace. *Modern Roses III.* Harrisburg, Pa.: J. Horace McFarland Company, 1947.

Nicholson, George. *The Illustrated Dictionary of Gardening.* London: L. Upcott Gill, 1885. This was the edition Florence Yoch owned.

Perry, Bob. *Trees and Shrubs for Dry California Landscapes.* San Dimas, Calif.: Land Publishing, 1981.

Sunset's New Western Garden Book. Menlo Park, Calif.: Lane Publishing, 1979.

Willis, J. C. *A Dictionary of the Flowering Plants and Ferns.* 8th edition. Revised by H. K. Airy Shaw. Cambridge: Cambridge University Press, 1980.

Glossary

ACROPOLIS A high plateau, raised part of the garden on a rocky site, like the fortified temple complex of Athens.

ALLEE A walk or road lined with trees or tall, clipped shrubs. Seventeenth-century French gardens trimmed hedges and trees into flat walls on each side of a path or road to achieve outdoors the architecture of a hallway. English gardeners a century later cut bridle paths, called "rides," through woodlands for a rougher version.

APSE A semicircular recess, formed by trees or shrubs, implying the curved conclusion of the nave or side chapel in a church or temple.

ARBOR A light garden structure, sometimes of pipe but more usually with wood or stucco columns supporting rafters or wires for vines to make a shaded retreat.

ATRIUM The central, formal court of a Roman house and by extension a light well in modern buildings.

AVENUE A road or walk lined with trees that define the edges and control the view. Italian and French gardeners most often used Italian cypress trees; English versions employed lime (linden), oak, chestnut, sycamore in ranks of as many as four trees on each side. American versions are usually less emphatic.

AXIS An imaginary line stretching from a viewpoint to a conclusion (sometimes) in a statue, gate, tree, bench, or vista. Along the sides of an axis, landscape designers organize walks, beds, shrubs, rows of trees. A cross axis, cut through the principal axis usually at right angles, offers alternative vistas. Italian and French axes were primarily straight lines. In the eighteenth century, English gardeners, perhaps imitating Oriental models, introduced curved lines.

BALUSTRADE A row of stone or wood posts, shaped like the pomegranate flower (Italian, *balaustro*), connected by a cap to form the edge of a terrace or a stair.

BORDER A formally marked bed devoted to flowers or shrubs.

BOSCO Woods, mock wilderness in a garden.

CAP A wall's top course, overhanging or otherwise defined.

COPSE A thicket of small trees and shrubs.

CORTILE An enclosed courtyard often surrounded with a covered walk.

DENTIL Small blocks that run beneath the projections of a cornice.

ELLIPSE A regular oval. In the sixteenth century Pirro Ligorio used an elliptical terrace for the Villa Pia behind the Vatican, and the shape was popular in Italian gardens of the seventeenth century. In contrast to the stability and simplicity of the single-centered circle, the two-centered ellipse is more dramatic.

ESPALIER To train a tree or shrub into patterns flat against a wall or trellis.

EXEDRA An outdoor conversation area, usually a bench in the shaded recess of a hedge or a garden pavilion.

FORECOURT Enclosed space for reception in front of a building.

HERBACEOUS BORDER A broad, linear bed planted primarily with perennials and usually placed against a hedge or wall. Used in monastic and Renaissance gardens, these became a major element in English gardens of the late nineteenth century, particularly for displaying the range of plants that William Robinson promoted or the painterly effects that Gertrude Jekyll achieved.

HERM A garden statue composed of a bust, often of the god Hermes/Mercury, atop a base that is either rectangular or tapering to the ground. The usual proportions are of a human figure. Herms resemble Terms, which display the head of Terminus, the Roman god of boundaries, on a column marking the limits of a garden.

LIMONAIA Lemon House for storing potted citrus trees in the winter; also the adjoining garden area where the trees are moved for the warmer months.

LOGGIA   A gallery or arcade, open on at least one side to the garden, for viewing, dining, conversation.

MIRADOR   A Spanish rooftop garden or pavilion for viewing.

MOTOR COURT   Parking area in front of a house.

ORTHOGONAL   At right angles. Calm, expected, comfortable. Contrasts with *oblique.*

PALAZZO   The Italian word for palace, a large building.

PANEL   A defined section within a larger field. A regular geometrical shape containing within a border a block of flowers or grass, like the raised panel of a door or wainscoting.

PARTERRE   A unified and enclosed series of garden beds in decorative shapes that include knots, brocade patterns, or simpler geometrical figures.

PARTERRE `A L'ANGLAISE   Garden beds filled with designs in cut turf. The simplest parterre imagined in French seventeenth-century garden manuals, which praised most highly the *parterre de broderie,* embroidering in flowers.

PATIO   A Spanish courtyard. The name for any informal, outdoor paved space, whether largely enclosed by buildings as in Moorish gardens (Alhambra, Generalife) or simply a spot for encampments in the garden. Less formal in use and smaller in scale than a terrace.

PAVILION   A light, decorative garden building for dining, amours, conversation, reflection. An outdoor living room, equivalent to the Roman *aedicula,* which the earliest Renaissance garden pavilions deliberately imitated.

PERGOLA   A set of posts or columns supporting an overhead structure and creating a passageway. Poles, trellis, or wires hold plants, which usually give shade and sometimes a crop of fruit or exhibition of flowers.

PLEACH   To interlace branches to form a natural arbor or pergola.

POLLARD   To trim a tree back to a knob on the central trunk to encourage a crown of new growth and to control size.

PORTAL   A gate or door, usually of dignity.

PORTE-COCHERE   A covered entrance for vehicles or an overhang between drive and house.

PUTTI   Cupids.

RAMADA   A covered porch.

RAMPART   A stone embankment or wall.

RILL   A small stream, runnel, rivulet.

RUNNEL   A narrow-channeled watercourse, particularly used in Mohammedan gardens to carry water from a fountain to basins around plants for irrigation. William Kent ingeniously altered straight irrigation runnels into the curved waterway for the garden at Rousham.

SARCOPHAGUS   A stone coffin, usually sculpted, sometimes inscribed, in classical Rome.

TERRACE   A raised, level garden area, sometimes paved, defined with hedges, trees, walls, or balustrade.

TRELLIS   A structure, usually of wood lath interwoven with diamond or square openings, that forms walls or roofs to support climbing vines.

TYMPANUM   A recessed space, often filled with statues, enclosed within a triangular pediment.

VERGE   Grass, herbal, or other edging along a path or flower bed.

VILLA   An Italian country house with a notable garden and, in the word, a sense of pretension to Roman grandeur. More elegant than *vigna,* a simple farmhouse, although *vigna* can be used in understatement for a great place in the same way that owners described Newport mansions as "cottages." Many great villas are resting spots for visits to farms and therefore preserve close ties with agricultural planting designs and incorporate vistas over the fields.

VISTA   A carefully controlled view, usually framed by trees and perhaps blocks of hedges that serve as shutters in a camera to organize perception of the outdoors.

VOLUTE   A spiral scroll, like those in an Ionic capital.

WELLHEAD   A fountainhead, usually stone, that caps a well. A crane or other device for raising water was originally part of the structure.

Index

Yews, "pet," 80–82

Yoch, Catherine Isch (mother), 5

Yoch, Florence: in Africa, xii, 94–98, 141; in Australia, 135; birth of, 5; in Carmel, 174–78; client requirements of, 22; commissions of, 181–85; and credit for "Tara," 102; death of, 27, 175, 179 n.1 (ch.2); early career of, xi; early life of, 4–9; final garden of (see Francis Doud house, project for); and Hollywood projects, 65–108; homes of, 157–78; and Howard Hughes, 50; influence of Europe on, 29, 34, 48, 50, 63; influences on (see Flandrau, Charles Macomb; Jekyll, Gertrude; Lutyens, Edwin; Munthe, Axel); and Lucile Coucil partnership, xii, 5, 20; in Mexico, 102, 141–43; and Monterey, xi; and movie moguls, 65–92; and movie set design, 93–108; in Pasadena, 158–62, 168–74; and patrician gardens, 29–64; persona of, 88; personal gardens of 157–78; professional philosophy of, 109–11, 131, 136–37, 164, 177, 178, 186–88; public-sector projects of, 139–55; researching "Tara" in Georgia, 104; in San Marino, 162–68; travels of, xii, 11, 94–98, 102, 104, 135, 141–43; at university, 9; and Villa Landon, 96–98; workforce of, 22–26 (see also Ross, James; Salcido, Alex); at work within limited space, 59–60; during World War II, 26–27; writings of, xii, 9, 27, 108, 109, 186–89, 205–16

Yoch, Joseph (father), 4, 5